KU-782-273

Ayrshire's
LOST
VILLAGES

Dane Love

Other books by Dane Love:

Scottish Kirkyards	Robert Hale
Pictorial History of Cumnock	Alloway Publishing
Pictorial History of Ayr	Alloway Publishing
Scottish Ghosts	Robert Hale
Scottish Ghosts	Barnes & Noble
The Auld Inns of Scotland	Robert Hale
Guide to Scottish Castles	Lomond Books
Tales of the Clan Chiefs	Robert Hale
Scottish Covenanter Stories	Neil Wilson
Ayr Stories	Fort Publishing
Ayrshire Coast	Fort Publishing
Scottish Spectres	Robert Hale
Scottish Spectres	Ulverston Large Print
Ayrshire: Discovering a County	Fort Publishing
Ayr Past and Present	Sutton Publishing
Lost Ayrshire	Birlinn
The River Ayr Way	Carn Publishing
Ayr – the Way We Were	Fort Publishing
The Man Who Sold Nelson's Column	Birlinn
Jacobite Stories	Neil Wilson
The History of Sorn – Village and Parish	Carn Publishing
Legendary Ayrshire	Carn Publishing
The Covenanter Encyclopaedia	Fort Publishing
Scottish Ghosts	Amberley Publishing
Scottish Kirkyards	Amberley Publishing
A Look Back at Cumnock	Carn Publishing
A Look Back at Girvan	Carn Publishing
A Look Back at Ayrshire Farming	Carn Publishing
Ayr Then and Now	The History Press
Ayrshire Then and Now	The History Press
The History of Mauchline - Village and Parish	Carn Publishing
The Galloway Highlands	Carn Publishing
The History of Auchinleck - Village and Parish	Carn Publishing

www.dane-love.co.uk

Ayrshire's
LOST
VILLAGES

With best wishes.

[signature]

2021

Dane Love

CARN PUBLISHING

© Dane Love, 2016.
First Published in Great Britain, 2016.

ISBN - 978 1 911043 02 7

Published by Carn Publishing,
Lochnoran House,
Auchinleck, Ayrshire, KA18 3JW.

Printed by Bell & Bain Ltd,
Glasgow, G46 7UQ.

The right of the author to be identified as the author of this work has been asserted by
him in accordance with the Copyright, Designs and Patents Act 1988.

All rights reserved. No part of this publication may be reproduced, stored, or
transmitted in any form, or by any means, electronic, mechanical or photocopying,
recording or otherwise, without the express written permission of the publisher.

Contents

List of Illustrations

Introduction

Many people in Ayrshire know that in years gone by there were former mining communities which no longer exist – the mines having closed and the residents rehoused. Often these communities comprised of rows of houses, built by the mine owners adjacent to their pits, so that the workers were on hand. Often the location of these houses was remote, and the occupants were truly isolated, in some cases there being no road to them for decades. Readers will no doubt have heard of places like Glenbuck and Lethanhill, two of the larger communities, both of which have been abandoned for many years now. A few former residents still survive, but their number is gradually dwindling.

However, this book also looks at almost fifty other communities which have passed into the annals of history. Most of them were former mining communities, varying in size from ten or so houses, to larger villages, with a population of over one thousand people. Some, like Darnconner, had schools, post offices, police stations, churches and co-operative stores, whereas others were little more than a single terrace of houses.

There are a few older communities, which were formed for agricultural labourers, weavers and rural workers. These include Loudounkirk, Alton, Montgarswood Bridgend and Old Rome, names which have basically been forgotten in modern Ayrshire. Even the site of the clachans can only with difficulty be identified on the ground.

As stated, most of the lost villages in this book were built for the miners. If we go back to the eighteenth and early nineteenth centuries, miners' houses were little different to agricultural workers – we can image them living in buildings like Burns' Cottage at Alloway. These were built of stone, roofed in thatch and had small windows in them. Some of these old houses were referred to as the 'Colliers' Row', and old maps indicate them all over the Ayrshire coalfield. Usually, there were only two or four houses in these rows, and they were randomly placed in the countryside in no formal pattern. There are also a number of small communities which comprised of no more than half a dozen houses, usually joined together to form a row of thatched dwellings, bearing names including the word 'coal', such as Coalhall, examples being near Neiphill (Kilmarnock), and Drongan, Coalheugh (Dalry), or Coalburn (New Cumnock).

The next development in miners' houses came about when the railways arrived and the mines became much larger, and consequently a great workforce was required. As the development of coal-mining expanded, the coalmasters found themselves establishing mines in places distant from the population, or else in places where there were not enough workers for their needs. To solve the difficulty, they had to build houses for their employees, but comfort and space was not high on their list.

One of the earliest forms of mining community was what are known as 'colliery squares'. These were small homes, all joined together to form a square, or more usually a rectangle, around a central courtyard. A number of old villages of this type existed in Ayrshire, including Kerse, Craighall, Mosshouse and Darnconner, although the latter was to expand further.

The next style of colliery village comprised rows of houses. Often these were built alongside railway lines, the sidings which served the pits themselves. The houses were close to the pits, and the coalmasters often assumed that the residents would not need to go anywhere else, for a number of the villages, such as Beoch, Lethanhill and Benquhat, did not have a roadway linking them to the outside world. As the pit next to the rows closed, the residents often found themselves employed farther afield, and either had to trek along the bed of the railway to the next pit, or else catch a lift on a waggon or carriage that was going that way. These workmen's trains were known as 'The Cairriages', and the first are thought to have started in the 1890s. On a number of occasions, they were also brought into use when a mining village football team was playing another, such as Burnfoothill to Rankinston, Glenbuck to Muirkirk, or Cronberry to Auchinleck.

The miners' rows were often lengthy, it being cheaper to build a long line of houses with only two gables than the same number of houses in shorter rows, which would require more gables. A number of rows were quite lengthy, but perhaps the longest in Ayrshire was the Common Row in Auchinleck parish, which had 96 houses in a single row, but one which took a curve, following the line of old bogey lines which served older pits. The next longest rows were at Benquhat (Dalmellington), where the rows had 32 houses, Carsehead New Row (Dalry) and Grasshill Row (Glenbuck), both of which had 36 homes, Tongue Bridge with 39, and Glengyron, which had forty.

Another style of building used by some of the earlier coalmasters was the back-to-back cottage, where the houses butted against each other, meaning that the only source of light was from the front of each house. A number of places had houses like these, such as Beoch, which was composed of nothing else, but also at Craigmark and Glenbuck. Very often these homes were described as 'Double End', often shortened to 'Dublin'. This name became so common that many people have erroneously assumed that the houses known as Dublin were so-called because of the large Irish influx of workers who often ended up in what was usually the poorer standard of house.

The construction of the houses changed over the years. Initially, many were built of stone and roofed with thatch. Internally the floors were either hard clay or quarry tiles. Later houses were built of brick, the coal companies often setting up their own brickworks to use the coal waste and convert it into another useable commodity. By this time the houses had slate roofs, but many were to have roofs of a tar-covered cloth, which disintegrated fairly quickly. These rows were invariably referred to as the 'Tarry' or 'Taury' Row.

The mining community at Pearston was established by Patrick Mure MacReadie to house mineworkers employed in his new Pearston Colliery. The houses were slightly larger than contemporary mineworkers' homes, being 18½ feet square. The main room, which served as the kitchen, was 18 feet 6 inches long, by 12 feet wide. To the back of the house were two small rooms, each 9 feet by 6 feet, often used for lodgers, or else for privacy. Each house had a window one foot wide by four tall. Internally the floors were better than the flattened clay used up to then, being a type of concrete mix of lime and gravel. Each house had a garden, where potatoes were grown, and these were surrounded with larch and spruce trees. There was a coal shed for each house. To encourage a better standard of labour force, MacReady offered 'a premium to steady men, by giving a house rent free'.

Conditions in the rows was something that was beginning to be taken notice of at the turn of the twentieth century. Miners were becoming more vocal, and the formation of the National Miners' Federation raised their concerns. The Ayrshire Miners' Union (formed in 1886) persuaded the Royal Commission on Housing to investigate the state of things in 1913. Thomas MacKerrell and James Brown, Agents for the Ayrshire Miners' Union, toured the county and visited many miners' communities, sending their report to Commission. Of the numerous villages they visited, twelve are featured in this book of lost villages.

James Brown was to stand for parliament, winning the South Ayrshire seat for the Labour Party in 1918, the first time it was to hold a seat in Ayrshire. He remained the M.P. until 1931. He was re-elected in 1935 and served the people until 1939. A memorial to his memory was erected in Annbank, where he lived much of his life.

Although the report was damming, parliament had little opportunity to do much about it. The outbreak of the Great War, or World War I as it was later to be called, stifled any progress or improvement for five years. Once peace had settled, and finances had improved, the building of new houses by burgh and county councils commenced. Some of the older council houses still survive, such as those at Polnessan, to the north of Patna. Similarly, the row of houses at Cronberry known as Riverside Terrace was erected by William Baird in 1924, allowing folk to be rehoused from both the old 'Taury Rows' in Cronberry itself, but also from the now lost village of Gasswater.

This book gives details of fifty old communities in the county. Others existed, but little is known about them. The list includes Loadingbank Row, which was located south of Kilbirnie, its site now built over by an expanding town. Loadingbank had 26 houses in a single row, owned by the Glengarnock Iron and Steel Company Ltd, followed by Colvilles. Plann and Hemphill rows were isolated communities to the west of Kilmarnock, near to Southhook. Davidshill was a small community of farm buildings, agricultural workers' cottages and a few other houses. It had the distinction of having a small hospital for a time, the building surviving as a private house. It was located by the side of the River Garnock, south of Kilbirnie. South of the River Irvine, to the west of Drybridge, was the community of Shewalton. There is still much research to be done!

Dane Love
Auchinleck, 2016.

Acknowledgements

As ever, I must thank all of those folk who have assisted in so many ways to make this book possible. As I have said before, sometimes they don't even realise it, or else are helping with information or pictures for other books, perhaps written some time ago. These folk will have been acknowledged at the time. However, to make this book possible, I must offer my thanks to the following people: Barbara Alexander; Burns Monument Centre, Kilmarnock; Doon Valley Museum, Dalmellington; Lilias Ferguson; Stephen Fisk (www.abandonedcommunities.co.uk); Friends of Loudoun Kirk; Carnegie Library, Ayr; Nairn Kennedy; John MacKenzie; North Ayrshire Heritage Centre, Saltcoats; Donald L. Reid; Ian Riggans and Louise Ross. Most of the maps have been supplied by the National Library of Scotland.

1

Alton

*

On 1 December 1941 a great fire ripped through the grand pile of Loudoun Castle, north of Galston. The mansion was about to be leased to the War Office as a military headquarters but the conflagration put paid to that. The building suffered considerably, the roof collapsing and many of the fine rooms being completely destroyed. Once the flames had been doused and the extent of the damage assessed the occupant, the Countess of Loudoun (the castle and estate had been sold to the Heritable Securities and Mortgage Investment Association Limited), was shocked to find that they had not paid their insurance for eighteen months. The family were left with little option but to lay off most of their staff, many of whom lived in a couple of local villages – Alton and Loudounkirk. The war, and the demise of the castle were two factors that were instrumental in bringing the life of the two villages to an end.

Alton was located on the road north from Galston heading towards Glasgow. The community was small, a veritable estate village where the occupiers of the houses were employed by the Earls of Loudoun. The houses were old – indeed by the time of the fire they were very much antiquated, but whilst they worked for the Loudoun family, the tenants were happy enough to call the buildings home. On Timothy Pont's map of Cunninghame, he lists the village as 'Oldtoun', a different spelling and less quaint, perhaps, but indicative that the community existed in 1654, and even then, the community was regarded as being of considerable vintage. General Roy's 1747 map names the village as 'Oldtown'. Some say that the clachan existed as far back as the year 1000, though the only evidence for this was the fact that when many of the tenants at Alton were digging their gardens they often found shards of Roman pottery, marbles and coins.

The site of Alton, or Auld Toun as it was sometimes referred to, appears to have been an ancient one. The Castle Hill is a rounded knoll, its original purpose unknown, though it may have been a Norman motte. Writing in *Prehistoric Man in Ayrshire* (1895), John Smith described the Castle Hill as being 'sixteen paces in diameter on top, and thirteen feet above the road, which skirts its south-east base. On the top there is a slight indication of a rampart, and on its south-west side faint indications of a ditch. On the north-east side there is a small dyke, and outside of it a hollow, or ditch, partly filled in with boulders.'

The houses at Alton were single-storey, with steep thatched roofs. At the end of each row the buildings had gables, and these sometimes had chimneys on them. Most of the cottages were joined to each other, and the front façade was little more than a door in the centre with a small window to either side. One account claims that there were from 30-40 houses in the community at one time.

1. Alton – the School row on right and Smithy row on left

By the time of the 1856 Ordnance Survey map, however, there appears to have been only twenty or so houses in the village. These were rather spread out, extending alongside the roadway from near Alton farm (which survives) to beyond the Castle Hill, alongside the Alton Burn. Access to the village was from the Glasgow Road at Alton farm, crossing the Upper Alton Bridge. Just to the west of Alton farm was a limestone quarry, the limestone being reduced to lime in a limekiln that was abandoned before the 1850s. No doubt, the lime was used for agricultural purposes.

On crossing the Upper Alton Bridge, the road swung to the left, to follow the Alton Burn onto the moors. At this sharp bend was the main part of the clachan. To the right was a row of five houses, all joined together. Abutting the end was a sixth building, which for a time served as a school. This still operated in the early 1890s. To the rear of the cottages were gardens, tended by the residents as a ready source of fresh fruit, vegetables and potatoes in season.

At the sharp bend was a second row of houses, rising gently across the hillside. There appears to have been about four or five houses in this row, with at least one other at right angles to it, on the Newton Road. At the east end of this second row was a smithy, which appears to have been a long-standing business. Around 1910 the smith was John Nisbet. A century earlier there was already a smithy at Alton, for an old stone that was in Loudoun kirkyard commemorated Margaret Reid, spouse to John Campbell, smith in Alton. She died on 27 December 1821 aged 65 years. On the stone was a verse as a warning to the passer by, a variation of a common old Scots epitaph:

> Time was I was as thou art now,
> Looking o'er the dead as thou dost me;
> Ere long thou'll lie as low as I,
> And others stand and look o'er thee.

In the middle of the row, one of the properties was occupied by James Shields, who had a joinery. He manufactured numerous timber implements and various goods for farmers and others on Loudoun estate.

A third row of houses was located alongside the Newton Road, probably three in number, with gardens around them. Perpendicular to the road was another building, perhaps one cottage, but it is difficult to determine now. It faced onto the roadway that led to the large field south of the Alton Strip of trees.

Facing the Castle Hill was a small row of three houses, again surrounded by gardens. Beyond this were a couple of semi-detached cottages, at angles to the road, and yet further, a second couple of houses, joined together. A footpath made its way around the western side of the Castle Hill to the Alton Burn, then across a footbridge to a well, the source of much of the community's water.

The residents at Alton shared common grazing in a field of forty acres, located below the village. Thus, each family was able to keep their own cow, used for milk from which butter and cheese could be made.

Writing in the *New Statistical Account of Scotland* in 1842, Rev Norman MacLeod, minister of Loudoun parish, noted that Alton or Auldton, contained around 24 families at that time. He further noted that 'in this village there are, 1 smith, 1 wright, 1 shoemaker, 1 grocer, 1 publican, and 1 teacher.' He also recorded that at Alton there was also one school-room and dwelling house for the teacher, provided by the Loudoun family.

In 1900 Alton was owned by the trustees of Lord Donington, as was much of Loudoun estate. By this time there were only ten houses which remained with a roof, and one of these was already uninhabitable. The occupants of the other houses were John Donald, labourer; Ronald Campbell, labourer; John Yeudall, teacher; John Meikle, woodsman; James Shields, joiner; William Ramage, roadsman; Mrs John Ferns; William Nisbet, blacksmith and Matthew Richmond, game watcher.

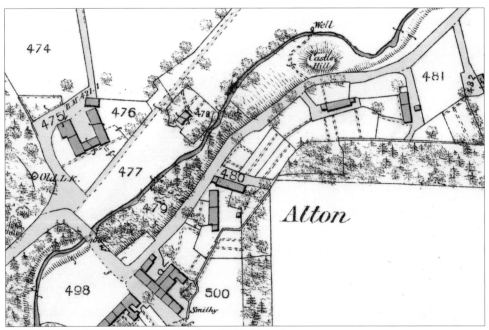

2. Alton from 1856 Ordnance Survey map
Reproduced by permission of the National Library of Scotland

One of the last residents of Alton was John McGill, who carried out considerable research into Loudoun estate. In his book, *A History of the House of Loudoun and Associated Families*, written under the pseudonym, Craufuird C. Loudoun, he recalls how 'within the white-washed, stone-built, thatched cottages the first memory is the huge, wide, open hearth, where burned a fire of peat, coal or wood, the only source of heating and cooking. There were hooks and hobs within the fireplace for utensils. Water was boiled in large pans hung over the fire. There was an oblong metal tub used for bathing. The fire was rarely allowed to go out winter or summer since hot meals were served throughout the year.' He also noted that the houses had no damp-proof courses and were damp for much of the year. Inside, the floors were paved with time-worn limestone slabs, whereas some buildings only had flattened clay. The roofs were thatched with dried bulrush reeds and straw.

Even within the last forty years of the nineteenth century, the community of Alton had started its decline. The two sets of paired cottages east of the Castle Hill row had gone from the maps. So, too, had the cottages on the roadway to the large field. One of the cottages in the school row had been demolished, and the school was by this time closed. The school building itself was demolished between 1895 and 1908.

When the fire in the castle rendered most of the servants jobless, they soon began to look elsewhere for work. As a result, they left their homes behind, and soon the cottages fell into disrepair. Many of the residents were decanted to other properties in different communities. The last two occupants were Mrs Susan Stewart and Robert G. Christie, ploughman. The other three houses which were still standing at this time were uninhabitable. To save paying rates, the thatch roofs were removed, and soon the stone walls collapsed. The last standing walls forming the old houses of the village were cleared away in 1947.

2
Annicklodge

*

The name Annick Lodge today makes one think of a grand country house, standing close by the side of the Annick Water, in a little glen to the north-east of Irvine. The house, which incorporates the remains of the ancient tower known as Pearston Hall, was erected around 1790 by William Montgomerie, second son of Alexander Montgomerie of Coilsfield. In style it has been described as Georgian Palladian, and with its landscaped grounds forms an important part of Ayrshire's architectural heritage.

However, across the Annick Water, and slightly to the west, was the mining community of Annick Lodge, or Annicklodge as it is represented on older Ordnance Survey maps. The contrast with Annick Lodge itself could not have been greater.

The first of the miners' rows were probably erected in the first half of the nineteenth century, laid perpendicular to the minor road that serves a few farms. As with many mining communities, the rows were built facing the branch railway that served the mine itself, at Annicklodge this being a loop from the Glasgow & South Western Railway line that linked Kilmarnock with Dalry. The branch passed between the houses and just as it crossed the minor road, it split into two sidings, serving the Annicklodge Colliery.

There have been a few different pits bearing the Annicklodge name. Annicklodge Number 2 was certainly working in 1852, for on 8 November that year Andrew Calligan was killed when he was struck by a piece of timber that fell from the surface. This mine was located to the south of the village, by the side of the farm road leading to Holehouse.

Annicklodge mines were owned by the Glengarnock Iron and Steel Co., the coal being taken to Kilbirnie for use in the steelworks there. Annick Lodge itself was occupied around 1900 by Robert Barclay Shaw, coalmaster, of 94 Commerce Street, Glasgow.

On the east side of the line was a long row of houses, built in a single terrace with no gaps. There were 26 homes, all similarly sized apart from the two at the southern end, which were larger. North of the long row was a second row of homes, this one having a shallow dog-leg in it, to follow the curving line of the branch line. This row had sixteen houses in it. The third original row at Annicklodge was located to the west of the railway. This row had twelve houses in it, with a larger L-shaped building attached to the northern end.

There was a high percentage of Roman Catholics living at Annicklodge. In 1870, when Father Thomas Keane of Irvine carried out a survey of his parishioners: he reckoned that there were 120 Catholics living there.

The residents of the community loved their sport, and participated in local quoiting and football matches. In 1864 the men of the rows accepted a challenge from the miners of Irvine to a game of 'rounders'.

3. Annicklodge

However, Annicklodge was noted for another type of mining – shale coal. Annicklodge was the last shale-oil mine to operate in Ayrshire, and it is thought that it may have been the largest ever in the county. The coal contained a high percentage of oil, and this was extracted by means of heating, after which the oil seeped from the coal.

Sometime between 1860 and 1890 a shale-coal mine was established at the northern side of Annicklodge, the principal works being located to the east of the branch line. The mine was closed and cleared by 1896, when the Ordnance Survey drew its updated plans. No surface buildings are shown, but two former bings are depicted to either side of the branch line.

In 1881 the local geologist, Robert Linton, unearthed a large slab of shale coal at Annicklodge, measuring around 3 feet in length. Most remarkable was the imprint of a fossilized skeleton on it, measuring around 31 inches in length. The appearance of the outline puzzled the geologists of the district, including Rev Dr David Landsborough (1779-1854) of Stevenston, who made a description of it. Not waiting to find out what the experts made of it, it is reported that the 'wise women in Kilmaurs declared [it] must be a monkey!'

The company was owned by the Baird family, and in the 1881 Census there is reference to twelve shale miners living at Annicklodge rows. Another reference prior to the Oil Company being established exists from 1884, when the Midlothian Oil Company Ltd refers to 160 tons of shale from its pits being sent to Annicklodge for testing. This was carried out in 32 Young & Beilby retorts that operated at Annicklodge. In 1885 the Valuation Rolls for the parish of Irvine refer to the oil works, having a rateable value of £60. The company also owned 25 houses in the community, as well as the store, school and schoolhouse.

The newly founded Annick Lodge Oil Company Ltd was established in January 1885 and acquired the oil works, pits, branch line, workers' houses, and ancillary buildings associated with the original Annick Lodge Oil Company. With this came the goodwill of the business, mineral leases and stocks of shale piled up. It was reported in *The Scotsman* of the time that the business made crude oil and sulphate of ammonia. 'The yield per ton of shale in daily working for the last eighteen months has been 37 gallons crude oil, 21 lb sulphate of ammonia; a result which compares with the richest shales in Scotland. The cost of working the shale is under 4s. per ton.'

Although the production of oil was profitable for the first few years, the Annick Lodge Oil Company Ltd was placed in liquidation in 1889. Perhaps the quantity of oil had reduced to unprofitable amounts, for it is noted that production had fallen to around fourteen to twenty gallons per ton. This crude oil had then to be transported to a refinery in the Lothians for finishing. On 7 October 1890 the whole works were put up for sale at auction on site. Advertisements for this indicated that all of the heritable and moveable machinery and plant was for sale, as were the workmen's houses, school-house, workshops, store and office. Amongst the machinery were horizontal and other steam engines, varying in size from 5-14 inch cylinders, steam boilers, pumps, retorts, condensers, waggons, weighing machines and lead-lined vitriol and other cisterns.

With the new shale coal mine being established at the end of the nineteenth century, a new row of houses was built. This was located to the east of the long row, fronting the minor road. Each of these new dwellings was L-shaped in plan, the terrace comprising of twelve homes. Around half-way along the row, on the opposite side of the road from the houses, was a water pump, allowing the occupants to draw water. A second pump was located further to the west along the minor road, opposite the end of the western row. To the rear of the new cottages was the luxury of a garden. The west row also had garden plots, located in front of the houses and between them and the railway.

The new row of houses was in part erected to replace some of the older cottages. The dog-legged row was demolished before 1896, as was the northern half of the long row, leaving just fourteen houses standing.

4. Annicklodge

The village had its own company store, the manager in 1888 being Andrew Wilson. Also in the nineteenth century the storekeeper was John Shanks. In 1871, when investigations were being carried out across Scotland to find out if any mining companies still held their employees in 'truck' to the company store, Shanks supplied information. He stated that he had formerly worked at Annicklodge but that 'there was then no compulsion to induce the men to deal at the store. When I was at Annicklodge there were no cases of men sloping. If there had been occasion perhaps I would have stopped their books.'

One of the local employees, Thomas Smith, added, 'There was no compulsion except expectation, but I have known men spoken to by the managers or foremen and told that they were expected to go to the store. That would be five or six years ago [i.e. 1865]. It was very common. I have seen placed up in the windows of one of Messrs Merry and Cunninghame's works, bills, stating that no person would be compelled to deal at the store, and just by the side of that, a bill stating that on certain days the men could get cash advanced. I considered that an indirect mode of compelling the bulk of the miners to deal in the store whether they would or not, and the men understood it so perfectly. Some of the people live three miles from the store at Annicklodge. They have to take their articles from the store on the day of the cash advance. At one time there was a cart in use to bring goods to the people.'

In 1900 the houses at Annicklodge were owned by James MacGavin Yuille and Andrew Turnbull of Kilmarnock. The West Row had twelve houses in it, plus a cottage occupied by James Adrain, storekeeper. The Store Row had eleven houses, plus a couple more in the Store Buildings. At the southern end of the Store Row was the co-operative store itself.

5. Class at Annicklodge School

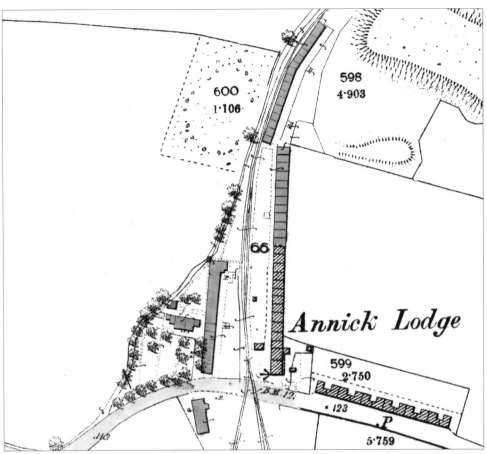

6. Annicklodge from Ordnance Survey maps (composite of 1860 and 1896 maps)
Reproduced by permission of the National Library of Scotland

At the start of the Second World War there were still twelve houses occupied at Annicklodge – forming the Brick Row. These were owned by John R. Howie, who lived in Annick Lodge itself. The occupants at that time were Peter Baird, Thomas MacLaughlan, Anthony Hamilton, John Gillespie, Henry Bennet and Hugh Kennedy (all miners); George Smith, railway worker; James Nixon, drainer; Agnes Gillespie, widow; James Downie, railway worker; and William Millings, labourer. Millburnside Cottage was occupied by Janet Gillespie, Hugh Gillespie and David Gillespie, the latter two running a garage and petrol pump nearby. There was also a school, run by Ayr County Council, and a teacher's house, occupied by James Stirrat, schoolmaster.

If one heads for Annicklodge today, then there will be little to see. The site of the old colliery is now an overgrown wood, as is where the rows facing each other across the railway siding stood. Only one building exists in the community – a cottage named Millburnside.

3

Barleith

*

The 'Railway Buildings' formed a small community at Barleith, south of Hurlford. Locally, they were better known as 'The Blocks' from the chunky double-storey buildings. They stood to the south of the Irvine valley railway line and were occupied by men who worked on the railways. The railway line from Hurlford Junction (or Galston Branch Junction as it was also known) was laid eastwards towards Galston in 1848, later to be extended through Newmilns and Darvel to link with the Caledonian lines in Lanarkshire. The railway, although it carried passengers, made most of its profits from transporting coal and ironstone.

There was in fact an older hamlet of Barleith before the Railway Buildings were erected. Just a few hundred yards to the south of the 'blocks' was a row of houses occupied by miners. These were located halfway between the Blocks and Barleith farm. Mining for coal at Barleith commenced in earnest in the early 1820s, when Robert Dunsmuir obtained the lease for minerals on Barleith farm. He already worked the nearby Skerrington pits. The pits were located on the edge of Riccarton Moss. Dunsmuir hauled the coal from Barleith to Kilmarnock, where he sold it from his depot in Portland Street. The pits were never too successful, and the miners' houses were abandoned before 1895. The Barleith Coal Company survived, but it had to close three pits in the Hurlford area due to a downturn in 1930.

To service the hundreds of trains that ran on the lines, Glasgow and South Western Railway Company constructed a workshop at Barleith, complete with a large engine shed and numerous sidings where engines and carriages were stored and serviced. Previously the company had their works in Kilmarnock itself, but there was little room for expansion, hence the decision to move to a new site, where there was nothing to hinder any possible extensions required in the future. The sheds were erected from 1876-77. The site became the principal servicing and maintenance department for most of the company's rolling stock, and at the peak time of operation, just around the First World War, the sheds handled over ninety locomotives. The business employed many men and, to provide houses for them, the railway company erected 144 houses in a self-sufficient community in 1877.

Nearest to the many sidings was a long row of 72 flats. At the front were outside staircases, leading to the upper residences. All of the community was built of brick, with different coloured bricks used to emphasise door and window openings. The roofs were of slate, and there were large chimney stacks with eight chimney pots on each.

7. Barleith Railway Buildings prior to demolition, looking west

Parallel with the first row was a second row of 70 houses. There would have been 72, to match the northern row, but the building near the centre was used as a school. It, too, was built over two floors, and facing north were three windows together, lighting up the classroom. The school provided education to the youngest children at Barleith, those over the age of nine moving on to the parish school at Hurlford, and then, perhaps, to Kilmarnock Academy. Barleith School was opened on 13 January 1879 under the headmaster, Mr D. W. MacNaughton. At the time 107 pupils enrolled, but the school building was soon to prove to be too small, so the former reading and recreation room in the flat above it was taken over, allowing room for 235 pupils. In 1887 the school received a grant of £146 15s. 0d. from the Scottish Education Department. The school was closed around 1948, the building being used for community purposes thereafter.

In 1930 the houses at Barleith were described as Block A, which had 30 houses plus two houses known as 17½ and 15½. Between houses numbered 29

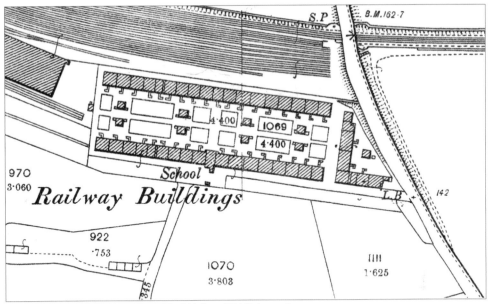

8 Barleith from 1896 Ordnance Survey map
Reproduced by permission of the National Library of Scotland

and 30 there was a Workman's Recreation Room. Block B had 28 houses, plus houses numbered 11½ and 13½. Block C had 32 houses, as did Block D. By this time the houses were owned by the London Midland and Scottish Railway Company Limited, which had taken over the Glasgow and South Western Railway Company in 1923. The houses were still occupied by their employees, and official records note their occupations as Guard, Fireman, Driver, Waggon Wright, Engine Driver, Goods Guard, Ash Filler, Shunter, Fire Dropper, Pointsman, Steam Raiser, and other railway-related titles.

Between the two rows were small areas fenced and walled off to form drying greens. There were also eight wash-houses, shared by the homes, built from the same brick as the blocks, and having a large chimney.

At the eastern end of the pair of rows were more houses, known as Block E, located in the triangle of ground between the rows and the public road. The block contained eighteen houses, plus numbers 3½, 11½ and 15½, laid out in an L-shape. Within this block one of the buildings contained a branch of the Hurlford Co-operative Association Limited. Previously, in 1914, this was a small grocery run by William Findlay Jr.

The community at Barleith had a number of facilities to allow the residents some form of leisure. There was a play park for the children, a football pitch, in addition to the worker's recreation room. To improve the education of the people who lived there, craft classes were organised for women. Ministers from Hurlford organised church services in the hall at Barleith. In 1887 Barleith Savings Bank was established, allowing the residents to save small sums of money. By January 1888 the total sum of £169 10s. 9d. had been deposited. Another savings group, the Barleith Friendly Society, was formed in 1882: it survived until the 1930s.

Although it wasn't created at the same time as the railway was laid, a station was to be established at Barleith. Originally there had been a small halt, with a wooden platform, used only by residents and workers at the site, being opened in June 1904. The halt was rebuilt, with platforms on either side of the double line that passed under the road bridge. Barleith Station opened to the general public in 1927, and was to serve Hurlford latterly, when Hurlford Station on the Dumfries line was closed to passengers on 7 March 1955. Barleith Station was closed to passengers on 6 April 1964.

Even as late as 1951 there were still 600 people living at Barleith. The *Third Statistical Account of Scotland* states that, 'in their time they were good substantial houses; but with their nearness to the sheds and the suggestion they give of the people being herded together they have never been very pleasing in appearance. With the passing of time they have grown more drab and out-of-date.'

A former resident of Barleith was Annie Mackie, born here in 1905. She became a socialist and was to enter local politics in 1956, becoming a town councillor in Kilmarnock that year. In 1971 Annie was elected as the first female provost of Kilmarnock, succeeding her husband. She died in 2003.

The railway works at Barleith were closed on 3 October 1966, and the need for workers ended. The residents were rehoused in new council houses erected in Hurlford, and in 1964 the Blocks were demolished. The site was taken over by the whisky blending company, Johnnie Walker, and huge bonded warehouses were built on the site in 1966, going into production the following year. The site was at one time to be the world's largest whisky blending facility. In 1986 Johnnie Walker was taken over by the Guinness group and the Barleith blending and bottling site was partially closed. In recent years, the remaining Johnnie Walker's warehouses were closed and these have been re-occupied by Glen Catrine whisky company and a haulage contractor.

4

Bartonholm

*

The sand dunes and low fields to the north-west of Irvine have seen folk living there for thousands of years. In 1875 a flint scraper was found by the local antiquarian, John Smith. It was no doubt one that had been used by stone-age man, but was buried under 10 feet of sand, the land hereabouts being susceptible to change. The scraper, which has a hollow side, was described by Smith in his book, *Prehistoric Man in Ayrshire*, as 'perhaps the most ancient article which has been found in Ayrshire.' In the same area, Smith also found an amber 'melon' bead, lying with a bone.

At the time of the find, it was just a few hundred yards from the village of Bartonholm, a place that no longer exists, having been cleared away around the time of the Second World War. Today, lorries filled with public refuse trundle past the site of the cottages, dumping their loads into the coup, which was established in 1969.

Bartonholm was created to provide accommodation for miners employed at the Bartonholm pits, and other collieries in the area. Mining for coal was commenced on the Garnock floods early on, and as far back as 1798 one of them had a 'fire engine' or steam-powered engine to pump water from the shafts. The lessee was William Taylor, who acquired the lands in 1797. He was something of a fly character, for by 1811 he managed to bypass the tolls on the road between the community and Irvine harbour by transferring the coal on a waggon way to barges in the Garnock and sailing them downstream to the harbour. Despite his acumen in by-passing some of the costs, and in expanding by taking over the Shewalton pits, he was to go bankrupt.

After Taylor, the coalworks at Shewalton and Bartonholm were taken over by Samson & Co., and in 1820 the village of Bartonholm was first established. It was named after a small farm that existed on the flat ground south of the Garnock. According to the census of 1821, there were 26 households in the village. At that time there were just three rows – two facing the road, and the third at right angles at the western end. The short row, the first reached on passing under the railway bridge, only had four houses originally – the middle part of the row was occupied by a smithy. This was later to be converted into two houses. At the time, the community was known as Bartonholm House.

There were a good number of mines on this flat stretch of ground, seemingly no-man's land, for a look at the parish boundaries reveals that the River Garnock had formerly described a large meander on the moor, both Stevenston and Kilwinning parishes extending south over the present course of the river. The Mid Pit was located immediately north of the rows, the Longford Pit within the former loop of the Garnock. The Engine Pit was located next to Deepdraught cottage. Two other old pits were located near to Bartonholm and Snodgrass farms, and a third behind the rows.

The 13th Earl of Eglinton had spotted the financial gains to be made from coal, and in 1854 he re-established the mines at Bartonholm. By 1874 the village had a population of 379. Of this number, Father Thomas Keane of Irvine reckoned that there were 70 Roman Catholics in 1870. At a later date, the coal works and houses here were acquired by the expanding William Baird & Company.

By 1895 there were five rows in total in the village of Bartonholm, four parallel and one positioned at right angles to the rest. The village was reached from Sandy Road by means of a track that passed through the railway bridge. Immediately on the other side was the first, shortest, row, with six houses in it. Just beyond an opening was a second row, comprising fourteen houses. This row faced directly onto the roadway that led to Bartonholm Number 1 Coal Pit.

At the end of this second row, striking back at right angles to it, was another row, comprising of eleven houses; this was known as the Single Row. Within the L-

9. Bartonholm – one of the back rows

shape formed by these rows was another, parallel with the first two, and containing sixteen homes. Parallel with this row, and backing onto the pit bing, was the fifth row, the largest of the five, with nineteen houses in a single terrace.

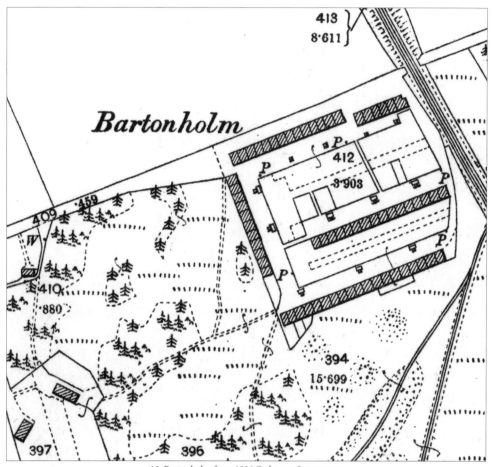

10. Bartonholm from 1896 Ordnance Survey map
Reproduced by permission of the National Library of Scotland

There were five pumps in the community from where water could be drawn, supplied from 1884 by mains water from the reservoir at Dykehead in Dalry parish. Within the square formed by the rows were a number of allotments. The village had its own store, from where provisions could be purchased. This was located in what was known as Number 1 and 2 of the Double Row, the first building reached on passing through the railway bridge, in what had been the old smithy.

Just west of Bartonholm rows were the three cottages of Deepdraught, thought to have been named from a deep drainage channel that passed nearby, or else from the deep draught available to boats in the Garnock, when it flowed past this location. The cottages appear on an Eglinton estate plan of 1820 and were originally single-storey buildings of two apartments, white-washed externally.

Bartonholm folk, though domiciled in Irvine parish, seem to have had more of an affinity with Kilwinning. Indeed, the Kilwinning war memorial from World War 1 lists eleven men from Bartonholm on its roll of honour. These are Robert Aitken, James Cairns, John Campbell, George Frew, William Mulholland, Frank Mullin, Henry Orr, John Smith, William Timpany, James Walker and David Young. As with many men at the time, they left their families behind in their miners' houses to fight in Europe, never to return.

Most of the houses at Bartonholm had two apartments, although there were a few with three rooms. In 1914, when James Brown visited the village, he noted that 'the rooms are very small, and the houses are of a poor type. They are built of stone, but many of them are very damp. Most of them are dingy and depressing.'

Around the houses were a number of pathways, described as being unpaved and often in a bad state. There were ash pits and wash-houses and one dry-closet for every eight families. Between 1895 and 1908 the small wash-houses were replaced with new, larger facilities, two to each row. Occupants of the houses paid six shillings and five-pence per month. In 1898 there was a small store at Bartonholm, operated by William Tyre.

The village had a population of 352 in 1914. At the time there were 57 families resident there, all tenants of William Baird Ltd, the largest colliers and iron manufacturers in Ayrshire.

Although accommodation at Bartonholm was tough, the residents still had time to enjoy themselves. The community was able to support its own football team, known as Bartonholm United. This team played in the 1920s, in season 1926-27 being successful enough to win five cups – Ayrshire Cup, Irvine and District Cup, MacAndrew Cup, Baird's Cup and the League Cup.

One footballer who doesn't seem to have played for Bartonholm United was Ronald Orr, born in the village on 6 August 1876. He certainly played for Kilwinning Eglinton, followed by Glossop North End and St Mirren. Just before his 21st birthday he signed for Newcastle United, playing as an inside-forward.

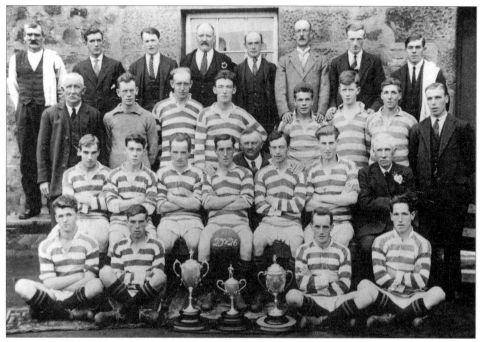

11. Bartonholm United Football Club, 1926

A stocky five foot five lad, Orr was a massive success at Newcastle, playing 180 games and scoring 69 goals. He assisted the team to win the 1905 and 1908 league championship.

In April 1908 Orr signed for Liverpool Football Club, and in his first game for the team scored the club's only goal against Aston Villa, though the team were beaten five-one. In season 1908-09 Orr was Liverpool's top scorer, with twenty nets to his credit. In all, he played for Liverpool 112 times, before deciding to return to Scotland in 1912. He then signed for Raith Rovers and finished his career at South Shields.

Ronald Orr played for Scotland on four occasions – and his only international goal came in May 1902 when he scored against England in a 2-2 draw. Ronald retired from football, living at Kilwinning, where he died on 21 March 1924.

Football was not the only sporting success to spring from Bartonholm – there were three significant golfers who lived there. Hamilton MacInally won the Scottish Amateur Championship in 1937, the first of three times. Later winners were James Walker and Jack Cannon.

Death by accident was something that small communities dreaded. On 4 June 1911 Alexander Haswell was swimming in the River Garnock when he got into difficulties. His uncle, Robert Haswell, jumped in to assist, but he too began to struggle in the attempt to save Alexander's life. To assist, William MacLachlan jumped in, and he was able to pull Robert Haswell to safety. Unfortunately, Alexander Haswell was drowned. Later that year, Robert and William, who were miners from Bartonholm, were honoured at a meeting in the Eglinton Ironworks Institute, when they were presented with certificates from the Royal Humane Trust. William MacLachlan received £10 from the Carnegie Hero Fund Trustees, Robert Haswell receiving £5.

Bartonholm pit was flooded in 1833 when water from the River Garnock burst into the mine and filled the shafts. The pit was abandoned and did not reopen until 1853. By this time the great meander of the Garnock had been removed, a cutting made at the neck, to shorten the river. Once things in the river had settled, the pit was pumped dry, and it commenced working again. Bartonholm became more populous, with the erection of two more rows of houses.

An explosion took place in Bartonholm Pit in October 1871, resulting in the deaths of four miners. Nine others were seriously injured. Reports in the papers of the time reckoned that some of the nine seriously injured men were not expected to recover. Apparently, the inspector failed to descend into the pit at the proper time to ascertain the state of working. When he did enter the pit, he allowed a number of men with naked lamps to accompany him, resulting in the explosion.

On Wednesday 11 August 1909 another explosion took place in the pit, at a point known as the Number 7 Drift. A fireman named Hugh Coulter, living at Bartonholm, was doing his rounds late on that evening when he walked into an accumulation of gas, resulting in the explosion. Coulter was burned about the face, arms and hands. Thomas Kennedy, of High Street, Irvine, was also burned in the incident. Two others escaped unhurt. At the time of the accident there were 27 miners at work below ground. James MacNeil was killed in the pit on 9 September 1919.

Bartonholm Pit closed in 1928, and soon the rows at Bartonholm were being abandoned. By 1938 eight of the houses in the back row had been un-roofed, and many other houses were empty. Nobel's acquired the ground, as part of an expanding facility based at Ardeer, and the residents moved out. By

1939, all of the houses were empty, apart from the Deepdraught House, owned by Nobel's but leased to Archibald Rae. Many of the residents moved to Dirrans in Kilwinning, a new council housing scheme. The new houses in Kilwinning were far superior in quality, and the residents were keen to enjoy the comforts of running water and toilets inside the houses, not to mention electric lighting and power for cooking. Others moved to houses at Girdle Toll, north-east of Irvine, living alongside neighbours from other former mining communities.

5

Benquhat

★

There's something about Benquhat that seems to attract descendants of villagers back to the remote moor where the rows of houses once stood. It is perhaps the lonely war memorial that does this, a solitary obelisk perched on the slopes of Benquhat Hill itself, overlooking a wide and bleak expanse of countryside, covered with gorse and heather, high above the Doon valley. Thus it was in November 2014 that Diana May, her husband and son came on a pilgrimage to the memorial, to pay her respects to her great uncles, whose names are chiselled into the stone. Her great grandmother, Agnes Wilson, had unveiled the monument in 1921. She wasn't the first person to return to the home of her ancestors, for annually the lonely roadway from Dalmellington is walked by others, keen to see the wild place that moulded their characters.

There must have been an old shepherd's cottage or croft around this area known as Benquhat that existed in the seventeenth century. It was here that Roger Dun (1659-1689) lived, the son of the farmer, James Dun. Roger and his brothers, Allan and Andrew, were to become supporters of the National Covenant. On one occasion they attended a conventicle at Craignew in Carsphairn parish but, on their return home, the soldiers apprehended the two brothers. They were never to be seen again. Roger managed to escape and had to spend much of his time in hiding, often in secluded Dunaskin Glen. On one occasion he met the soldiers searching for him, but as they didn't know what he looked like, he was able to act as though he was someone else, and assisted them in their search! Dun made a number of other escapes, the most notable being at Caldons in Glen Trool. When a prayer meeting was attacked by the dragoons, Dun managed to make his way to Loch Trool, where he submerged himself in the water. Although Dun survived the 'killing times' of the Covenanting period, he was actually shot dead by someone who was intent on killing another. This was at the time of Carsphairn Fair, and his body lies in the kirkyard at Carsphairn, where a small headstone marks his grave.

In 1847 a new village was created on the southern slopes of Benquhat Hill by the Dalmellington Iron Company. The village was located on remote moorland, bare of trees, and stood over 1,000 feet above sea level. The name given to the village, Benquhat, came from the hill below which it was located, but the locals preferred the simpler spelling of 'Benwhat'. Though this variant appeared on the Ordnance Survey Six Inch map of 1860, in general the spelling Benquhat was insisted upon by the authorities.

At first only one row was built, with 34 single-apartment houses, constructed from the handmade Dunaskin brick. This row was named the Laight Row, after the castle ruins which existed lower down the glen. To the east of the row a school and store were built, also by the Dalmellington Iron Company, but stone from the Dunaskin Quarry was used in their construction.

Sometime between 1870 and 1874 a further four rows of 98 houses were erected, located behind the Laight Row and contouring along the hillside. Behind Laight Row was the Stone Row, of twenty houses. East of this was the Store Row (of twenty houses), so-called because it stood behind the Co-op. Next again was the Post Office Row with thirty houses, one of which contained the small post office. The last row of 28 houses was called the Heath Row, so-called because it overlooked the remote moor. The Stone Row was built of Dunaskin stone, the other three rows of Dunaskin bricks. The Store Row was sometimes known as the Middle or Brick Row, perhaps implying that the four rows were not erected simultaneously, with the Stone Row erected first, the Heath Row last. On the south side of the rows were the gardens.

The houses at Benquhat were let for 2s. 3d. per week for a room and kitchen in 1875. At that time there were no closets or ash pits in the community, but the water supply appears to have been fairly good.

Benquhat, like many other mining communities of the time, attracted folk from all over Scotland and beyond, all in search of work, and a better lifestyle than they hitherto enjoyed. Thus, Benquhat was to become home to exiles from Ireland, the Highlands, Cornwall, Wanlockhead, Cumbria, Lincolnshire, Wigtownshire, Argyll, Renfrewshire, and many other locations. In most cases, the local industry or agriculture had taken a turn for the worse, resulting in hundreds being laid off. Such was the case in the Highlands, where folk were still being removed from the land, Cumbria, where the lead mines were in decline, Cornwall, where a similar tale existed in the tin mines, and Ireland, where the potato famine and agricultural decline were still having a severe effect on the population.

The population of Benquhat in 1881 had risen to 772 people, housed in 131 dwellings. This was probably the largest it ever reached, for by 1891 it had dropped to 523. Gradually, as the mines closed on the high moors, families were keen to move out of the community, there being twenty empty houses in 1914. By 1951 the population had dropped to 460.

As the years passed, basic facilities were provided at Benquhat. A water pipe was laid across the back of the houses, and residents were allowed to ask blacksmiths to connect cast iron pipes to the water main and run the water into their homes. Prior to this, water had to be obtained from pumps, of which two existed per row. Alternatively, water from springs and wells could be used, and Campbell's Spoot and Squibbie's Well were such sources.

Electricity didn't arrive to Benquhat until 1933. A power station had been constructed at Waterside in 1917-18 by the iron company for use in the local pits, brickworks and workshops. As surplus power was generated, cables were strung across the moor to the village, and residents had the opportunity of connecting to them.

At Benquhat the Dalmellington Iron Company erected a school sometime in the early 1870s, located south of the Post Office Row, at the top of the Store Brae. Built of Dunaskin stone, the school had three classrooms. At the time its roll was around 200, but only about 140 pupils attended. In 1879 the roll was 140, taught by two assistants and one pupil teacher. One classroom was divided by a glass screen which was removable. This was often done to allow various functions to take place, from weddings to tea dances. Pupils of primary age were taught here - they had to travel to Dalmellington for secondary education.

The school proved to be too small for the population, and in 1926 a new school was erected at the west end of the village, between the rows and the bing of Corbie Craigs Number 4 ironstone pit. In addition to the usual classrooms, the school had a new domestic science room, where sewing and cooking was taught, a gymnasium and a woodwork room. A unique feature was the introduction of water closets, the only ones that ever existed in the village. In 1930 the roll was around 120 pupils, dropping to 80 by 1950. Headmasters at Benquhat included Alex MacArthur, appointed in 1909. As the village was cleared, the school roll plummeted. When it was finally closed in 1951 there were only three pupils still attending – Doreen Atkinson, Jean MacHattie and Maureen Wilson. The last teacher, Mrs Paterson, only worked there for a few months.

The store at Benquhat was operated by the Dalmellington Iron Company. A railway siding was laid to its side, which allowed pugs to arrive with provisions. The store had two halves, one which sold groceries and general supplies. The other sold beer, but not spirits, which was the iron company's decision. Among the storemasters who ran the shop was John Talman.

A number of women, often widows, ran small shops from their homes. Among those which existed at times were Maggie Fisher's – she sold 'cough cakes' and other sweets; Mrs Dick had a post office which also sold confectionery and mineral waters; Mrs Moffat sold cigarettes and Granny Hainey sold a variety of sweets, mostly homemade. George Park, who spoke at Benquhat Re-union in 1967 recalled that he would 'watch her make her famous stalks and candy – a pennyworth lasted Saturday and Sunday. She also made Boston cream and Burdock Stout which went down well in the hot summer days we had then.'

12. Benquhat – the old school (right) and the store (left)

There was no church established at Benquhat, but the minister, Rev George Hendrie from Dalmellington, travelled up the hill every fortnight to hold Sunday evening services, held in the former school building. In 1917 a joint communion service was initiated, run by the parish church and the United Free Church. In addition to formal services, there were fortnightly 'kitchen meetings'.

The workmen banded together to form societies which were instrumental in improving conditions for their members. Among those formed in the nineteenth century were the Benquhat and Lethanhill Aboveground

Workmen's Society, Benquhat and Lethanhill Underground Workmen's Society, Dunaskin and Doon Aboveground Society, and the Jellieston and Drumgrange Friendly Society. For the men, two cottages at the end of the Laight Row were converted into a Miners' Institute, or reading room, where many of the meetings were held. Boys aged fourteen or over, if they were in work, could join. Among the games and pastimes on offer were cards, dominoes, billiards, skittles, snooker, summer ice and carpet bowls. There was a small library with books supplied from Dalmellington, in addition to daily newspapers. To be a member, the men had four pence per month deducted from their wages.

The Hope of Benwhat Tent of the International Order of Rechabites was founded on 7 July 1906 and the juvenile branch, the Ark of Safety Juvenile Tent, was established in 1907. In 1913 there were 86 state members of the Hope Tent, plus 80 order members and 43 juvenile members.

The Benquhat Silver Band was founded either in 1869 or 1871 depending on which source is used. It may even have existed in 1867. Certainly, it was up and running by the latter date, entertaining the villagers and performing at every main social function in the community, from Sunday School trips to weddings. The band survived the demise of the village, latterly merging with an Ayr band to form the Ayr-Benwhat Silver Band. In 1971 the band celebrated its centenary, at which long-standing conductor, James Armour, was honoured for his fifty years as bandmaster, most of which was with Benquhat.

Little changed at Benquhat from the Victorian era until the rows were eventually cleared after the Second World War. The post office was operated by Mrs Jane Dick for over thirty years until she retired. It was then taken over by Mrs MacHattie, who was born at Burnhead farm nearby and who married Andrew MacHattie, son of Adam MacHattie who lived at 1/2 Corbie Craigs, two houses converted into one. Mrs MacHattie closed the post office in 1951. In the late 1930s work had commenced on rehousing the residents of the rows at Bellsbank and Dalmellington, but this scheme was temporarily abandoned following the outbreak of war.

The Benquhat war memorial was unveiled on 31 July 1921. The memorial was sculpted by James Vallance of Prestwick from Kemnay granite and it stands 13 feet 6 inches tall. It was erected on the slopes of Benquhat itself, so that the memorial was visible on the horizon from the village. On it are the names of 22 residents who set off to serve in the First World War but never returned.

As with most miners' rows, the sport of football was followed with considerable seriousness. A football pitch was created on the old hearth of Corbie Craigs Number 5 pit, and here Benwhat Heatherbell played in their light blue tops. They were to win the Ayrshire Junior Challenge Cup in season 1899-1900. The club temporarily folded during the Great War. When the Ayr and District League folded in 1926 the club joined the South Ayrshire League. In 1928 they achieved one of their greatest goal records, beating Lugar Boswell Thistle 9-2 at home. They did not survive much longer, folding in the 1930-31 season. In that year they only played five games, winning two and drawing one. One of their defeats was 8-0 at Cumnock Juniors. At the January 1931 meeting of the club it was announced that it was to fold.

13. Benquhat Heatherbell Football Club, 1895

Another keen association was the Doon Harriers, established in 1927 as a cross-country running and athletics club. The members took part in many events across the county, their strength in cross-country running being developed with running across the moors and hillsides.

About half a mile to the south of Benquhat was a row of ten single-apartment houses known as Corbie Craigs. This was officially classed as a separate village, but its proximity to Benquhat and the fact that the residents shared all the facilities of the larger village, meant that most residents regarded themselves as being part of the same community. Corbie Craigs dates from the

1850s. The houses were built for the workers who were employed in the operation of the railway incline from Waterside up to the Corbie Craigs pits. This line was erected at the same time as the houses. each house had one main room, of 20 feet by 12 feet, plus a small scullery of 9 feet by 8 feet, which projected to the rear, or north. On the south side of the row were the tenants' gardens.

When the incline was closed in 1866 it became a pathway commonly used by Corbie Craigs and Benquhat residents. The community at Corbie Craigs was probably intended to be larger, but the Dalmellington Iron Company decided to erect the village of Benquhat instead. It had few facilities, the water obtained from nearby burns, sanitation limited to dry closets located in wooden huts. The rent was 1s. 9d. per week. Though there were only ten houses, the 'village' had a population of around 50 people. Latterly houses numbered one and two were joined to create one unit.

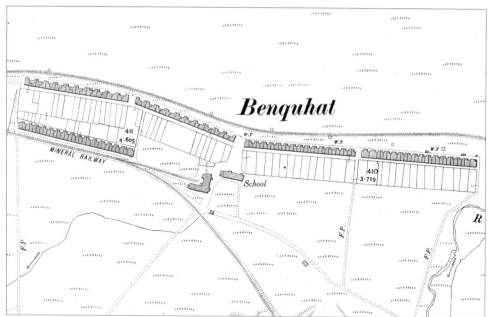

14. Benquhat from 1909 Ordnance Survey Map
Reproduced by permission of the National Library of Scotland

When the coal mines were nationalised in 1947, Benquhat became the property of the National Coal Board. They were keen to off-load many older properties, and the fact that the houses did not meet modern standards meant that they were subject to the slum clearances. Ayr County Council built new houses in Dalmellington, and also established a new community on the outskirts of the village, named Bellsbank. Most of the Benquhat residents were evacuated in 1951, when 460 residents were to make the journey down from the hill and into the valley below. The last family to move out of Corbie Craigs was Mr and Mrs Joseph Thomson, he being a miner. At Benquhat the last resident was John Reilly. He was such a noted resident that he was nicknamed the 'Provost of Benquhat'. The village was demolished, but the foundations of many of the buildings can still be made out on the ground.

The Benquhat name survived, however, for Benquhat Burns Club continued to hold Burns' Suppers long after the village had gone. The club was founded in 1941, and joined the Burns Federation in 1944. It had its roots as part of the Discussion Club, which originally met in the school. When the village was abandoned, the club moved to Dalmellington's church hall, which meant that the suppers were dry, something of a novelty among traditional Burns' Suppers. The club usually had 160 attending the suppers, but by 1970, twenty or so years after the village was demolished, there were still fifty folk attending. Another group with Benquhat connections was the annual Benquhat Re-union, which was instituted in 1965, inviting speakers such as John P. Kennedy, manager of Minnivey Colliery.

In 2015 a memorial stone was erected at the site of the village by three men, William McCluskie, William Rowan and Scott Filson. The granite boulder was sculpted by Kevin Roberts and bears the legend *Benwhat Village 1860-1952 Erected by S. Filson, W. McCluskie, W. Rowan.*

6

Beoch

*

The Kyle Forest is an extensive commercial plantation of Sitka spruce, larch and other pine trees, extending south-west from Cumnock towards Dalmellington. The land it covers is high moorland, originally acres of moss and heather, with low hills rising out of the vast expanse. The only real summit is Ben Beoch, a rocky eminence, the cliffs of which are formed of basalt rocks.

The Beoch Lane is the name of a watercourse that drains the moss north-east of Ben Beoch, the term 'lane' being an old Scots word for a stream or river, more common in Galloway than in this part of Ayrshire. About one mile from the source of the lane lay the community of Beoch, a single row of houses a few hundred yards from the stream. Today, the site of the village is lost in the forest, only the little steading of Upper Beoch surviving.

The Nithsdale Iron Company was formed in 1845 to work the iron ore and coal seams around New Cumnock. An ironworks was erected at Connelburn, and workers' houses were built for the benefit of the employees. One of the rows built by this company was Beoch.

The houses of Beoch were different to most mining rows in that they were erected back to back. The row had fourteen houses on one side, with a further fourteen butted immediately on the rear. Around the houses was a rough path, and the only pedestrian access was by way of a track from Upper Beoch farm, and from there across the hill via old ironstone tramways to Waterhead in Nithsdale. Between the houses and the Beoch Lane was a mineral railway, off which was a short siding, terminating at the eastern end of the cottages, used to collect and return the mineworkers. A second siding to the west of the row enclosed the row in the gusset of the two lines.

Beoch was quite different also, in that the four end houses were double-storey in height. Built of stone, these had two houses facing one way, and two the other. Dominant on the moor, their extra height meant that they looked a bit like bookends. In the later 1800s there was a store at Beoch, run by the coal company. It was a time when the truck system was popular, and the miners were paid in vouchers, redeemable at the company store. An early incident took place at Beoch when a miner, Joseph Wadsworth, was issued with a voucher for four shillings. He added a one in front of the four, and obtained fourteen shillings' worth of goods from the store. His fraud was detected, however, and he was sentenced to four months in Ayr jail.

The supply of water may have originally come from the adjacent stream, but later a well was sunk to the immediate west of the row. A footpath from the row to the well was well-worn. At a later date the water was piped from the well to a water tank that was located at the western end of the row. In front of the houses most cottages had a barrel, in which water from the roof was gathered.

The remote location of Beoch was troublesome for the residents, who found themselves very isolated from the rest of New Cumnock parish. The height above sea level resulted in worse weather than the rest of Ayrshire, an Ordnance Survey bench mark on the row being 893 feet above sea level.

Around 1900 the old railway lines were no longer required, so the rails were lifted, and the old track-bed formed a roadway that could be used by the residents to access the outside world. In 1894 there had been a proposal to lay

15. Beoch – looking north east

a passenger railway line from Cumnock, up through the Glaisnock valley to Nithsdale, and thence via Beoch to Dalmellington. Beoch, the little row of houses, was to have its own station! The line, of course, came to nought.

Around 1875 a timber school building was erected at Beoch. This was located closer to the old railway gusset. A small building, it was T-shaped in plan. Inside it had two 'classrooms', separated by a curtain. The school was known as Beochside Public School, operated by New Cumnock School Board, but was usually referred to as the Beoch School. In 1914 Miss Eaglesham was the schoolmistress, Mrs Park holding the post in 1929. The teachers taught a fair-sized roll, the highest being 58, dropping to 38 in 1926.

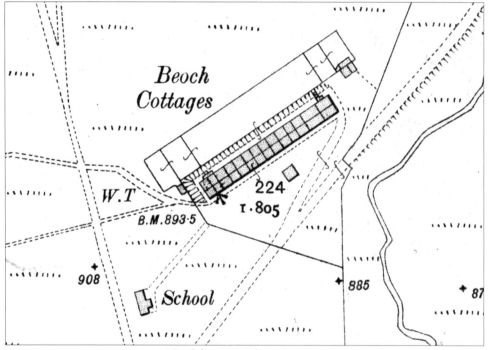

16. Beoch from 1909 Ordnance Survey map
Reproduced by permission of the National Library of Scotland

The school soon proved to be unsuitable for the children, and proposals were made in 1926 for new premises. This was agreed to in 1928. This was also to be a timber building, faced of lapping weather boards and roofed with red slates. It had a brick-built toilet block, which was to survive longer than the village of Beoch itself, being used for many years as a store by the local farmer. Within the school were two classrooms, each holding three year groups.

As with most mining communities, the church was keen to serve the residents. Beoch Sunday School was attended by most of the children, and ran for many years. At Christmas, Jean Walker of Camlarg House, the local landowner, would supply the village with a Christmas tree from the grounds, plus £2 in cash, six Bibles, six books, sweets and an orange for every child. At the summer picnic, similar gifts were bestowed.

17. Beoch – another view looking north-east along the row

Although Beoch was a small community, there was a local branch of the Order of Rechabites aimed at children. The Rowantree Juvenile Tent was established at Beoch in 1911, associated with the adult tent at Dalmellington.

Most of the men at Beoch worked in the local mines that littered the moor. The oldest mine, the Beoch Number 1 Colliery, was sunk in 1850 by the Nithsdale Iron Company. This was to supply coal for use in the iron works that were located at Bank, lower down Nithsdale near New Cumnock. The company was financed by English businessmen. Coal from Beoch was transported to the Bank furnaces by a standard-gauge railway, the waggons hauled by horses, assisted by steam-powered rope inclines.

In 1870 the Nithsdale Iron Company, which had failed, was taken over by the Dalmellington Iron Company. They expanded work on the moor at Beoch, sinking Beoch Number 2. This was the handiest colliery for the residents, which was located a few hundred yards to the west of the community. Perched about 1,000 feet above sea level, Beoch Number 2 operated until 1912. In 1924 a new Beoch Number 2 was sunk (the original mine becoming known as Number 2A), and this produced coal until 1950. Beoch Number 3 was sunk in 1910 and operated until 1937. Beoch 4A was sunk in 1924 but this was not a success and was closed the following year. A new Number 4 was sunk in 1936, though at the time it bore the name Benbain Number 5. It was renamed Beoch Number 4 in 1938. Being 1,068 feet above sea level, the mine had the distinction of being the highest coal mine in Scotland. The underground workings associated with Beoch numbers 2, 3 and 4 were connected with each other. The Beoch pits eventually closed in 1968.

The Auldnaw mine was another pit where the residents of Beoch found employment. This pit was famed for its smithy coal, much in demand for forges in smithies all over southern Scotland. Old residents often recalled the number of horses and carts that made their way to Auldnaw from Galloway to collect a load of this coal. Apparently, the farmers who owned the carts had an agreement with the smiths that they would collect a load of coal at their own expense from the pit and transport it back to their local smithy.

Death in the mines was never far away, even in a small community like Beoch. In 1853 there was a small explosion in the pit when John O'Neil's oil cap-lamp ignited the methane gas that had accumulated. On 13 July 1917 Walter Riggans was killed in Beoch Mine at the age of eighteen years. He lived in the row at Beoch. James Wallace was accidentally killed at North Beoch on 2 November 1901 at the age of 61 years. He is buried in Dalmellington cemetery.

Beoch was occupied for around one hundred years. By the 1930s the little houses were well-past their lifespan, and the residents were desperate to leave. All of those who remained were eventually re-housed in Dalmellington from 1937-38, and Beoch ceased to exist as the Second World War broke out.

7

Borestone

★

The village of Borestone was located on the south side of the road from Dalry to Kilbirnie. Heading north from Dalry, the first row one came to had eight houses in it, facing directly onto the public road. Centrally placed in front of the row was a wash-house, shared by all of the eight families. Immediately following the first row was a second row of homes, again facing directly onto the main road. This was longer, there being eighteen houses in it.

After the second row was a gap, where a minor road passed to the right, heading past Pitcon House and a mine to cross the Rye at a ford and arriving at Kersland. Just beyond the roadway was a third row of houses facing the main road. This had seven houses in it, as well as an eighth property at the north-eastern end, occupied by a public house. The inn at Borestone was a larger building than the rest, with a small area of garden to the front, and an enclosed yard to the rear.

A fourth row of houses at Borestone faced onto the main road. These were perhaps the oldest houses in the community, and they appear to have been built of various sizes, whereas most of the other houses were fairly regular in size. This row had nine houses in it. The last property was almost triangular, sandwiched between the roadway and Burnside Bridge. One of the rows at Borestone was known as MacDonald's Row. Within it was a store, where residents made their purchases, and a community hall.

Across the Pitcon, or Mains Burn from the main community of Borestone was a small row of four houses, named Burnside. This was located at right angles to the public road, sandwiched in a plot of land between the Pitcon Burn and the branch line serving some of the numerous pits and mines south-west of Kilbirnie. In one of the gardens was a well, from where the residents drew their water.

The longest row of houses at Borestone was located immediately behind the first two rows and ran parallel to it. The gap between the houses was narrow. This row originally had twenty houses in it, but at the south-western end one of the cottages was converted into a school room. The school at Borestone had been established by Merry & Cunninghame a number of years prior to the Education Act of 1872, when it transferred to Dalry School Board. At the north-eastern end of the back row was a larger building, occupied by a smithy.

In the triangle of land between the road to the Garnock ford and the Pitcon Burn, were three more rows of homes, tightly packed together. Facing the road were two rows, the first, nearest the junction, having eight houses in it. The second row also had eight houses in it.

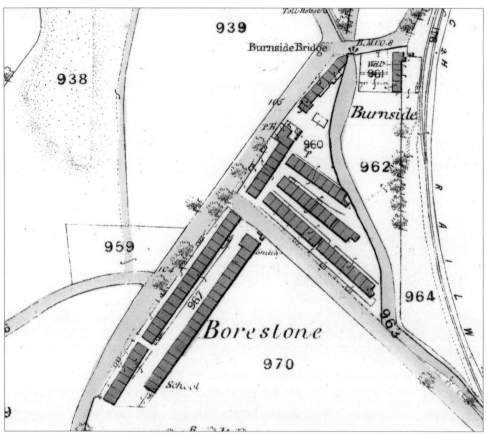

18. Borestone from 1858 Ordnance Survey map
Reproduced by permission of the National Library of Scotland

Behind these two rows was another row, with ten houses, though there appears to have been a narrow pend through one end of the row, aligned with the gap in the two rows in front. At the back of the middle row was the back row, containing eight houses.

Writing in *Ayrshire Streams* in 1850, William Wyllie discussed some of the problems experienced in the rows by the occupants, many of whom had come from Ireland in search of work:

Too often has the presence of the people from the sister isle acted prejudicially on the native population. They have eaten up our public charities, crowded the calendar of crime to fill our prisons and destroyed the character of Scottish villages. Shadows have darkened into sullen gloomy clouds. Subsisting on the coarsest diet and paucity of apparel, the Irish offer their labour at a lower rate than the Scot. … Filth fills the atmosphere with a miasma sufficient to pollute the breezes from the hills. Heaps of ashes and pools of water stagnate at the doors where half-clad, stunted children play around.

With the Irish Catholic population being fairly strong locally, many of the protestant miners at Borestone were involved in a thriving flute band.

The Catholic community had its own football team, which kept to stereotype by being named Borestone Celtic F. C. Naturally, all of the players were usually from the Catholic families, but John MacLean often played for them. His background was Church of England. To outsiders, Borestone Celtic was often described as 'ten Papes and wee Johnnie MacLean'.

The school at Borestone was run for Roman Catholic children, originally meeting in a larger house. One of the head teachers at the start of the twentieth century was Peter Daly, whose ability was not particularly high. He walked with a limp and used a stick. When he asked a pupil to read, and they became stuck at a difficult word, if it was one that he didn't know himself, he would announce, 'That's a big town in Ireland. You or I will never be there, so just pass it by'.

It was also at the school at Borestone that the story of Mary MacCann is said to have occurred. She arrived at school one day and her body odour was rather repugnant. The teacher sent her home to get a wash, but her mother brought her back next day and shouted at the teacher, 'Oor Mary's nae rose. Ye're peyed tae teach her, no' smell her!'

In *Mining Lays, Tales and Folk-Lore*, written in 1916 by Arthur Wilson of Dalry, but published in Australia, to where he had emigrated, there is an amusing tale about a couple of the MacDonald's Row residents. Paddy Coleman and Dennis Casey were brought up in a village in Ireland near to Wexford. They were very close friends, being seen everywhere together. During the potato famine, both men emigrated to Scotland, finding work at the mines near Dalry. They both got houses in Borestone. Unknown to each other, both had a liking for an Irish lass, Nora Kelly. Casey wooed her, unbeknown to Coleman, and they were married in June 1876. Coleman was never married, and had a reputation of blowing his monthly pay on alcohol. Some said this was as a result of some Irish lass refusing to leave the Emerald Isle and join him in Ayrshire. At length, in March 1881, Casey was killed in Greenbank Pit by a fall of blaze from the roof. Coleman made his way to Nora Casey's house in MacDonald's Row, where she was busy washing clothes in a tub, and her two children, Mickey and Aileen, were blowing bubbles through their father's clay pipe. 'Good morning, Widow Casey, is it washing ye're doing?' Coleman blurted out. 'Sure, can't we see that it's washing I'm doing, and none of yer imperence to me, Paddy Coleman. I'm no' a widow, I'm a ----.' 'You are, Nora – you are a widow. They're bringing Dinny home now. God forgive me, Nora, for being so brutal-like; I didn't mean to offend ye, I'm real sorry for Dinny – he was my best friend – I'm sorry for you, and the childer, Nora. Shure I'll marry ye the moment you're ready, and I'll drink no more. Will ye, will – ?' The outcome of the proposal is not recorded in Wilson's Tales!

Another Borestone character was James Ewing. He was born in Argyll in 1859 and came to Ayrshire looking for work. He settled in Dalry in the early 1880s, finding accommodation in the model lodging house. He was to find a local wife and they set up home in MacDonald's Row at Borestone. Locally Ewing was known as the Dodger, which was probably descriptive of his work ethic. However, he was no slouch when it came to exercise. According to the *Ardrossan & Saltcoats Herald* of 1887 he left Dalry Cross one Monday morning with the intention of walking to London and back, pushing a wheelbarrow all of the way. He told the large crowd of well-wishers that he would be back in 42 days. The object of the exercise was to raise money for himself and his wife, he having been out of work for some time. Ewing reached London in fifteen days, whereupon he turned around and started for home. According to the *Herald*: 'A great stir was caused in Dalry on Saturday evening, the occasion being the return of James Ewing, who had walked to London and back in the record time of 33 days. He was met by a large crowd of several thousands, and, proceeded by a brass band, was marched to the Public Hall, where a concert on behalf of Ewing and his family was held. The proceeds, after expenses had been met, were

£13 9s. 3d.' Seven months later Ewing announced that he was going to walk to the summit of Ben Nevis and back, proposing to carry out the 'sponsored walk' in eighteen days. He took just eight to walk to Ben Nevis, scale the mountain and descend to Fort William.

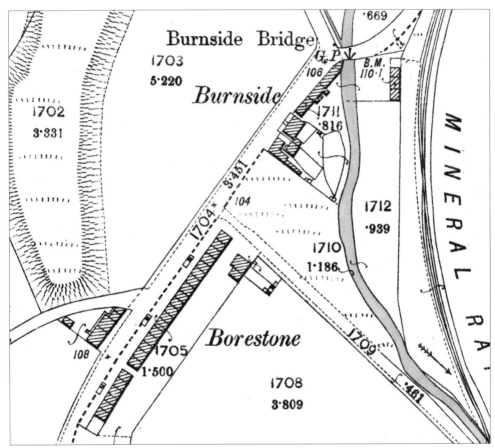

19. Borestone from 1897 Ordnance Survey map
Reproduced by permission of the National Library of Scotland

By 1939 most of Borestone had been cleared away. At that time there were still a few houses occupied, and there was one shop, occupied by David Boyd. At Burnside there was only one of the six houses still occupied, by Malcolm MacManus, a labourer. Today, there are just a couple of houses in the community, plus a car repair business. By the side of the main road, opposite Swinlees Road, one can see the remains of some of the houses, the bricked-up windows and doors of former homes surviving in a wall.

8

Burnbrae

★

It is said that a photographic competition held in Glasgow in 1901 had an entry which depicted a village called Burnbrae. It was taken from the pathway that led from the school down to the village, with the Enterkine Viaduct and the woods of Enterkine House in the background. The judges deemed it to be the best entry, and it brought some attention of the community, a place which to Glaswegians appeared to have survived from a time long forgotten. Postcard manufacturers produced similar views thereafter, and even a china manufacturer, Grafton, included the scene on some of its tea-sets.

The village was located on the road from Annbank to Gadgirth Bridge near to the farm of Crawfordston. A couple of modern cottages are located by the side of the road, their gardens occupying the ground between the roadway and the wooded burn-side. These cottages are built on the site of the ancient clachan of Burnbrae, a village that predates Annbank and Mossblown by many years.

In the 1850s Burnbrae comprised of fifteen cottages, all of which were thatched. These were arranged in three rows by the roadside. The walls were constructed of stones held together with compressed clay, covered over with a whitewash.

One of the rows faced directly onto the roadway. This had five irregularly-sized houses in it. At the southern end stood the ruins of what may have been a sixth house, though it must have been rather small. The building may have been used for some other purpose. The cottage at the northern end of the row faced onto the main road, its front doorway having a window to either side. A tiny window on the gable faced up the brae. The four other cottages in this row faced east, towards the back row, each having a small window facing the main road. This row was thatched.

Immediately behind this row, running parallel with it, was a second row, again containing five homes. The cottages were not equal in size and, unlike most rows, the facades were not even built in line, with projections to the front and rear, no doubt additions to the homes. Again, the houses had thatched roofs. By 1895 there were a number of small buildings added to the south of the rows, perhaps containing wash-houses and other facilities.

The third row at Burnbrae lay further south, at right angles to the road. Again there were five houses in this row, all of various sizes. This row had gardens to the south of it.

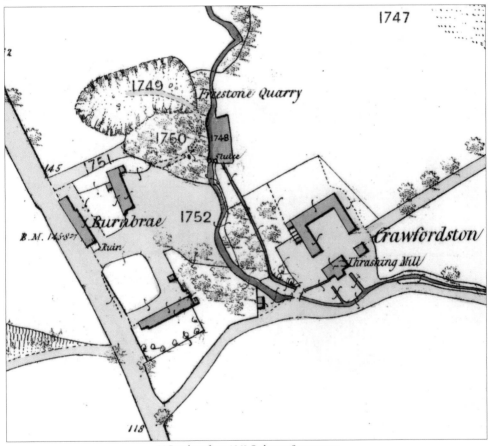

20.Burnbrae from 1860 Ordnance Survey map
Reproduced by permission of the National Library of Scotland

There were a number of shallow pits in the Burnbrae area, and the miners may have lived in the houses. In 1842 Rev David Ritchie, writing in *The New Statistical Account of Scotland*, makes reference to the 'Weston or Crawfordston colliery', which produced coal of excellent quality, sold at the pit for six shillings per twenty hundredweight.

Burnbrae may also have been established as a clachan where quarrymen lived, for the 1860 Ordnance Survey map indicates a Freestone Quarry immediately to the north of the village, with the access track passing from the rear row. The quarry was never of any great size, and by the time the 1895 map was being surveyed, it had been abandoned and filled in. The residents had by this time no doubt become coal miners, a coal mine being in operation on the opposite side of the road, a few hundred yards uphill from the village.

By 1900 the rows at Burnbrae had gained names from long-time residents. Martin's Row, Cree's Row and Wilson's Row recall the names of some of the occupants. The Martins became well-respected residents, and when the village of Annbank was constructed at the top of the hill above Burnbrae, Allan Osbourne Martin was honoured when two streets were named after him – Martin Avenue and Osbourne Avenue.

21. Burnbrae from west looking to Enterkine Viaduct

In the 1850s the children from Burnbrae and surrounding farms were educated at Weston School, which was built on the hillside above the village. Originally a long building with a porch, by 1895 this had been demolished and a new school building was erected, L-planned in shape. The school was closed in 1903 when the new Annbank Public School was opened.

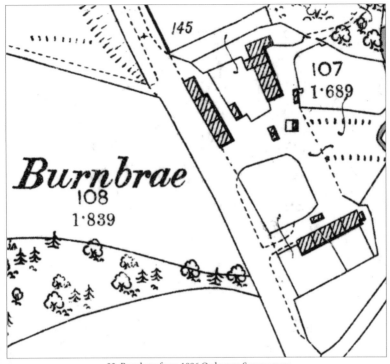

22. Burnbrae from 1896 Ordnance Survey map
Reproduced by permission of the National Library of Scotland

Although Burnbrae may pre-date the coal-mining boom, the houses were certainly occupied by miners latterly. Much of the community was owned by the Annbank Coal Company. According to a report in the *Glasgow Herald* of 1875, the conditions endured at Burnbrae were abysmal. The community was occupied by fifteen or sixteen families. The cottages had roofs of either slate or thatch, but internally suffered from low ceilings. The stone walls were thick, and the windows were small, preventing much light from entering. The floors were of stone, and the doorsteps were in many cases below street level, allowing water, during periods of heavy rain, to flow into the houses. In warm weather the houses were filled with 'battalions' of insects. There were two sources of water for the residents, a spring well which supplied water 'sparingly in winter and not at all in summer', or else from a field drain, which only ran in the rainy season. Life at Burnbrae could be hard. In 1919 the clachan was struck by a flu epidemic, in which Janet Martin died.

23. Burnbrae cottages being demolished

The old houses at Burnbrae were deemed unfit for human habitation, and most of the residents were to be given new tenancies in Annbank. The old community was demolished in 1928, the thatched roofs being hauled down and burned, then the walls flattened. A photograph of the houses being demolished appeared in some newspapers, including one as far away as Manchester, where the *Manchester Guardian* reported that the houses were 'made of stone bound together with clay instead of mortar.' One of the old legends associated with Burnbrae was that the stone used to build the houses had been collected from the bed of the River Ayr.

9

Burnfoothill

★

In 1846 Messrs Houldsworth of the Coltness Iron Works in Lanarkshire purchased the mineral rights to much of the Doon valley and set up their ironworks at Waterside. A new community was established there, to house the ironworkers. To the east of the new village, on the high moorland plateau, they sunk numerous small coal and ironstone mines, the source of their primary ingredients. The new industry required hundreds of workers, something that was in short supply in what had been a quiet valley, filled with sheep farms and little else. Undeterred, the company advertised for employees and word of mouth brought hundreds from Ireland, where times were hard, or from the highlands of Scotland, which was still reeling from the Highland Clearances. There was also a number of men who travelled north from Cornwall, the coal and ironstone mines offering them a better life than the tin mines they had left behind.

The workers needed housing, and Houldsworths erected dozens of houses in new communities. They didn't worry about amenities, or attractive locations. The decision as to where the new houses were to be located was based on where the pits were. Thus, on the moorland uplands new communities were built, such as Corbie Craigs, Lethanhill, Benquhat and Craigmark. Another was Burnfoothill, which was to be little more than a single line of houses all of the time of its existence. It stood near to Lethanhill, just 250 yards or so separating the nearest buildings in each community, but officially it was a separate village. To locals, however, it, Lethanhill and Corbie Craigs were collectively known as 'The 'Hill'.

Burnfoothill comprised three terraces of houses, all built facing onto a mineral railway that made its way from the valley at Waterside, up the steep incline, and across the hillside to the pits on the hill. Between the railway and the front doors of the houses was a narrow walkway, totally unpaved. Behind the houses were their gardens, difficult plots to cultivate, having been formed on the moor. The houses were officially known as Polnessan Row, the eastern one being built of stone. All of them were erected in 1872. In 1891 the population of

Burnfoothill was 332. In 1913 there were 22 families living in what had been thirty single-apartment homes, but, as with most mining communities, a number of the houses had been knocked through to form one larger house.

24. Burnfoothill – Polnessan Row

In 1875 the rent for the houses at Burnfoothill was 3s. 6d. for double houses (a large room and kitchen), the single apartments cost 1s. 9d. per week. Although the houses were only three years old at this time, some of them were damp. Nevertheless, they were of a better standard than many miners' homes, having wooden floors, high ceilings and largish kitchens. To the rear of the houses were coal houses, often converted into washhouses. However, there was no closet or ash pit and rubbish was strewn across the back yards.

Housing Inspectors visited Burnfoothill in 1913 and measured the interior of the houses. In the Stone Row they found that the kitchen measured 18 feet by 11 feet, with a scullery 9 feet by 8 feet. Where two houses were knocked into one, the house had two of these rooms, being converted into bedrooms.

Facilities were poor. It was also noted that 'there is no washing-house, but generally there are boilers in the sculleries, but bought by the tenants. There are no coalhouses, the coal usually being placed below the bed. There are no closets in the proper sense, but a tenant may apply to the Company, who may give him a wooden erection, readymade, not much larger than a sentry box. This is set up, but nothing more, for the tenant has to place in his own pail and to empty them, and as there are no ash pits the matter is either scattered among the ashes or put on ground called a garden.'

The second row was built of brick. Again, the row originally had single-apartment houses, but many were linked together to make a larger house. To make the merge more permanent, many of the original second front doors were bricked up. The row originally had thirty houses in it, but by 1914 this had been merged to form 23 homes. The third row was also built of stone. Originally there were thirty houses, but again many were joined, so that by 1914 there were twenty homes.

Residents at Burnfoothill were able to draw water from public water taps that were located to the rear of the houses, one each for each row, positioned around the centre. The water in these came from a pipe which drained water from Pit Number 9, but it was noted for turning broth and porridge black in colour. If a pail of it was left overnight, a scum formed on the surface. In the winter the water pipes were often frozen.

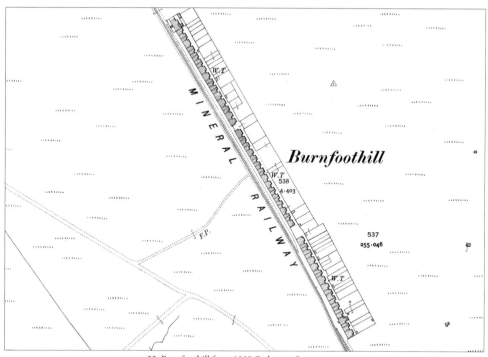

25. Burnfoothill from 1909 Ordnance Survey map
Reproduced by permission of the National Library of Scotland

For many years, access to Burnfoothill and its neighbour Lethanhill was by walking up the incline from Waterside, or else by a number of rough paths across the moor. No roads meant that the residents had little contact with the outside world, and most of the supplies were purchased from the village store, which was controlled and run by the proprietors. Eventually, a new road was constructed from Patna Station Bridge to the village in July 1921. This allowed mobile shops to visit, and the arrival of a number of services.

The village was large enough to support a football team, playing in the junior leagues. Burnfoothill Primrose was founded in 1908, playing in the Vale of Doon League before joining the Ayr and District League. They were league winners in 1915 and 1917. Dormant during the latter part of the war, they were to have their greatest season on the resumption of peace. They won five trophies, including the Ayrshire Consolation Cup. They won the South Ayrshire League West Section in 1926-27, but were beaten by Lugar Boswell in the overall final. The club dropped out of junior ranks in 1929, but continued in juvenile leagues for another five years or so, winning most of the competitions they entered. The club folded for good at the outbreak of the Second World War. A few Primrose players were to move up to the senior ranks. Among these were Willie Bell, who signed for Kilmarnock and a couple of English clubs, and Jimmy MacDowall, who was capped for Scotland in a match against Ireland.

A new football team was formed in 1946, named Burnfoothill Hearts. Playing at juvenile level, the team benefitted from a relaxation of the minimum age rule, which had existed during the time of war. However, in 1948 this was reintroduced, forcing the team to fold after only two seasons.

When the number of occupants of Burnfoothill dropped for a time, two houses, numbers 16 and 17, were converted into the village Reading Room or Institute. A committee was formed to run it, and members could play skittles, dominoes, or summer ice. There was also a fair-sized library and most of the national newspapers were available to read. The front of the institute was extended with the addition of a porch, the only one in the long row, making the building more distinctive. To the rear of the institute an extension was added to allow two billiards tables and carpet bowls to be played. At a later date the front room of one of the institute houses was converted into a small confectionary shop.

Within the institute the local order of Rechabites established a juvenile group, named the Star of Hope Juvenile Tent. This was opened on 7 September 1912 and by the end of December that year had 42 members.

The institute was also probably the meeting place of the local brethren. Burnfoothill assembly was formed sometime before 1874 and existed until 1951 in which year the assembly moved into Patna, meeting in the Ebenezer Hall.

The clearance of Burnfoothill commenced in 1947 and continued until 1954. The residents were offered houses in Patna as soon as they were built. A system of identifying who was most in need of removal was devised by the council, and this was adhered to. The last person to leave the village was James Stevenson, who lived at 18 Burnfoothill. He was moved into his new house at Hillside, Patna, on 31 August 1954. The Burnfoothill Reading Room trustees still had a fair bank balance once the rows were demolished. They joined the Lethanhill Village Hall committee and together organised trips to Girvan until the funds had ended.

For over fifty years the foundations of the rows at Burnfoothill were visible on the ground. Here and there stones, bricks or quarry tiles protruded through the grass, indicating that at in times past man had made his home here on the open moor. Then, when the opencast coal miners arrived, the site of the community was blitzed. The foundations were dug up with the rest of the surrounding countryside, and virtually every indicator was removed. Then, when the opencast was being restored, a new roadway was created where once the front street of the village once ran. The settling ponds used by the opencast to clean the silt-laden run-off waters remain in front of the former street, and the square stand of pine trees survives at what would have been the north-western end of the street. Today, the only physical remnant of old Burnfoothill is a small stand of hawthorn bushes, originally perhaps part of the hedge surrounding one of the gardens at the south-eastern end of the village. The trees look rather hoary, and perhaps they, too, will not survive for much longer.

10

Byrehill

★

Byrehill was a small community located to the south of Kilwinning, named after Byrehill farm. At the junction of the Irvine-Kilwinning and Irvine-Stevenston railways (Byrehill Junction), two rows of houses were built, almost due east-west, to the north of Byrehill Road. At the west end of the community was another railway line – serving local mines. The longest row was erected alongside the public road, with tiny rectangular gardens located in front of each house. This row had 25 houses in it, numbered 2-26, all joined together in one length. Whether there was a Number 1 is not known – it may refer to Byrehill farm. Every five houses in the front row shared a wash-house, located to the rear of the homes, across an open yard.

The second row at Byrehill was located parallel to the front row. This only had eight houses in it, again all joined together, and stretching west from the railway embankment. Again, two wash-houses existed for the eight houses. Between the two rows were allotment gardens.

Byrehill was erected in the late nineteenth century, probably by William Baird & Company, who were mining in the Kilwinning area and who had opened the Eglinton Ironworks in 1846. The company became very prosperous and iron from Kilwinning was used far and wide. Residents of Byrehill could reach their work at the ironworks by walking under the railway bridge at the east end of the rows, following a path alongside the railway, crossing the mineral line that served the ironworks, and reaching the ironworkers' cottages which were located adjoining the ironworks. Here too were the local school, football ground and ironworks co-operative store.

Sometime between 1895 and 1908 the old wash-houses were demolished and four new wash-houses were erected to serve the needs of the community – three of these served the front row, the fourth for the back row. There were also four water pumps located by the side of the yards, from where the villagers obtained their water.

The Eglinton Ironworks were closed in 1924, resulting in many local men losing their jobs. As a result, Byrehill was in decline by the start of the Second

World War, but the outbreak of hostilities held up the final evacuation. In 1939 the community was still owned by Bairds & Dalmellington Ltd, William Baird & Company having merged with the Dalmellington Iron Company in 1931. Houses numbered 2-9 were all empty. Houses 10-26 were still in the main occupied by miners, labourers, widows, etc., apart from numbers 23, and 24/5. Houses numbered 27-35 (the Back Row) appear to have been demolished, and those numbered 36-43 were at this time empty and uninhabitable.

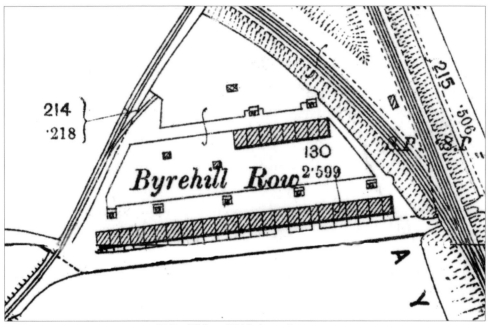

26. Byrehill from 1896 Ordnance Survey map
Reproduced by permission of the National Library of Scotland

Some of the houses in Byrehill remained in occupation until after the Second World War. By that time it was realised that the houses were no longer fit for modern living, and over a period of time the residents were given new council houses in Kilwinning. The rows were demolished in the late 1940s. Today, the site of the community is just a rough stretch of ground, forming a triangle between the railway and Byrehill Road, a byway from Kilwinning to Stevenston. The name survives in the local West Byrehill industrial estate and Byrehill Avenue in nearby Blacklands.

11

Cairntable

★

Travellers on the B730 road between Drongan and Patna will pass a rounded granite boulder by the side of the road. It is located on the north side of the highway, just beyond Knockshinnoch farm's road-end, three and a half miles from Drongan. The stone has a simple inscription: *Cairntable Village 1914-1963. Erected by J. Dunn.*

The stone was placed there in 2007 by Jimmy Dunn, a former resident, who was born at 26 Cairntable Terrace in 1931. He often returned to his childhood home to reminisce, and one day thought that there should be some form of permanent marker. Being a lover of the countryside he knew of a granite boulder on Skeldon estate, near Dalrymple, which he obtained permission to take. The stone was inscribed by Patna monumental sculptor, Kevin Roberts, and installed on site, just where Dunn's front door had been. There was a flaw in the granite, and a black mark was adapted into a carving of a small mouse.

The houses at Cairntable were erected by the Cairntable Gas Coal Company in 1914 to house the miners employed in the Kerse pits. The company gained its name from the high hill at Muirkirk, in which parish the firm had its origins. They had mines at Auldhouseburn and Glenbuck. The company took over the pits of Messrs Thomas Barr & Co., who owned some of the mines in Dalrymple parish. The company owned Kerse Number 1 and Number 2 pits, but these were to close in 1915. The Cairntable Gas Coal Company was later to be taken over by the Coylton Coal Company.

Many of the residents of Cairntable were employed at Littlemill Colliery. This stood almost due east of the village, almost one mile along the railway line. The pit was operated by the Coylton Coal Company Ltd up until 1937, when it was taken over by Bairds & Dalmellington Ltd. Whether or not the change of ownership resulted in a lowering of health and safety standards in the pit can't be told, but in December 1938 four men were killed by an explosion. These were John Leslie, James Graham, William Brown and Robert Howie. None of the dead hailed from Cairntable, being resident in nearby Rankinston, but following the explosion in the pit, there was a message sent to Cairntable asking for assistance. Most of the men who were there at the time went to help and managed to get a good number of injured miners out. The residents hadn't been so lucky earlier in the year, for William Wallace, aged 41, who resided with Henry Walters, 33 Cairntable, was killed by a fall in Littlemill Colliery, on the morning of 25 August 1938. Littlemill pit was closed in July 1974, with the loss of 314 jobs

27. Cairntable – memorial stone

The houses at Cairntable were arranged in two main rows, on either side of the roadway. On the northern side was the main row, divided into two equal parts, totalling forty homes. These houses were single-apartment homes, with one bedroom, a kitchen which doubled as a living room, which also had a bed in it, and a small scullery.

On the south side of the road, at the bottom end of the hill, was another row of houses, numbering eight homes, which were larger in size, having two rooms. This row, from its length, was known locally as the Wee Row. Cairntable had the advantage of having electric lighting from an early period. Soon after the resumption of peace in 1945, the county council installed three street lights in the village. Although there was electricity in the houses, the residents had to use outside toilets, located in the gardens behind the terraces, and these were shared with neighbours.

28. Cairntable – sketch of village from north

One larger cottage, known as Rowanbank, located at Knockshinnoch, was also owned by the company, and was tenanted by the manager of the pits, William Adam, for some time. The forty houses of the same size paid a rent of £6 16s. per year in 1927. The eight larger houses paid a rent of £10 5s.

Cairntable Terrace was occupied by miners, with others having trades such as oncostman, fireman, roadman, engineman, labourer, joiner, bencher, machineman, screenman, pitheadman, blacksmith, shaftsman, electrician and under manager. Houses numbered 30-31 Cairntable Terrace, which had been joined to form a larger dwelling, were occupied by James Jamieson, police constable.

The village had its own shop for a time, located in a wooden hut. This was positioned at the upper end of the village, at the end of the long row. The shop was run by Robert Deans who sold general groceries. He also had a number of hen houses in his garden to the rear, and was able to sell freshly laid eggs. A second small shop was located in the Wee Row, run by Elspie Knox, which mainly dealt in confectionary.

Just after the First World War the terrace at Cairntable was partially empty, there being little work in the district for miners. Of the 48 houses in the rows, ten houses remained unoccupied. At that time Rowanbank was occupied by John S. Burt, manager.

29. Cairntable – sketch of village looking south-west

Cairntable was in decline after the Second World War. Most of the residents were being rehoused in either Drongan or Dalrymple, and the houses were left empty. The last tenant moved out by July 1963 and it wasn't long before the diggers arrived to pull the buildings down. Apart from an old water tank at the top of the Big Row, virtually everything that existed of Cairntable has gone.

30. Cairntable – the half-demolished rows

73

12

Carsehead

*

Carsehead was a small mining community located to the east of Dalry. The oldest row was known as the Stickit Row, originally comprising eleven houses built in a single terrace on the southern side of the roadway from Dalry to Beith.

At a later date two additional rows were built to the west and east of the Stickit Row. To the west, between Carsehead Bridge and Stickit Row was the 'First Row', so-called because it was the first row reached on leaving Dalry. This contained thirteen houses, built in a slight dog-leg to follow the line of the roadway. The First Row was built of stone and contained a series of two-apartment houses. Inside these the kitchen measured 14 feet by 11 feet. The room measured 6 feet by 8 feet. In addition, there was a large cupboard in which was found a set-in bed.

The First Row tenants shared six dry-closets, but in 1913 they did not have the luxury of a door. The houses, which were owned by William Baird & Company, did not have any wash-houses or coal houses, but the residents had in many cases fashioned ones for themselves. When inspected in 1913, the row was very dirty – it was difficult to use the closet without soiling your boots, and the pathways were unmade, being very muddy and with dirty cesspools all around. To live in these houses, the tenants paid one shilling and sixpence per week.

The Stickit Row itself was also built of stone, again of two apartments each. The kitchens here measured 12 feet by 10 feet, the room 12 feet by 9 feet. The rent payable was five shillings and sixpence per month. Again the conditions endured by the tenants of this row were poor – the closets had no doors, there were large ash-pits, no wash-houses were provided, and the tenants complained of the rats and dampness.

Adjoining the east end of the Stickit Row, higher up the brae, was the Wee Stickit Row. This had nine two-apartment houses in it, again constructed of stone. Inside the houses were two rooms – a kitchen measuring 12 feet by 11 feet, and a room measuring 10 feet by 9 feet. Again, the rent was five shillings and sixpence per month. Two dry-closets were provided for the nine homes, again not having any doors. In front of the houses, facing the roadway, was the ash-pit.

A New Row was constructed at Carsehead sometime before 1895. This was located on the opposite side of the main road from the original rows, built at an angle across the foot of the hill below Carsehead farm. Although newer, the houses here weren't to be much better. They were small, and there were 36 houses joined together in one long terrace. On the roadway in front of these houses were six wash-houses.

Most of the floors in the older rows were finished with brick tiles, many of which had become broken and twisted over the years. Many of the homes at Carsehead were over-occupied, in 1913 the inspectors finding one house with twelve people living in it, four of them adults.

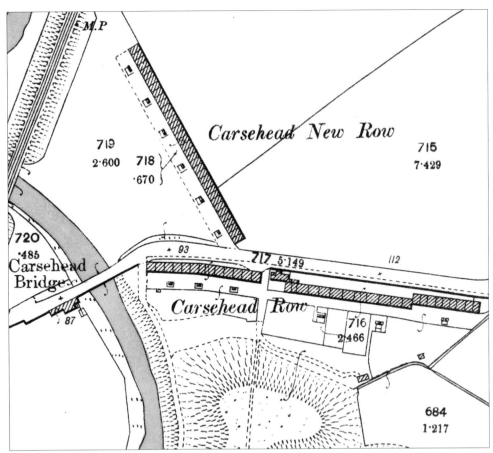

31. Carsehead from 1896 Ordnance Survey map
Reproduced by permission of the National Library of Scotland

The folk who lived at Carsehead worked in the local mines, indeed the large bing associated with Carsehead Number 2 Ironstone pit rose up immediately to the south of the rows. This pit was ordered to be closed in January 1891, the contractor going there to carry out his orders. Eighty miners employed at the pit were laid off and the pit itself was dismantled. The rails were lifted from the surface and the ponies who worked underground were taken elsewhere. The closure was a result of a lack of demand for coal, the iron works being on strike at the time, and most of William Baird's miners were put on short time. A good number of the Carsehead residents moved away from the district at this time.

In 1898 the Carsehead Number 2 bing was identified as being a suitable source of material for brickmaking and a new brickworks was erected at the site. This was established by Messrs D. Logan and Sons Ltd, of Glasgow.

By 1931 the New Row had been demolished and the ground on which the

32. Carsehead – the rebuilt rows used as part of a foundry

houses had stood returned to nature. The Old Row remained in occupation, still the property of William Baird & Company. Most of the houses were still lived in by miners, colliers, labourers and one or two widows. The row was still occupied long after the Second World War.

The residents of Carsehead were offered new council houses in Dalry, and gradually the community was abandoned. The houses remained standing for a good number of years, gradually succumbing to the elements, until the last houses were demolished in 1988. The last resident had moved out only months before. Today, only the foundations of the old rows survive, and at the west end of the site a foundry, operated by Arthur McLuckie, was built on the site.

13

Coalburn

★

Laigh Coalburn was a miners' row located in New Cumnock parish, midway between Benston and Dalleagles. It was known as Laigh, which means low, from the fact that Old Coalburn was positioned further up the hillside, where the large Coalburn Quarry was long used to excavate yellow sandstone. The row at Laigh Coalburn was located in the gusset of roads formed by the junction of the Dalgig and Dalleagles roads. Built on an elevated position – there was an Ordnance Survey benchmark chiselled into the wall which indicated 834 feet above sea-level – the houses afforded a wide panorama over upper Nithsdale.

The houses at Laigh Coalburn were probably erected sometime between 1841 (for they are not listed in the Census returns of that year) and 1857, when the Ordnance Survey plotted them in their detailed maps. The minerals at Coalburn had been leased to a couple of short-lived developers, followed by John Nisbet and James Sloan. Sloan left the partnership, leaving Nisbet to carry on alone from 1857. He also operated the Guelt coal works (near to the lost village of Grievehill). In 1850 the firm employed nineteen men, five boys and three carters. He was succeeded by Richmond & Clarkson, who passed on the lease to James M. Nicol by 1874. He was a local coalmaster who also worked limestone at Benston and produced clay for drainage tiles at Wellhill. Nicol was also the proprietor of the Cumnock Pottery Company, manufacturer of 'Scotch Motto Ware' for many years. He died in 1886.

A new Coalburn Colliery was sunk up the hill from the houses, but it was never one of the larger pits in the New Cumnock area. Robert Nisbet (1880-1924) was manager of Coalburn Colliery from 1908 and he oversaw the sinking of the new Coalburn Pit in 1912. Up to 1928 it was leased by William Nicol Ltd from the Marquis of Bute, but in that year it was acquired by The New Cumnock Collieries Ltd. Many of the other miners who lived at Coalburn worked at Bogside Colliery.

The houses were occupied by colliers, there being numerous small coal pits in the immediate vicinity. Perhaps the oldest houses in the row were those at the northern end, where the first edition of the 25-inch Ordnance Survey map, surveyed in 1857, shows a couple of irregular-shaped buildings by the roadside, facing the entrance to Auchencross farm. To the south, and adjoining these buildings, was a row of cottages. The houses at either end of the row were larger than the others, probably a double-storey structure, with an external stair leading to the upper flat. Between these two book-end houses were twelves houses. To the rear of the cottages was an area used for gardens, in which were three wash-houses, shared by the residents. Water was available from a small well that was located a few hundred yards across the field in front of the houses, by the side of the small Auchencross Burn.

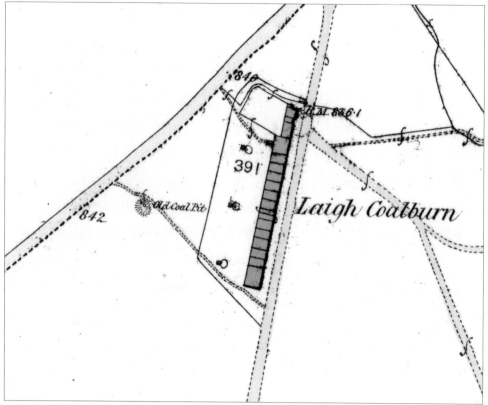

33. Coalburn from 1860 Ordnance Survey map
Reproduced by permission of the National Library of Scotland

Despite being a small community, the residents of Coalburn were keen on their activities. In 1893 a Band of Hope was instituted in the village, the membership in 1898 being forty. There was also a thriving Sunday School, local Sunday School teachers being assisted at times with visits from parish clergy.

By 1895 the older cottages at the north end of Laigh Coalburn were demolished and little remained to indicate their existence. In 1904 major developments were taking place nearer New Cumnock with the sinking of the new pit near Riggfoot. New houses were built at Connel Park, and soon most of the Coalburn residents were moving there. By 1907 the row was basically empty. When the Ordnance Survey map-makers returned in 1908 the row had been more or less abandoned. All of the cottages, apart from the northernmost one, were shown as being roofless. No doubt this last cottage was abandoned soon after. The site of Laigh Coalburn remained as a small field for years thereafter, before it was merged into the adjoining larger field. With the creation of Greenburn surface coal mine the site of the village was totally obliterated.

14

Commondyke

✱

There is only one real physical survivor from the lost village of Commondyke. A mile and a half east of Auchinleck, on the road towards Cronberry, passing motorists sometimes spot a sandstone cross standing in a small field to the east of the road. Few stop to visit, and those that do sometimes find the inscription difficult to decipher. In fact, it reads:

> AT A DISTANCE OF EIGHT FEET IN FRONT OF THIS SPOT THE REVD SISTER LAURIENNE WAS ACCIDENTALLY KILLED ON THE 7TH DAY OF AUGUST 1888. 'BEHOLD,' MY BELOVED SAITH UNTO ME, 'RISE UP, MAKE HASTE, MY LOVE, MY DOVE, MY FAIR ONE, AND COME AWAY.'

The cross commemorates a nun, Sister Laurienne, whose death by a train on the branch line which served Commondyke Number 1 pit stunned the local Roman Catholic community. Sister Laurienne had been the principal of the catholic school which stood across the road, but she had to resign her duties in the spring of 1888 due to an infection which left her deaf. She went to Girvan to convalesce and her position as headmistress was taken over by Sister Columba.

Sister Laurienne was given the task of looking after the sick and needy in the district. She undertook this task with vigour, but on 7 August 1888 she was knocked down by a railway waggon as she was crossing the railway, being killed almost instantly. Within two hours hundreds of people, including non-Catholics, were at the convent to offer their services to the Sisters, or were praying in the chapel. Over one hundred offered to guard the corpse through the night. Father Murphy, who had been at Rothesay, returned as soon as he heard the news, to conduct the service prior to her burial at Girvan. Commondyke Station had to be closed when the corpse was taken away, for too many people were trying to get onto the platform.

Father Murphy wrote to the Mother General at Girvan:

> The sad death of dear Sister Laurienne is a calamity for all of us in this parish. Oh! what a holy sister she was! Her sanctity was above the ordinary and I knew her soul sufficiently well to vouch for that. You and your congregation have suffered a heavy loss through her death, but it will be a consolation for all to know that she was a faithful, religious person right to the end and that she gave her life in an actual accomplishment of her duty - striving to procure the salvation of souls.
>
> I have never witnessed such a display of grief at the loss of anyone. The entire parish, men, women and children, came to pay their last tribute to her. It was heart-breaking to see so many men in tears! Such sympathy has helped to lighten the cross that God has sent to us.
>
> May God bless you and may He give us sisters to continue our good work here and may He preserve the peace and happiness which reigned here in our little convent.
>
> Very respectfully and sincerely in Jesus Christ,
>
> [signed] P. Murphy.

Father Murphy's wish did not come to be, however, for in a short time Sister Columba Fogarty became seriously ill and had to return to Girvan. The remaining sisters' health began to show signs of failing, so they withdrew their services from Birnieknowe and returned to Girvan on 31 July 1889.

Commondyke was for many years the centre of the Roman Catholic community in the parishes of Old Cumnock, Auchinleck and Sorn. Before this, a chapel of sorts existed in Cumnock, but in 1855 the priest, Rev John O'Dwyer, started raising funds to build a proper chapel. He collected donations from all his parishioners, as well as £50 from the Eglinton Iron Company, and obtained a site near Commondyke for the church from Lady Boswell. She allowed him the use of a nearby quarry and sandpit and with volunteer labour he supervised the erection of a church and presbytery.

The church was a simple, but dignified, gothic building, with porch to the north and an apse to the south, opened in 1867. Father O'Dwyer died in 1873 and for the next year Rev John MacGinnis took charge. He was succeeded by Rev Patrick Wright in 1874. Father Wright was responsible for establishing St Patrick's School at Birnieknowe, opened on 15 August 1878 behind the presbytery. Lord Bute had donated a considerable sum to aid its erection, and it soon had 150 pupils in attendance. Father Wright was the school manager, Miss Somerville the principal teacher, with the Misses MacGuinness and Jordan as pupil teachers. Father Wright died in 1881 and was followed by Rev John O'Neil (d. 1922), who remained until 1883.

In 1883 Rev Patrick Murphy took over at Birnieknowe. On 21 August 1882 Lady Boswell had sold a strip of ground adjoining the chapel to the Marquis of Bute upon which he erected a convent, opened on 1 March 1885. The first recorded confirmations to take place at Birnieknowe occurred on 10 August 1885 when Bishop John MacLauchlan confirmed 120 males and 97 females.

Many of the miners' rows across Ayrshire had a high percentage of Roman Catholics living in them, often as a result of the influx of workers from Ireland. Relationships were not always cordial, and there are many accounts of the arguments and struggles between the two groups. A slightly more comical tale took place at Commondyke.

Francis Collins lived in the small thatched cottage known as Habbie's Howe, which was located across the Auchinleck Burn from Commondyke village. His sister had married a Roman Catholic and set up home in the High Row, Commondyke. In old age, and knowing she hadn't long to go, she told her brother that she did not want to be buried as a Catholic. She predeceased Francis, but a Catholic funeral was arranged by her husband, so Collins went

34. Commondyke – Long Row (right) and Dyke Row (left) from above the railway station

to her house and asked for her corpse to be given to him. The priest requested that he be allowed to bury her, but Collins threatened the priest with his gun and demanded the corpse, which he got. For years afterwards he and his family were known in the district as 'Steal the Coffin'!

The size of Commondyke never really changed over the years. In 1857 there existed the High Row of 24 houses, the Long Row, later called the Store Row when the company store opened there (23 houses plus store), Dyke Row, later called the Chapel Row (six houses), Birnieknowe Row, adjacent to the farm, with six houses, and the Commondyke Row, known as Kilpatrick's Row, also of six houses. In 1878 the village had a population of 332.

35. Commondyke – Sister Laurienne's memorial

As with most mining communities, Commondyke had its own football team. Commondyke Celtic played on the old hearth of the Commondyke ironstone pit, which operated from 1878-1881. The hearth had previously been used as the local quoiting rink, and this had to be moved to the old hearth at Dykes Number 2 Ironstone Pit, which was located across the road from the High Row, but the players and spectators complained about the open aspect of the rink, which left them frozen.

Another team, Common Thistle, was founded just a few years before the turn of the new century, a close rival to their neighbours, Darnconner Britannia.

The club played in a field at Barglachan, known as 'Barglachan Park', with a clubhouse in existence in 1911. In 1900 Common Thistle took the Cumnock and District Cup, Darnconner having won it previously. They won the Mauchline Cup in May 1905, beating Glenbuck Cherrypickers 1-0. A year later Common took the Ayrshire Consolation Cup following a 1-0 defeat of Kilbirnie Ladeside. The team failed to win any great prizes thereafter, the club folding in 1913 and not being reformed after the war. They had opened a new pavilion on 25 July 1902. The club was officially wound up in January 1918. The pavilion was sold for £6 and even the goalposts were up for offers!

36. Commondyke – Our Lady & St Patrick's R. C. Church

Commondyke Station was created adjacent to the miners' rows, access to the platforms being from the new road bridge over the railway. This station was opened on 9 August 1848. It was never a very busy place, the miners rarely affording travel by rail, but it continued until it was closed on 3 July 1950. The line from Cumnock to Muirkirk itself was closed to passengers in 1951.

On 5 December 1914 the Housing Committee issued a report. They found that at Commondyke extensive repairs were being made on Baird's 52 houses. Wood lining was being affixed to cover damp walls, new window sashes, doors and floors were being installed. Outside, the ash pits were being cleared away, and new toilets, coal-houses, wash-houses and small ash pits erected. Though noting the improvements with delight, the committee recommended that water be piped into the washrooms.

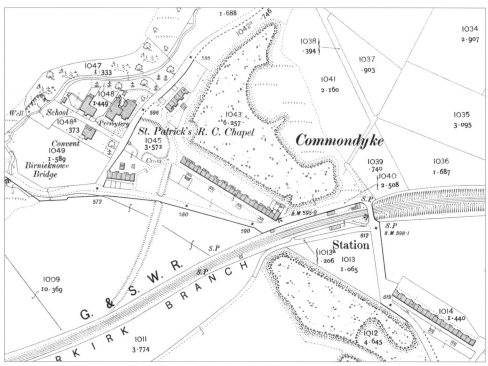

37. Commondyke from 1909 Ordnance Survey map
Reproduced by permission of the National Library of Scotland

The rows did not last much longer. Many of the residents were moving elsewhere, and gradually the houses were emptied. This took longer than planned, for the outbreak of war held up the rehousing process. Eventually all of the residents were given new council houses in Auchinleck, but some were rather ungrateful of their new homes, claiming that the council was charging higher rents than they were due to pay under the Slum Clearance Act. Many went on rent strike, but when their case went to court they were found to be in the wrong.

The chapel and school remained at Commondyke until 1964. By then a new chapel had been erected in Auchinleck, and in 1966 a new primary school for the Roman Catholic children was opened. Both buildings were demolished, leaving only one house that had formed part of the original village – the old convent. This survived much longer, becoming a private house, but this, too, was eventually demolished, having been burned down in 1990. Its site is now occupied by a modern dwelling, Lochnoran House, and next door is another new bungalow. The foundations of the various rows can still be seen on the ground, and the old platform walls of the station can be made out in the railway cutting, next to the bridge. The site of the old football ground was in 2016 built over when Commondyke poultry farm was opened.

15

Craigbank

✶

New Cumnock's noted junior football team, Glenafton Athletic, were building a new pavilion in 1960, having moved their home ground from Connel Park to Loch Park, in the centre of the village. Once the new field was laid, the facilities for fans were planned, and the new pavilion was to be one of the largest in junior football grounds at that time. The roof was built using trusses salvaged from six former miners' houses that were being demolished at the village of Craigbank.

Where once the village of Craigbank stood, today is just trees and open ground. Lying to the south-west of New Cumnock, on the road towards Dalmellington, the village was one of a number that was established to house miners in the local pits. Some of the communities strung along this route still survive, all-be-it in various stages of decline or rebuilding, such as Legate, Connel Park, Bankglen, Lanemark, Burnfoot, Burnside and Dalleagles. Most have lost much of their population, but in each of these cases newer bungalows have often been erected on the site of older houses, meaning that the community is still changing, and there is still some sense of population in each.

Craigbank was erected by the Bank Coal Company but was later acquired by New Cumnock Collieries Ltd. The first houses were erected in the middle of the nineteenth century, and by the time the Ordnance Survey surveyors reached the village in 1857 to survey for their detailed maps there were six rows built. Four of these formed an irregular square, or trapezoidal shape, their front doors all facing outwards.

The row facing the main road originally had thirteen houses in it, the front of the buildings sitting directly on the roadside. The houses were double-storey in height, and each home had a door and window facing the street on the ground floor, and a single window on the upper floor. At a later date the north-eastern end of this row was demolished and the buildings rebuilt to form a store and inn. This row was later to be officially named Front Row.

The grocer's shop at Craigbank was originally run by Andrew Gibson and latterly by Gavin Lawrie. He was also the proprietor of the inn, erected on the corner of Front Row and Plantation Row. This was the only building in Craigbank that had any architectural pretentions. The walls were constructed of coursed sandstone, the quoins and corbie-stepped gables, lintels and door surrounds being of a lighter stone. The inn stood two storeys in height, with further rooms in the attic.

38. Craigbank – Front Row prior to demolition

At the New Cumnock end of the Front Row was a roadway striking east, facing which was a row of seven houses. This became known as Plantation Row as it faced a triangular wood on the opposite side of the road. Part of this was to be later cut down. By the roadside, within this wood, was a well, where most of the villagers had initially to obtain their water.

The row at the eastern side of Craigbank's square comprised ten houses to start with, but at the southern end a couple of houses were rebuilt to form a school. This was to serve the youth of the village until the new Bank School was erected in nearby Bank Glen in 1874. Mr Kay was the teacher for a number of years. This row was known as the Stable Row.

The southern side of the square had twelve houses in it, built facing onto the roadway. As this road was built on both sides it had a more enclosed feel about it, and thus it gained the name Blair Street.

On the other side of the street was a second row, again comprising twelve homes. The houses in Blair Street, as with most of the older houses at Craigbank, had two apartments, one built above the other to form double-storey buildings. The kitchen was located on the ground floor, with the room above.

The sixth row at Craigbank was located further to the south, and was built at an angle to the main road, but parallel with the other rows. This row was named Peesweep Row. Between this row and Blair Street were gardens. Peesweep Row was actually the oldest row at Craigbank.

Sometime between 1895 and 1908 a seventh row was erected at Craigbank. This was built facing the main road, to the north of Plantation Row, in line with the Front Row. This row of houses had eight dwellings in it and one of the houses was actually built over the old well. By this time, however, water was obtained from a water pump at the corner of Front Row and Blair Street.

39. Craigbank – Front Row prior to demolition

Craigbank was built by John Hyslop of Bank House (1817-1878). When the Nithsdale Iron Company went bankrupt in 1855 he inherited the buildings and works they had established, as the properties reverted to the landowner as no-one was interested in buying the business. Hyslop was quick to realise that there was still potential for mining coal, and thus kept Bank Number 1 pit operating. A second Bank Pit followed, and in 1861 he was sinking Bank

Number 3. With the increase in his business, he needed more homes for the workers, and Craigbank was created.

William Hyslop (1854-1936) succeeded to Bank and was an enlightened landowner. He served for some time as chairman of the parish school board. Each year he organised a picnic for the residents in the summer, and in the winter a social soiree was held. The picnics were held in different places each year, perhaps in Glen Afton or up the Connel Burn. As the group set off from the village, the local brass band led the march, adding to the children's excitement. Races were organised for all of the family, and the scones and buns supplied were much appreciated.

The winter social was often held in New Cumnock Town Hall. In 1904 it was noted that 700 people were packed into the hall to enjoy the entertainment. The socials and picnics stopped on the outbreak of the First World War.

William Hyslop extended the family estate with the proceeds from the sale of coal. In May 1905 he was able to buy the Afton Estate from the Gordons for £26,000, at the time comprising of five farms.

William's brother, Thomas Hyslop, was to emigrate to Natal in Africa, where he was a successful farmer at Howick. He was elected to the colonial parliament and was colonial treasurer for a time. He was to be knighted in the New Year Honours of 1911. He died in January 1919.

The population of Craigbank varied over the decades. In 1891 it had 345 residents. In 1913 the population had fallen to 247. However, this was to grow to around 1,000 in 1930 and 1,030 in 1951.

The miners who lived at Craigbank worked in the Bank mines. Around 1890 a new mine was sunk just across the road from the west end of Peesweep Row. A branch line with a couple of sidings came into the pit from the south, and a low bing was formed with refuse from the pit. The mine was closed by 1908. In 1931 the community celebrated when new pithead baths were opened at Bank Colliery, meaning that the men-folk could return home clean.

As with all mining communities, many of the families lived in fear of receiving a knock at the door with the terrible news of a fatality in the mine. At Craigbank one who was killed was John Monteith, who was removing a prop in Bank Number 1 Pit on 15 August 1918 when the roof collapsed, pinning him under piles of stone. When the debris was removed he was found to be dead. Another was Robert MacDicken, aged 20 years, who died on 14 October 1925 following an accident at Afton Pit. John Brechney, aged 24, was seriously injured with thirteen others by burning in Bank Number 2, dying in Kilmarnock Infirmary on 19 December 1929. Two others were also to die. In April 1938 the rope hauling the miners in hutches to the surface at Bank Number 6 Mine broke, allowing the train to hurtle back downhill for half a mile. Five miners were killed, and a further 21 were injured. Among the dead was John Mackie, aged 27, who lived in Stable Row.

Craigbank had its own quoiting rink, as did most mining communities. The village was home to an annual competition which took place up to the First World War. William Gray donated a trophy which the winning rink would keep for the year. In 1916, despite it being the middle of the hostilities, the competition attracted 101 entries. To keep young boys amused, in 1911 a local Scout troop was formed.

Like most mining communities, Craigbank had a keen number of footballers, the local team being Lanemark, which played in the senior leagues at the end of the nineteenth century up to 1920, when it appears to have folded.

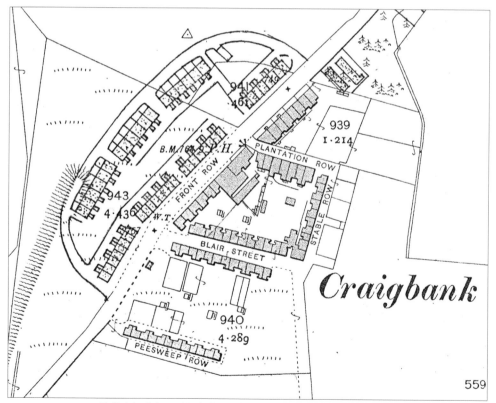

40. Craigbank from 1896 Ordnance Survey map with new houses sketched in

Hugh Monteith was born at Craigbank in 1874 and worked in the local pits. He was a goalkeeper and won a Football Association cup winner's medal with Bury in 1903, beating Derby County six-nil – still a record winning margin in the final. Another local miner was Colin MacLatchie, who was born at Mansfield, near New Cumnock, but moved to Craigbank. He was to win an English First Division Championship medal with Sunderland in 1902.

When the inspectors visited Craigbank in 1913 to see what conditions the miners had to endure they were taken aback at the lack of toilet facilities. They wrote of the Stable Row: 'The back row of this square has two earth closets, one of which has no roof. No one can ask friends to come here. How the people who are condemned to live here manage to exist is a mystery. It is alleged that one lady visitor lately had to go out into the open moss, no other accommodation being available. She is not likely to repeat the experience.'

In 1913 a number of new houses were being erected at Craigbank to try to alleviate the conditions. These houses were described as being of a 'superior character'. They had two rooms and a kitchen, the kitchen measuring 12 feet by 12 feet, and having an oven grate and a sink. Each of the rooms measured 12 feet by 10 feet. In addition, each of these new homes had a bathroom, water-closet, and a coal-bunker, all within the same house. The houses were built for the New Cumnock Collieries Company by a Strathaven builder and had been financed by a loan from a lawyer in that town. The cost of this was regarded as being too expensive by the general manager, James Jack, who started to investigate how best to finance new properties. Accordingly, the Workmen's Dwellings Acts were applied and when the plans for fifty new houses were sent to London, the company was offered a loan with repayments at a reasonable rate, payable over thirty years.

The new houses were constructed of brick and were located across the main road from the original community. Four rows of eight houses were built facing onto the main street, opposite Front Row. This made the Front Row more street-like in appearance, the open fields on the opposite side being hidden. Behind these new homes were three rows of houses, six homes in each, which were arranged to form a crescent. These houses had baths – something of a novelty at the time, but no great advantage. The water had to be heated elsewhere and carried into the bathroom in buckets to fill the tub.

In 1916 the residents of the village complained to the council sanitary inspector about the poor supply of water in the village. He investigated the matter and came to the conclusion that the supply was insufficient. He blamed the recent introduction of sinks in each house, plus the new water closets that replaced the dry privies meant that the demand for water had increased, and that the local supply could not cope with it.

The first houses to be demolished at Craigbank were those forming the Peesweep Row. These had disappeared by the Second World War. After the war was over, evacuation continued, and soon Craigbank was emptied and demolished. Many of the residents moved to the new council houses at Afton Bridgend, the southern part of New Cumnock.

16

Craighall

*

Craighall was a small compact community of nineteen houses, built on an elevated part of Auchincruive estate. The owner of the properties were the Oswalds of Auchincruive.

The village was an old one, for General Roy's Military Survey of Scotland, executed in 1747-55, depicts Craighall as a rectangle of houses, much as it was to remain for the next two centuries. Looking at current maps, one gets the impression that the road into Craighall must have been a dead end, petering out into a track down to the side of the River Ayr soon after where the village was. However, studying old maps show that the road passed through Craighall, climbed up to Mount Scarburgh, skirted the wood, and then dropped down to a ford across the Ayr, where the present Oswald's Bridge is located. With the steep climbs to either side causing difficulty for transport, a new road was created further west, skirting the hillside, but by-passing the hamlet.

On the first detailed Ordnance Survey map of 1857 the community is shown as being rectangular in plan and, to the east at the top of the track that led down to the River Ayr, was a secondary row of four houses. The northernmost row, which had three houses in it, was demolished before 1895, leaving the community more like an open 'U' shape.

The western side of the courtyard had five houses in it, as did the southern side. The eastern side had six houses, making it slightly longer. These three sides were all joined together with no spaces between the rows. All of the houses were single storey, latterly roofed in slate, and each home had a front door facing outwards, away from the central courtyard, and a solitary window. The principal distinguishing feature of Craighall was the tall chimneys that indicated each house.

At one end of Craighall was a spot known as 'The Paling', from the up-ended railway sleepers which formed an enclosure. This spot was the village's equivalent to the St Kilda 'parliament', where the menfolk gathered to discuss the politics of the day, both national and local.

There also existed a local group of young men called the 'Black Gang', who formed a society said to be run on similar lines to the freemasons. As with many such groups, there were initiation ceremonies, one of which involved being blindfolded and strung up from a tree at Broadwood Toll, south of the village.

Some accounts claim that Craighall was at one time a stable courtyard for Auchincruive estate, and that the cottages were fashioned from them. Nearby, on the other side of a low hill separating the communities, is Barrackhall, another small hamlet, but where a number of houses survive. The name Barrackhall hints at army accommodation, leading to speculation that the soldiers were based at one place, their horses at the other. Of this there is no proof, and it is more likely that the communities were established as homes for miners, when small pits existed all over Auchincruive estate. The location of Craighall, in a hollow behind Mount Scarburgh, would mean that the Oswald landowners in Auchincruive House wouldn't need to see the small cottages and the squalor that the mine-workers had to endure. Reference is made in the *New Statistical Account* of a coal mine at Craighall, one of three in Coylton parish when the account was written.

41. Craighall – remnants of original houses

At the time of the *New Statistical Account*, compiled in 1841, Craighall was one of the more important villages listed in the parish. Joppa, now part of the present village of Coylton, was the largest village in the parish, with a population of 173. Laigh Coylton, where the old kirkyard is, had a population of just 40, whereas Craighall had 100 residents. Ten years later, when the 1851 Census was taken, the village had twenty houses, with 90 residents.

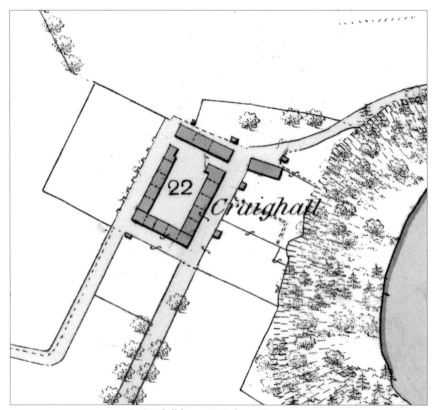

42. Craighall from 1857 Ordnance Survey map
Reproduced by permission of the National Library of Scotland

Studying the Census, one can identify the type of residents in the community. Of the heads of the households, eleven were employed as mineworkers, two worked on farms, usually as agricultural labourers, but there was also a shoemaker, three paupers, a blacksmith, a surgeon and one resident, John Hutton, was a farmer of 35 acres. Two of the houses had nine residents in them, one of them being Charles King's household. He was a miner, aged 37. His wife was 34, and they had three sons. Also in the house were four lodgers.

Francis Stewart lived at Craighall with his wife and children. One of the boys, James Stewart, was accidentally killed on 19 February 1915. His father died later in the same year, and both are interred in Coylton cemetery. The family appear to have left Craighall and emigrated to the United States, Francis Stewart the younger dying there in 1953. Another memorial in Coylton cemetery commemorates James Dykes, who died in 1941. He had left Craighall by that time, but he had two wives, both of whom died at Craighall. The first was Agnes Stewart, who died in 1912 aged 56. The second was Mary Cuthbert, who died in 1933 aged 65. At the turn of the century another resident, Francis Lees, was noted for his skill as a racing cyclist.

By 1923 eight of the nineteen houses at Craighall had been joined together to form four larger dwellings, more suitable for modern living, these being numbers 1 and 2, 3 and 4, 11 and 12 and 18 and 19. These were occupied by Andrew Jess, miner, and his family; Hugh Paterson, miner, and his family; Francis Stewart, miner, and his family, and Hugh Keggans, miner, and his family. These householders paid £6 per annum in rent, those who just had the single cottage paying £4 per annum.

Auchincruive estate was acquired by the Board of Agriculture for Scotland in 1927, and with it came ownership of the village. The department established Auchincruive as the West of Scotland Agricultural College, where students were taught animal husbandry, agriculture, and other rural industries.

The college authorities decided that many of the older cottages on Auchincruive estate were no longer regarded as being fit for human habitation, and thus, over the period 1930-1950 many were demolished. In 1930 the cottages at Craighall were still all occupied, in the main by miners, who probably travelled to Mossblown or Glenburn collieries for work. Another who lived at Craighall worked as a railwayman, plus there was one spinster and one widow.

The miners had to walk to their work for many years, and the distance travelled got further and further as the small local pits were closed. Henry Corrigan, in reminiscing about the time when he lived at Craighall, noted that, 'the way the men-folk going to the pits got out of [Craighall] on a winter's morning, to walk to Drumdow, five miles distant, Number 11 at Stair, the same distance, and the Sundrums, was a thing to be wondered at. They had no flashlights then, just a small, naked light. And how some of the men kept it in!'

The steep brae leading into the clachan was something of a problem for villagers. Henry Corrigan continues, 'The children [who had to walk to either Annbank or St Quivox schools] were all well-shod; they had to be, for the road into the place baffled description, and going up the big brae on a winter's night was a nightmare! While coming down was a thrill never to be forgotten – especially when the river was in flood! Taking coals to the clachan was an ordeal that Pundy Wilson was not sweet on; there were no motor cars in those days, and even the doctor would not have been averse to giving it the go-by; grocers, bakers, butchers and milkmen did not look with favour on visiting it.'

And yet Craighall did get visitors. It seems to have attracted 'gangrel bodies', keen to earn a penny or beg for charity. Among those who did make it up the brae were Mick Rooney, pushing dishes for sale in his barrow. An old sailor used to call for food – he had suffered frostbite, and had deformed legs. There was also a man who carried his fiddle beneath his coat until, on his arrival, would bring it out and busk among the cottages.

By 1933, however, only two houses at Craighall still had residents. The *Ayrshire Post* of November that year recorded that the village 'is shortly to disappear.' The last couple of residents were to be rehoused in Annbank. Within months, they had moved to their new council houses and the houses at Craighall were pulled down, the community obliterated from the landscape.

The residents were not to forget their homes for long, however, for soon the Craighall, Barrackhall and Tarholm Reunion was started. The first get-together took place in January 1937, meeting in the New Hall, Annbank. At the reunion, and that of 1938 and 1939, there were over 200 in attendance, desperate to meet friends and former neighbours, and to listen to anecdotes of life in the old hamlets in days gone by. The outbreak of the Second World War brought the reunions to a close, and despite the claim that 'although the houses have all been pulled down, and the grass and moss are growing over what were the streets of the homely, thriving clachan, the village will always occupy a warm spot in the hearts of the old inhabitants,' the old inhabitants themselves are now being forgotten.

Today, the rectangle that formed the village of Craighall contains one modern cottage on it, with little to indicate that the village ever existed. Part of one former house has been converted into a garage.

17

Craigmark

*

The name of the village of Craigmark survives in Dalmellington's junior football team. Craigmark Burntonians links two mining community names – Craigmark, which is a lost village, and Burnton, which survives as a small community of houses located immediately north of Dalmellington. The football team was founded in 1929 and played initially on Smithfield Park at Burnton, before moving to their present Station Park in Dalmellington. Prior to the formation of Craigmark Burntonians football club there had been an earlier team in the village. Craigmark Thistle played in the local football tournaments.

The community at Burnton was built to rehouse the residents of Craigmark, for by the 1920s the old houses were no longer deemed of a sufficient standard for modern living. As the houses at Burnton were finished, the folks of Craigmark moved out, and their old homes were pulled down. The first of the Burnton houses were erected in 1924 by the Dalmellington Iron Company. A total of 88 were built to either side of Burnton farm and the Craigmark residents were all re-housed by 1938. They had the wondrous benefit of running water in the kitchens, flushing toilets and by 1933 had been connected to the electricity supplied from the power station at Waterside.

Today, all that remains of Craigmark is the former store building, which in the 1960s was sold by the National Coal Board and subsequently converted into the Running Dog Saloon, a Wild West themed pub. It gained some publicity in the press and on the television as a result. It was later to become the Craigmark Country Inn. There are also the remains of the old Minnivey mine, for a number of years used as an industrial railway museum.

The oldest building at Craigmark was a long row, lying north-south, built on the higher ground between the Chalmerston and Caldwell burns. This is shown on the 1857 Ordnance Survey map, but by the 1894 revision it had virtually gone, leaving only one building, formed from the north end of the row. This was the remains of Craigmark farm, which had existed for centuries before the new village was erected.

Most of Craigmark was built around 1847 by the Dalmellington Iron Company to house many of its workers. The whole community was completed by 1853 and was to be the first village built in its entirety by the iron company. The stone came from Dunaskin Quarry. The village comprised of six rows of houses, all built back to back to each other, a format that was popular with many early miners' rows. This type of building was often referred to as a 'Dublin', a name which was later erroneously attributed to the high percentage of Irish immigrants who lived in the village. The name actually derived from 'double-end', descriptive of the back-to-back style of the rows. At one time there were almost 100 houses in the community. In 1875 rent for a house at Craigmark was 1s. 3d. per week for a single apartment, 1s. 6d. for a double apartment.

43. Craigmark from south

Most of the menfolk in the village were employed in the pits that surrounded their community. These were Sillyhole, Minnivey and Craigmark. The six Sillyhole pits were some of the earliest sunk after the formation of the ironworks, located north-west of Dalmellington and to the south of Craigmark. They operated from 1852 until 1862. The three Minnivey pits were sunk in 1848-52, and similarly closed in 1862-3. They were located to the west of Craigmark. There were four pits named Craigmark. Craigmark Numbers 1 and

2 were the oldest, the former sunk in 1866, the latter in 1879. Craigmark Numbers 3 and 4 were sunk in 1913.

In 1913 there were a total of 73 houses in the village, 52 of which were two apartment dwellings, the other 21 being single apartment. The village was accessed by a road that meandered alongside the Chalmerston Burn from Dalmellington. The first row encountered by the visitor was the largest, located on the left side of the road, between it and Caldwell Burn. It was referred to as the Laigh (meaning Low) Row. Sometimes it was also referred to as the Laight Row, an error, but seemingly plausible considering a local farm has this name. This row had eighteen houses in it, nine facing the roadway, the others built back-to-back with them and facing the burn. These were known respectively as the Front and Back Rows of the Laigh Row. Built of stone, the exterior was often white-washed to try to give it a cleaner appearance. Each house had at least one door and one window and within was a room and kitchen. The roofs, which

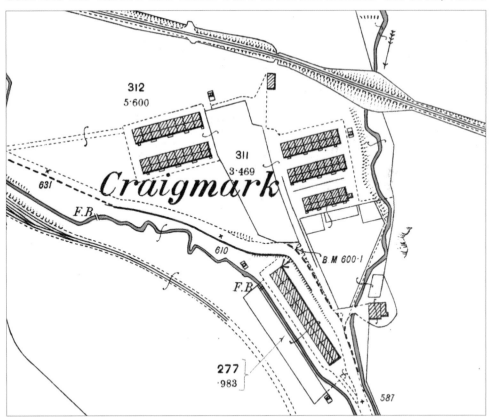

44. Craigmark from 1896 Ordnance Survey map
Reproduced by permission of the National Library of Scotland

were slated, had chimneys half-way up them, rather than on the apex. These houses latterly had gardens located across the burn from the row. The burn had been straightened and a footbridge gave access to the plots.

Climbing a roadway to the right, one came to three rows built parallel with each other, lying almost east-west. Officially, these were known as the Single Rows, from the fact that each house was just a single apartment in size. Unofficially, however, they became known as the Derry Rows. The first row had twelve houses in it. The row behind had sixteen houses in it, as did the back row. All of these houses were single-storey, with slated roofs, and again the chimneys were located half-way up the roof. As years passed, the smallness of these homes was recognised, and many families were able to take on the lease of neighbouring properties, removing part of the dividing wall to create a larger dwelling.

The last two rows were parallel with the three rows, but they lay further to the west, beyond a small burn that developed into an open sewer. The front row had sixteen houses in it, as did the row behind. These house were two apartments, or double-apartment, resulting in them gaining the nickname 'Dublin' Row. The name Derry Row is thought to have derived from the Irish place name as a contrast.

The interior of most of the houses was originally much the same as far as finishes went. The floors were mostly laid with bricks or stone blocks. On this was fixed the built in beds, under which hurley beds were rolled. The fire was located in a small fireplace, equipped with a Dover Stove, where most of the meals were made. The fire remained lit all day, providing some heat to the houses. The coal for burning was originally kept safely below the beds, but in later years the iron company provided coal-houses outside, giving the residents more room inside.

Craigmark appears to have been fairly well supplied with water during its lifetime. At the end of each row were water taps, or 'spickets' as they were termed locally, probably supplied from a spring on the hillside. The Laigh Row had the additional bonus of an open brick-lined water channel that ran into the Burnton Burn at the back of the houses. Thus, dirty water from closets and sinks could be poured into it and it was quickly flushed away.

To serve the children of Craigmark, a small stone-built school building was erected just to the south of the village, in the glen of the Chalmerston Burn. A simple building, this was established before 1857 and was operated by the

Dalmellington Iron Company. Around 1870 the school roll was about 220, of which around 180 attended regularly. By 1879 the roll was 198, taught by the schoolmaster, his wife and four pupil-teachers. The first schoolmaster, Robert Kidd, had an assistant teacher to help. Kidd used to send well-behaved pupils to the small copse of wood that grew alongside the Burnton Burn opposite the school to select a hazel stick from which he fashioned a cane, used to control and chastise the unrulier pupils. William Tavendale was schoolmaster up to his death in 1880, aged 50. Originally the school did not have a toilet, but an outside lavatory was later erected alongside the burn, on the opposite side of the road. Craigmark School was extended to the south, and was to outlive the community, latterly serving Burnton. It was closed in 1927, after which local children had to walk to Dalmellington. Thereafter the building was converted into a workmen's institute. This continued as the Burnton and Dalmellington Social Club.

The Royal Commission on Housing inspectors who visited Craigmark in 1913 were fairly complimentary of the community. They noted that:

> Although the frontage is unpaved the pathways are fairly clean. Each house has a water-closet and a coalhouse, with a washing-house for about every four tenants. All the houses are built of stone, and are between 60 and 70 years old. The rents are – double houses 2s. 3d. per week, and singles 1s. 9d. There are two inset iron beds in the kitchens, but some of the houses are rather small. One kitchen might be described as a lobby, as it measures 14 feet by 8 feet. The room was equally narrow, and this house contained 11 persons. Many of the people complain of the lack of repairs, and some of those we saw were indeed greatly in need of attention. The sewage arrangements, too, leave much to be desired. The arrangement consists of what seems to be a settling tank, and we were informed that it was never cleaned and was very offensive in hot weather. Some repairs and some attention to the sewage would greatly increase the comfort of the people.

The population of Craigmark peaked in the 1870s. In 1851 there were 459 residents. At the census of 1861 there were 543 inhabitants. A decade later the population had risen to 616, before it commenced its decline, dropping to 383 in 1881 and 371 in 1891.

Most of the Craigmark men worked in the various pits and mines on the hillside above. The mines were all owned by the Dalmellington Iron Company, and the miners often moved from pit to pit as they closed and opened.

Craigmark had few community facilities. On the east side of the Laigh Row, across a footbridge over the Chalmerston Burn, was Craigmark Stores. This was a branch of the Dalmellington Ironworks Co-operative Society. It was two storeys in height, the only building in the village with an upstairs. This was where the manager had a flat. It sold almost everything a villager could want, from groceries, butcher-meat to clothing. At the back of the store was a small inn, where beer and porter was sold. The iron company did not allow spirits to be sold. At one end was the pay office, where miners received their wages, less any debts due to the store or ale store. Amongst the store managers were Samuel

45. Craigmark from west

Heron and Alexander Rankin. The latter was to be the manager in the store for many years. He received his appointment in 1919, soon after he returned from war service, and he retained the position until he retired in 1964. There was also a smithy, run by blacksmith James Murdoch. Craigmark did not have a church or place of worship, as with the other iron company villages. It was felt that the churches and chapel in Dalmellington were within walking distance and the residents could go there on Sundays. In the 1860s Craigmark had its own brass band.

During the 1921 miners' strike the residents of Craigmark struggled to make ends meet. With no income from work, many miners resorted to poaching to find food with which they could feed their families. Heating in the houses was also a problem, and unless they could get wood from a farmer, the houses remained cold. To try to help, two young girls dug a small coal seam by the side of the Caldwell Burn. They had found an old tunnel left by the miners, but as they picked at the coal the embankment collapsed, trapping them. Their predicament was spotted by others digging coal further up the glen and soon a rescue of some size was commenced, many of those assisting using their bare hands. Unfortunately, one of the girls was found dead. She was Mary Hastie. The other girl survived. The lifeless corpse was carried by the miners back to her home at 3 Laigh Row. Her funeral was arranged by Matthew Wilson, leader of the local Rechabite tent, to which her family belonged.

46. Craigmark from south-west

The houses at Craigmark were deemed by Ayr County Council to be unfit for habitation under the Housing (Scotland) Acts of 1925-1935, and on 28 May 1936 the Craigmark Clearance Order was confirmed. The houses were to be emptied due to 'disrepair or sanitary defects unfit for human habitation, or are by reason of their bad arrangement or the narrowness or bad arrangement of the streets injurious or dangerous to the health of the inhabitants of the area'. At the time there were 72 households in the community, and they were given one month's notice to vacate their homes. The residents were rehoused in either Dalmellington or Bellsbank.

18

Darnconner

★

There has been a farm on the low hill at Darnconner for centuries. A rounded knoll protrudes above the wet surroundings of Airds Moss, its soil dry enough to grow grass and other crops. In the seventeenth century it was home to the Gibson family who were supporters of the National Covenant. A Covenanting minister, Rev David Houston, held a conventicle, or field-meeting, on the farm of Polbaith, near Kilmarnock, on 16 January 1687. Hugh Gibson in Darnconner attended. He probably took all of his family with him and it is thought that his young child was baptised at the event.

The government dragoons were sent out in pursuit of those who had attended and a number of Covenanters from the Auchinleck, Sorn and Ochiltree areas were captured and imprisoned. Among them was Hugh Gibson who was seized at his home. Apparently he had a number of illegal arms, including a gun and gunpowder. He also had in his possession a collection of books which were regarded as being seditious, and he was caught trying to dispose of them when the soldiers arrived. He was taken to Ayr for trial, which took place before Captain Douglas on 21 January 1687. The charge read:

> Heuge Gibson in Dargoner, Watersyde's tenant in the parish of Auchenfleck, baptised tuo children with the indulged minister of the Sorn; refuises to tell where his youngest child was baptised. There was a gune and halfe a pund of pouder found in his house; he says the gune was his goodfathers; his wyfe gott pairt of the pouder from the dragounes for rubbing his cattell; these rebelliouse books were found betuixt his house and his cottars throune out of ane window.

The case appears to have been un-proven and we next find him appearing before the Earl of Linlithgow and Foulis of Colinton in Edinburgh courthouse. There the charge laid before him was that:

Hewgh Gibsone in the paroch of Auchinleck, in Watersyde's land, depones he wes not at any of these conventicles, and never wes in any armes against the King; lives regularlie, and swears he will never be in armes against him; owns his authoritie and prayes heartily for him, his long life and prosperous government; and depones he cannot write.

Gibson appears to have been set free thereafter.

The lands of Darnconner were acquired by the Alexander of Ballochmyle family in the late eighteenth century. They were expanding their estates at the time, having made profits from the new cotton mills at Catrine and foreign plantations. Darnconner appeared to be a rather strange purchase, being but a small farm steading on a rounded knoll surrounded by peat bogs, but the potential of minerals below the ground had been recognised.

The first coal workings on Darnconner lands appear to have been sunk in the early 1800s, for by 1843 the *New Statistical Account of Scotland* noted that shallow seams of around 3-4 feet in thickness, approximately 50 fathoms (300 feet) below ground level, were dug. Approximately twenty to two dozen men worked in each pit, producing coal that earned around five shillings per ton.

An old map belonging to Ballochmyle estate, dating from the mid-1850s, shows Roundshaw, Darnconner and Common farms. There are five small mines depicted on the south-eastern part of Darnconner farm, west of the Mill Dam, and at the foot of the dam is Common Row, an early line of miners' homes. No village existed at Darnconner itself, but the potential for mining coal was pencilled in – a proposed railway line from the Auchinleck to Muirkirk line is shown, called the 'Shiells and Hilliar Branch'. This was never constructed, but a different mineral siding was laid across the moss at a later date, positioned a bit further to the east.

It was alongside this second railway line that the first part of Darnconner village was created. Two separate blocks of housing were constructed, formed into the High and Low Squares, totalling 34 houses.

William Baird, the coal- and iron-masters, extended the community by erecting new rows to either side of the two existing squares. North-west of the High Square two rows (the Railway Rows) of 24 single-apartment houses were built parallel to each other. Next to the Low Square, in which the Co-op operated by Baird was located, were the new Store Row of six houses and a School Row also of six houses.

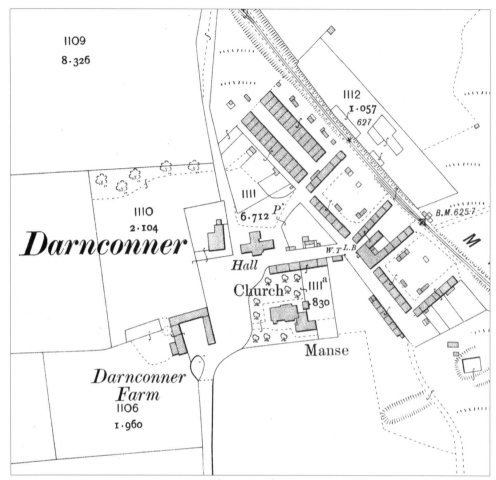

47. Darnconner from 1909 Ordnance Survey map
Reproduced by permission of the National Library of Scotland

The school was located north east of Darnconner farm and had five rooms. The building was erected in 1853 by the Eglinton Iron Company who deducted a monthly fee from its employees in order to pay the school-master an annual salary of £50. It had been erected at the instigation of Rev Dr Chrystal, minister of Auchinleck. Over the years it was added to a few times. On 5 January 1875 William Tweedie was appointed headmaster, previously being assistant teacher at Lugar. He was paid a salary of £150, and had the assistance of five teachers, some of them pupil teachers. Tweedie married Margaret Paterson in 1885 but she died soon after (on 13 August 1886) aged 28.

48. Darnconner Parish Church

On 1 November 1887 Darnconner, Lugar and Cronberry schools were transferred to the School Board who took over their running. At Darnconner William Tweedie continued until after the Great War. In 1899 he moved into the new schoolmaster's house which the board erected next to the school.

The school at Darnconner was leased from Bairds, but by the turn of the century it was deemed unsuitable for educational purposes, and if it was not brought up to standard then Scotch Education Department grants would be withheld. Accordingly, in 1904 it was resolved to have a replacement erected, capable of holding 300 pupils. James Hay, architect, of Kilmarnock, drew up plans for a new building, erected at the southern end of Common Row, a more central location to cover Darnconner, Common and Commondyke villages. The first sod was cut in the spring of 1905. The mason and plumbing work was carried out by Messrs Melville & MacPherson of Newmilns; the joinery work by Cook of Catrine; H. & T. Morrison of Cumnock did the slating, and M. Taylor of Cumnock the plasterwork. Opened on Monday 15 March 1906 by Robert Angus, the new school had cost £3,934 16s. 1d. to build. A gold key was gifted to Mrs Angus by Mr Hay and a banquet was held in one of the classrooms. The new school building was erected with terracotta bricks, with dressed stone at the doors, windows and gable tops. The roof comprised green slate. The main entrance was located at the west end of the building, reaching a lobby that ran through the centre of the building. There were seven classrooms, each with 'Boyle's patent air pump ventilators'.

49. Darnconner School in 1906

The school board instructed the headmaster at Darnconner that no pupils residing in Sorn parish should be admitted to the new school when it opened in 1906. Prior to the school's erection the board had been in contact with the Sorn parish board to discuss the possibilities of a joint school, but the Sorn board turned this down and refused to offer the Auchinleck board any money in respect of its residents educated at Darnconner. When no Sorn pupils were allowed into the new school the board at Sorn quickly contacted the Auchinleck board and agreed to grant some funds to assist in the running of Darnconner School. Most of the Sorn parish pupils resided at Burnside Row, just 1,500 yards from the school. The roll at Darnconner in 1917 was 195.

William Tweedie retired as headmaster in July 1919 after over fifty years of service. Tweedie himself lived until 4 November 1926 when he died aged 74. He was buried in Auchinleck. At Darnconner he was followed by Mr W. Rattray (1919-1926), after which the school was closed.

Darnconner Store was the principal shop in the immediate district, the store at Commondyke being smaller. In 1861 the storekeeper was John Provan. Adjoining it was a bakery. There was no butcher's – meat being brought by horse-drawn van from the main Baird store at Lugar. Baird's employees were expected to buy all their requisites in the company store, indeed they often bought items on tick, to be paid for from their next wage. At Darnconner an office next to the store opened for a couple of hours each Wednesday to allow employees to draw out a little of their wages if required. In April 1913 fire ripped through the store at Darnconner, destroying the building and stock, and causing some damage to neighbouring properties. John Dempsey managed to photograph the fire-ravaged ruins and sold postcards of the scene soon after. The manager at the Ironworks Co-op branch at the time was Robert Thomson. At the end of the Great War John MacDonald was the manager of Darnconner Co-op branch and he remained until the shop closed in 1931.

50. Darnconner School class

The post office at Darnconner was run by Mrs Annie Rae, postmistress, until 1911 when she retired. David Brown was postmaster until he died in November 1927. Postmen were Andrew Mitchell, who lived at Common Row, and Hugh Mullen.

The village had a police station in one of the rows, to which constables seem to have been appointed for a short period. These include George Smith (1878), John Innes (1881), James Mowat (1885) and G. R. Mair (1887). The village constable at the turn of the century was James Wilson. By 1928 the Darnconner Nursing Association existed.

By 1900 the new Common Row (or Commonloch Row) was built at Darnconner, the original Common Row of six houses becoming known then as the Stable Row. The Common Row was built alongside the old tracks which were laid to the Common Coalworks of the early nineteenth century, facing across the road to the Common Loch. To reduce the cost of erecting houses, the row was built continuous, with a total of 96 houses forming a dog-leg. Built of stone, some of the materials were brought from old houses which Bairds owned at Dalry.

Behind the Common Row was the much shorter Walker's Row of twelve houses, located perpendicular to the roadway into Darnconner farm. This row was owned by the William Walker Coal Company, hence its name. Also owned by Walker's were the Ballochmyle Rows, two rows of 24 houses each, on both sides of the road between Common and Glenshamrock farms. These probably date to around 1876 when the Ballochmyle Pit was sunk. Outwith the parish was the Burnside Row, of twelve houses, better known as 'The Poverty' from the fact that the residents were some of the poorer in the district, which was also owned by Walker.

On 11 November 1914 William Baird gave up the lease of Darnconner and ownership of the houses passed back to Ballochmyle estate. The estate did not really want much to do with the houses, and it was noted that no repairs were carried out on them thereafter.

Over the lifetime of the village, Darnconner's population rose and fell. At the 1871 census there were 928 residents. By 1881 this had fallen to 550, but it was to increase again by 1891, when 1,198 people lived in the community.

Darnconner continued to be an active community in the new century even although most of the local mines were beginning to be closed. The population in 1901 was 457. In 1914 there were 80 houses in the various squares and rows. By 1925 Darnconner and Commonloch rows were owned by James Clark of Carskeoch, near Patna.

Thomas MacKerrell visited the village as part of the survey into miners' housing in 1914. At Darnconner were 94 houses, 17 each in Low and High Squares, 48 houses in the two Railway Rows, built back to back, and six each in the School and Store rows. The total population was around 400. In the Low (or Laigh) Square there were no washing-houses, but a few boilers stood in the open air. Two doorless closets served the seventeen families who lived there, the open ash pits overflowing with stinking refuse. The condition of some of the coal-houses was such that a few tenants kept their fuel beneath their beds. The High Square had similar conditions, and the 'glaur' was inches deep at the house doorways. The Railway Rows, let at five shillings per month, were very damp, the floors made of broken brick tiles. The closets had no doors, some surrounded by a sea of human excrement. The School and Store rows likewise had poor amenities, the Store Row having no closets and needing to share those in the School Row. The village also had a church and store, the whole owned by William Baird and Company.

Although the population of Common Row stood at 506, there was not a single wash-house and only seventeen doorless closets for the whole row. The smell from the closets was described as abominable, the floor being covered in human excrement. The pathway in front of the row was unpaved, and the inspectors could not walk along it without going up to the ankles in dirt. The sewage passed down an open syvor before being discharged into the Auchinleck Burn.

Ballochmyle Rows stood to either side of the road which separates Darnconner and Barglachan farms and, like the Common Row, were owned by Bairds. There were 24 houses in each row, let at two shillings per week, the total population 227. When the Ballochmyle Colliery was closed one of the buildings was converted into a branch of the Auchinleck Co-op to serve this community.

The Stable Row, owned by Sir Claud Alexander of Ballochmyle's trustees, had only six two-apartment houses and one single apartment. There were 37 people living here, the rent £5 per annum. There was a single wooden closet for the six houses, and no ash pits or wash-houses. The sewage ran into a ditch to the nearby burn. This row stood at the southern end of the Common Loch.

A mission station of the parish church had been established at Darnconner in 1874, but the 'more airy than comfortable' corrugated-iron shed in which the villagers worshipped was blown over in a storm. On 14 March 1897 a new Gothic church with adjoining manse was erected with funds provided by Robert Angus of Craigston. Built of red Ballochmyle sandstone externally, internally it was finished in white Kilwinning freestone. It comprised a nave, small transepts and chancel, the latter floored with small tiles. The architect of the kirk was Robert S. Ingram and it was built to accommodate 300 worshippers at a cost of £3,000. The opening service was conducted jointly by the Revs Chrystal and Hill.

The church at Darnconner had a number of ministers over a short time, amongst these being Rev Benjamin Brown (nephew of Rev Dr Chrystal), Rev A. D. Scott MA, and Rev James Higgins. The latter's first charge was at Darnconner, where he married the infant mistress at Darnconner School, Grace Johnston Girvan, on 21 April 1910. They had four children. Higgins was later to serve as the minister at Rendall, Orkney, in 1910. In 1919 he was translated to Orphir, also Orkney, and in 1926 moved on again to Amulree in Perthshire.

Another minister for a time was Rev William Eadie, and Rev William Petrie performed baptisms in 1913. Latterly the parish minister visited to perform baptisms, the weekly services being conducted by 'missionaries'. These were James Eaglesham, W. Ross and George Laird. Traditionally, only one wedding was ever to take place in the church. The last baptism performed at Darnconner was of Hendryna Dickson (born 16 September 1937) which took place on 5 June 1938. She lived with her parents at 116 Peesweep Row, Lugar. As the rows in Darnconner were being abandoned and the villagers rehoused in Auchinleck, the church was closed in 1939 but stood for many years thereafter.

In addition to the local Church of Scotland congregation, there was an assembly of brethren which met in a former house at Ballochmyle Row. The brethren were formed in 1891 and continued to meet until 1929. At Darnconner there were many busy groups, including the Rechabites, Free Gardeners, and the Darnconner Branch of the Independent Labour Party which held an annual social and dance from 1910. The Rechabite movement was established at Darnconner in 1896, the juvenile branch the year following. The membership in 1913 was 76 state members, 107 order members and 69 juveniles.

Other groups which were represented at Darnconner included the Boy Scouts and a branch of the British Order of Ancient Free Gardeners, known as the Heatherbell Lodge. In 1901 Darnconner Airds Moss Burns Club was established, becoming federated on the roll of Burns clubs in the Burns Federation as number 122.

By the end of the First World War the community at Darnconner was in decline. Messrs Baird's tenancy of the houses expired at Martinmas 1920 and the tenants were told to leave by December that year. In 1920 many of the houses in the Squares, Front and Back rows were empty. Only squatters occupied some of the houses, or at least those who failed to leave by the due date were termed squatters. Ownership of the houses returned to Ballochmyle estate, who became liable for the rates. The estate claimed that the houses were uninhabitable, and therefore should not be subject to rates, and that anyone still living there had not been asked for rent and had paid none. At the Lands Valuation Appeal Court in Edinburgh in February 1922, Ballochmyle estate was deemed responsible for the houses.

In 1926 a group of labourers built rough homes for themselves in the side of the former Common Pit Number 10 bing, half a mile from Darnconner itself. These were partially dug into the side of the bing, and rough stone walls were constructed to support the sides as well as the roof of timber and turves. The semi-subterranean community stayed here for a number of years, in 1929 there being nine occupants occupying the dwellings. One of the residents, Michael Mulryan, was murdered by three other men. Mulryan, who was 57 years of age, was known locally as 'Mad Harry'. Charged for the murder were Hugh MacNaughtan, James Kelly and Joseph Donnelly.

By 1930 the Ballochmyle, Walker's and Stable rows were uninhabitable. Ownership of them had passed to Mrs Christina Gordon of Carskeoch, near Patna, who bought Darnconner and Common farms from Ballochmyle estate. She also owned the Common Row which was abandoned in 1928. In the 1930s a start was made by the county council on rehousing the remaining occupants in new houses at Auchinleck. By 1932 only 27 families remained at Darnconner.

In 1933 many of the tenants from Darnconner and Commondyke went on a rent strike in their new Auchinleck homes, claiming that Ayr County Council were charging them rents in excess of what the Slum Clearance Act allowed. Twenty-one court summonses were issued by the council in December 1933 and at court the tenants were found in the wrong, having agreed to the new rents prior to their moving.

In the year the Second World War broke out, both the school and the church were closed, each building becoming stores, the former for the council, the latter for the farmer. In 1940 the Common Row was demolished, the final row at Darnconner to be removed. The school was demolished in 1955, the church in 1979, leaving the manse standing. In 1958 the belfry had been removed and the bell gifted to Catrine Congregational Church. The font was gifted to the Peden Kirk in Auchinleck. J. L. MacArthur came to Darnconner after the Second World War with the job of demolishing the church, but found it so attractive that he bought it and the manse and resided there for many years.

Playing football at Junior level was Darnconner Britannia Football Club, existing from around 1888 to 1900. Their field was known as Pablin Ground, their colours red, white and blue.

In the late twentieth century open cast coal mines were developed at Darnconner and Common farms (the former from 1985, the latter from 1990). The open cast mine at Darnconner produced over 600,000 tons of coal before 1991. Darnconner was also used for the extraction of clay for brick-making. Brick-making collapsed, and so the site became abandoned. It was sold to a waste management company for landfill purposes, planning permission for it being granted in 1996. However, the site was never used and permission for dumping expired. The hole had also filled with water, creating a lochan of around 30 acres in extent. The site was subsequently subject to a variety of semi-restoration schemes, whereby the loch would be retained and the surrounding mounds landscaped to reduce their impact on the countryside.

51. Darnconner – last resident

Today, the site of Darnconner village has mostly been obliterated by surface coal mining, and much of the land has been infilled and planted with trees. Only the former schoolhouse and manse survive, alongside Darnconner farmhouse itself.

19

Doura

*

The village of Doura was located north-east of Irvine, just over half a mile along the Glasgow road from Sourlie. One of the older mining communities, it developed and waned over the years. There were quite a number of small pits in the countryside hereabouts, many established in the late eighteenth century, and by the time the Ordnance Surveyors arrived in 1856 they were abandoned.

However, mining is first noted on some scale in 1686, when Irvine Town Council commenced a coal works in the vicinity. A 'coal ingineer' named John Wallace was hired to survey the district and sink a pit where he found suitable coal. At Doura, which borders Irvine and Kilwinning parishes, he found coal, but not before the burgh council had to pay to entertain him at an inn in the town, which included 'aill and brandy, tobacco and pipes'. Further bills were forthcoming whilst he remained in the town, but by the time he left in the autumn he had discovered a suitable place for a coal mine. Workers from the town were hired to 'set doune the first shank of the heugh'. Food was supplied by the council, and extra ale on 7 September 1686 when the first coal was dug. The magistrates attended that day, but instead of ale they were given brandy to drink. Various seams were discovered, but the works appear to have been abandoned quite soon after.

Other mines were to be sunk, and rows of houses were built for the miners, perhaps the oldest being built in the last couple of decades of the eighteenth century. Certainly, at that time there were from twelve to sixteen colliers employed in the mines. The houses were mainly located alongside a farm road, originally leading to Laigh Doura farm. The farm was probably incorporated in a larger farm, perhaps Doura Mains, and the buildings were converted into miners' houses. Adjoining the old farm buildings was a row of around eight or nine houses. These faced onto the roadway and had gardens to the rear. They were rather small properties, however large families had to live in them.

Across the track, facing the row, was a shorter line of houses. This only had six houses in it. Again, the houses faced the roadway and had gardens to the rear.

Back towards the main Barrhead and Glasgow road was a second long row, located on the north side of the track. This row had twelve houses in it. Across the track from the terrace were the miners' gardens.

In line with the Laigh Doura roadway was a short access route located across the main road. Here was a row of seven houses, known as Whinniebrae. Behind the houses were gardens, however to the front was one of the old pits to which Doura owed its origins.

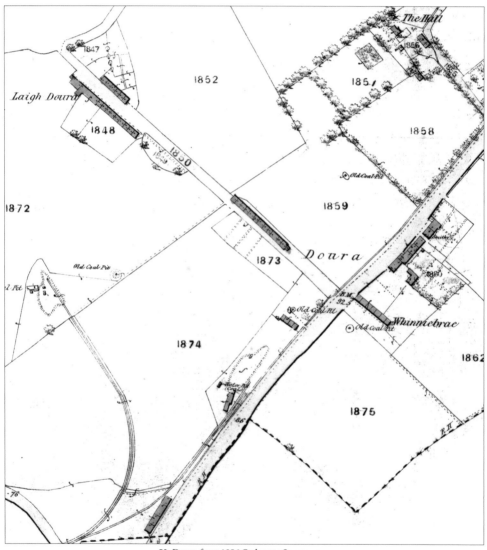

52. Doura from 1856 Ordnance Survey map
Reproduced by permission of the National Library of Scotland

Behind the row of Whinniebrae was a group of seven or eight houses, their irregular size and shape an indication of their antiquity. In one of the buildings at the north-east end of the row was a smithy.

A further row of houses existed, located nearer Irvine by a few hundred yards. This row stood at the side of the road, just north of the nearby junction. There were originally seven homes here. Immediately behind them was the mineral railway that led from the main line towards the pits at Doura. In 1856, one of these pits was still in production, located along this siding, between the rows.

By the middle of the nineteenth century, the miners' rows and pits at Doura were the property of John Barr, who leased the mineral rights. He was to serve as Provost of Ardrossan for some time. In 1900 the community, and its pits, were the property of Sir Thomas Montgomery Cuninghame, 10th Baronet of Corsehill, but they were leased to Robert Armour, fireclay manufacturer, Irvine.

Writing in *The Annals of the Parish*, John Galt described the coal coming from 'Douray' to Irvine, ready for sale or export. He explained that the coal came by the public road to Girdle Toll, then down the old road north from Irvine, known as the Glasgow Vennel. 'The coal-carts from the Douray moor were often reested in the middle of the causey, and on more than one occasion some of them laired altogether in the middens, and others of them broke down.' At Girdle Toll a fee of one penny was paid per cart load of coal that passed through, and a further charge was made if it was to be exported.

In addition to the deprivations of living in poor quality houses, and the permanent fear of accidents in the pits, the residents of Doura were to suffer considerably in 1832. At the time the cholera epidemic was spreading across Scotland, killing thousands of people in its wake. In February 1832 a woman came from Glasgow and passed through Doura, spreading the disease amongst the residents. A total of thirty villagers were to suffer death from the disease.

By the time the Ordnance Survey returned in 1895, Laigh Doura farm buildings had gone. The row adjoining it was also in ruins, the roofs removed and only the walls standing. Across the track the northern row survived. The row of twelve houses had also been demolished. Adjoining where it stood was a new row of houses, eight in number.

Across the track from this new row was another new row, containing six houses. The houses at Whinniebrae had been abandoned and their roofs removed. The old houses with the smithy were still much the same, though the smithy had closed.

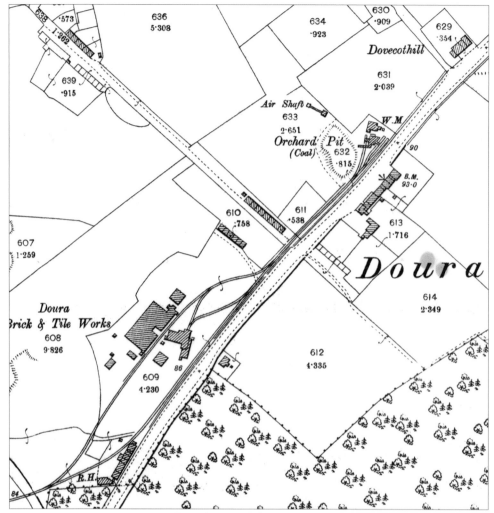

53. Doura from 1896 Ordnance Survey map
Reproduced by permission of the National Library of Scotland

Thirteen years later the map-makers returned to Doura, and again the village was noted as being in further decline. The old row of six houses at Laigh Doura was still there, but the new row of eight houses was already being abandoned – three of the houses having been demolished, and two of them being joined into one.

The population of Doura in 1841 was around 200. This grew to around 350 in 1874. In 1870, when Father Thomas Keane of Irvine was surveying the parish, he reckoned that there were 60 Roman Catholics living at Doura.

A school was erected at Doura for the children of the village at the sole expense of the Earl of Eglinton and Winton sometime before 1840. It had a 'large school-room and a house for the teacher, with a play-ground and garden attached to it'. This was taken over by Kilwinning School Board in 1872. In 1898 the schoolmaster was John Dunlop.

Ayrshire Constabulary had a police station at Doura, still open in 1931.

The last real pit at Doura was the Orchard Pit, which mined coal. This was sunk in the late nineteenth century, across the road from the smithy row. The old mineral siding was extended to the new pit.

The site of the old Water Pit coal mine was by 1895 converted into the Doura Brick and Tile Works. By 1908 this was renamed as the Doura Fireclay Works.

Most of Doura was demolished by the 1930s. Little remained, apart from two houses in the Store Row, plus the store itself. Two houses remained in the Haw Row, plus a further six at High Doura. These six houses were still occupied by mineworkers. Ownership of this part of Doura was still in the hands of Sir Thomas Cuninghame, 10th Baronet, of Corsehill. Elizabeth Kerr owned three houses in another part of the village, and William Wilson owned five.

20

Drumsmudden

★

The name 'Drumsmudden' is a bit like one of those twee, probably made-up, Scottish place-names that appear in music-hall variety and pantomime shows. Brigadoon, Barbie, Auchterturra and Drumsmudden are archetypically Scottish-sounding rural villages, used in novels and non-fiction stories. There was even a book published by the Ayrshire Post in 1892 entitled *The Annals o' Drumsmudden*, written by Anera MacDougal. Extending to 150 pages, the *Annals* are filled with many humorous Scottish dialect stories. However, there was a real Drumsmudden, a small Ayrshire village, home to coal-miners and their families.

The Drumsmudden Colliery was established in 1882 by the Dalmellington Iron Company. It stood on what had been a green field lying between two low hills on the farms of Drumsmodden (as it is spelled today) and Crawsland, itself now a lost dwelling. The Ayr and Cumnock branch railway was constructed between these hillocks, providing a ready opportunity to export the coal mined from below the green fields, and a series of sidings with 'lies' and loading hoppers for the waggons were built. Two shafts were sunk into the ground and the usual group of surface buildings and horrals were constructed to service the pit. The shafts, which were 40 yards apart, were 202 fathoms (1,212 feet) in depth. The pit produced coal of a top quality from the Lugar Main seam, but it was hampered by many faults. Often miners working at a face would discover that the coal disappeared, to be replaced by rock. Many hours and days were lost in prospecting up and down these faces to try to find the seam once more. This cost the company thousands of pounds, and the pit had only really covered the expense of sinking itself by the time it was closed in 1904. Maps of 1908 indicate that the surface buildings were quickly removed, leaving only three bings to indicate the existence of the colliery.

As with almost every colliery in the country, accidents far below the ground resulted in deaths that left the local community devastated. Drumsmudden was no different, although there appears to have been fewer deaths there, compared with other mines. Nevertheless, on 15 April 1886 James Paterson was squashed when the roof and sides of the area where he was working collapsed. He was only 26 years of age.

An unusual occurrence took place in Drumsmudden pit on the morning of Wednesday 21 November 1888. A severe thunderstorm broke out in the area, and a large flash occurred when the ascending cage was almost 20 yards from the surface. The engineman was made powerless by the electricity, but was able to throw himself on the brake lever, stopping the engine. On recovery, he felt pains in his arms, neck and shoulders. A report in the *Transactions of the Mining Institute of Scotland* gives details of the further problems:

A heavy charge descended the conductor on the stalk, uplifting the earth and ashes at the bottom, but otherwise doing no damage. The pit bottomer of the winding pit heard a loud, cracking noise, and saw a clear, bluish flame on the crowns on the roof at the pumping pit. The signal boy was terrified, seeing fire running and leaping between the haulage rope and the rails. The chainman was engaged at the time taking down the empty race, and was sitting on the last hutch, with his feet on the chain. When about 40 yards down he felt a shock through his legs, and was pitched on to the road, and lay stunned for a time. Twenty yards beyond the foot of the slope dook, or 320 yards from the pumping pit bottom, and 240 fathoms from the surface, two boys were standing, one having his feet on the rails and his head almost touching the electric bell wires. He got a shock, turning him round about and both were terrified by seeing fire flying between the rails and wire. They ran off to find the oversman. When they found him they were white with fear, and said fire was flying all through the pit. Fortunately, no serious injury was done to any of the workmen or property by the above strange occurrence.

Drumsmudden Pit was a good three miles from the parish village of Ochiltree, and slightly farther from the nearby community of Coylton. To provide a ready workforce, the firm established its own small village, two rows of houses built alongside. These were the Skerrington and Drumsmudden Rows. Built of brick, the houses were small.

The name Skerrington came from Lord Skerrington, who owned much of the surrounding countryside. Born William Campbell on 27 June 1855, he was educated at Edinburgh Academy and Edinburgh University. He was married in 1880 to Alice Mary Fraser, second daughter of the Hon. Patrick, Lord Fraser. Campbell was admitted to the Faculty of Advocates in 1878. He became a Queen's Counsel in 1898 and Dean of the Faculty of Advocates from 1905-8. In 1908 he was appointed as a judge of the Court of Session, entitling him to take a title. He adopted the name Lord Skerrington after his Cumnock estate, which at the time comprised of five farms. In Ochiltree parish he owned Drumjoan, Drumsmudden, Reidston and Whitehill farms. Lord Skerrington was to be the first Roman Catholic appointed as a judge in Scotland, resulting in some Protestant opposition at the time. In 1919 he was given the honour of Knight Commander of St Gregory the Great by Pope Benedict XV. Lord Skerrington retired from the judicial bench in December 1925. He died at his Edinburgh home after a long illness on 21 July 1927.

Although the land was owned by Lord Skerrington, the colliery and rows were sold to the Dalmellington Iron Company. When the colliery at Drumsmudden was closed, the rows no longer had any real need to be there, so the Dalmellington company leased the houses to the Coylton Coal Company, and miners employed by them were able to stay there, though they had to travel further to their work.

The Drumsmudden Row was built adjoining the pit, six houses in a terrace. It was often referred to as 'Number 2 Row'. The front doors faced northwards, overlooking gardens towards the woods and shelterbelts on the knoll occupied by Crawsland. Running along the northern side of the gardens were two railway sidings from the colliery, meaning that pugs and coal carriages often drew along in front of the houses.

The rear of the row had projecting wings on each of the houses, and between these wings were outside toilets. These homes were the better quality of the two rows, being larger in size. Here the pit manager and other 'gaffers' lived.

A second, much larger, row of houses existed at Drumsudden, officially named Skerrington Row but often referred to as Number 1 Row. The row had fourteen houses in total. This was located at right angles to the road linking Drongan with Sinclairston, near to where the four houses of Drumjoan Terrace stand today. The front of the houses looked to the south-east, the rising field blocking distant views. Along the front of the houses was a track, running the length of the row. To the rear the houses also had a projecting wing, but the houses were different in layout to the other row. Here the houses were either L-

or T-shaped, repeating alternately, the buildings fitting together in a rather strange way, a bit like a tesselated pattern. These homes simply comprised of a room and kitchen.

The kitchen measured around 21 feet by 13 feet, doubling as a sleeping area, there being two large built-in beds located along one side, and a press, or cupboard just inside the door. Within the 'room' there was a further set-in bed.

Linking the two rows was a track across the field. By the side of this path was the source of water for the village. The 1894 Ordnance Survey map indicates this as a pump, whereas by 1908 it was shown as a well. The supply of water to the rows always appears to have been something of a problem, for this pump often dried up. When this happened the residents had to walk a mile and a half to a former test bore, the 'Diamond Bore', from which water flowed continually. Another source of water that was used when possible was the water tank at Belston railway junction. This was normally used to fill the tanks of the steam engines, but it could be made to overflow and run into the burn that flowed past the rows. The men of the community would then scoop the water up and fill the barrels that stood by the rows to collect rainwater from the roofs.

The rows at Drumsmudden, although fairly new and of better quality, became surplus fairly quickly. By the start of the First World War in 1914, of the twenty houses there, thirteen were sitting empty. The Drumsmudden Row had three tenants – Mrs Bennet, a widow, and two workers' families. These were James MacGarvie, labourer, and John Rodger, pitheadman. In Skerrington Row there were four houses occupied, one of them by Mrs Kernachan, widow. The other three were lived in by John Wilson, James Wilson ad William Hodge, all miners.

To try to improve the quality of life at Drumsmudden, and encourage new tenants, in 1918 new drainage, water closets, coal-houses and sinks inside the sculleries were constructed at the High Drumsmudden Row. Previously there had only been two dry closets for the full row of fourteen houses. Dirty water was poured from the basins in the houses and closets into the small stream that flowed to the back of the rows. To keep the 'sheugh' as free-running as possible, at one time a young man was sent from the pit every Saturday and he had to brush it clean.

One of the families who lived at Drumsmudden was an old Irish couple known as John and Katie Bell. Every 12 July they travelled back to Ireland to take part in the festivities. The Bells were known for their pet monkey, but most locals were frightened of it, for when you approached it, it bared its teeth in a threatening manner.

A social spirit thrived in the rows of the district. The Coylton Drumsmudden Friendly Society existed for a number of years, providing a means of saving and boosting the welfare of its members. In August 1895 the president of the society, Thomas Watters, was presented with a mantelpiece clock 'for his long and faithful services, having acted as president for the last eighteen years'. Members of the society paid around threepence per week from their wages. Should the wage-earner turn ill, the society would pay the family an income for around five to six weeks.

54. Drumsmudden – Alex Linwood

In 1921 Ochiltree Parish Council agreed to rent 2½ acres of land on Whitehill farm as a recreation ground for the residents. This was located east of the Bardarroch Road between the railway and the small burn that drained the nearby fields, as well as the rows' drains.

The field was noted for being rather rough, but it didn't stop the local children from playing on it. One who used the field often was Alexander, or Alex Linwood, born in the rows on 13 March 1920. At the age of fourteen he, like most other boys of the time, went to work in the pits, but his love of football led him to sign for Muirkirk Juniors in 1938. He was to become a notable player, signing for St Mirren in October later the same year. In 1943 the club won the Summer Cup, beating Rangers by one goal to nil in the final – the boy from Drumsmudden scoring the only goal. Linwood's cousin was at the controls of a Lancaster bomber when news of the win came through. Local tales claim that he raised his arms to celebrate, causing the bomber to plummet several hundred feet before he regained control! He was signed by Middlesbrough, followed by Hibernian, Clyde and Morton. In November 1949 Linwood was picked to play for Scotland against Wales, his only peacetime cap, but he managed to score. He retired from football in 1955, living in Renfrew, before he died on 23 October 2003.

55. Drumsmudden – Robina Linwood

Life in the rows could be hard. During the General Strike of 1926 there was much hardship for many of the miners living there. Ochiltree parish council offered relief to families, children being fed and vouchers issued for a time, before it was suspended as being unaffordable. The residents from Drumsmudden and Drongan marched to the parish inspector's office in Ochiltree where they held a mass meeting in the recreation ground. Two prominent local Labour men, James Brown MP and Alex Sloan were among those who addressed the crowd.

56. Drumsmudden – Linwood family of Number 12

Although not a native of the miners' rows at Drumsmudden, the novelist George Douglas Brown was born in Ochiltree. He was born George Douglas on 26 January 1869 at the house known as the 'House with the Green Shutters'. He was the illegitimate son of Sarah Gemmell and a local farmer, also George Douglas Brown, who had purchased Drumsmudden farm around 1861, previously staying near Sorn. Brown wrote the novel *The House with the Green Shutters* as an antidote to the kailyard school of writing, which it killed virtually stone dead. The book was a great success, but Brown was dying. He died in London on 28 August 1902 at the untimely age of 33 years. He was buried in the Holmston Cemetery, Ayr.

Another man who lived at Drumsmudden for a number of years was Davie Bell. Born David Ernest Thomlinson Bell at Brydekirk in Dumfriesshire in 1907, he moved to Drumsmudden in 1934 when he got married. He later moved to Prestwick. Like many of his time, he was a keen cyclist, and he joined the Arran View Cycling Club in Drongan until it was disbanded in 1936, after which he joined the Ayrshire Clarion Club, also based in Drongan.

Bell cycled all over Scotland and beyond, from 1932 writing articles which appeared in the *Ayrshire Post* under the pen-name, 'The Highway Man'. These ran in the paper until his death in April 1965, at the age of 58. His readers

57. Drumsmudden – Davie Bell, 'The Highway Man'

collected money to erect a memorial which was built at a spot he loved on the hill road between Newton Stewart and Straiton, unveiled by his widow, Georgina, in 1966. In 1970 many of Bell's articles were collected into a book, entitled *The Highway Man*, which went into a second edition. A further collection of articles appeared in *The Highway Man Again* in 1990.

Tales from Drumsmudden were not always so pleasant. Around 1892 there was a national miners' strike across Scotland. A man and his wife, perhaps surnamed Bunyan, came to Drumsmudden and obtained a house at the end of the row. He was a mining student, and had been offered a job in the local pit if he didn't go on strike. The other miners regarded him as a 'blackleg'. One Sunday evening, the residents formed a flute band and they marched to the front of his house where they burned an effigy of both him and his wife. They also acted out the reading of his letter from the mine-owner. The young man, from the way he had been treated, left the area. However, the striking miners were to get their come-uppance when he returned around 1901 as the manager of the pit!

By 1951, when the *Third Statistical Account of Scotland* was written, Drumsmudden's houses were 'much overcrowded'. The community of Drongan was then being developed by Ayr County Council to rehouse miners from Trabboch and other communities, and gradually the residents of Drumsmudden were given new homes there. The old rows were demolished in 1958, so that today there is little to indicate their former existence. Even the pit bing was partially removed and landscaped when a firm dug away much of the mound to make it into bricks. Nearby, today, are four houses forming Drumjoan Terrace, built around 1950 as agricultural workers' houses.

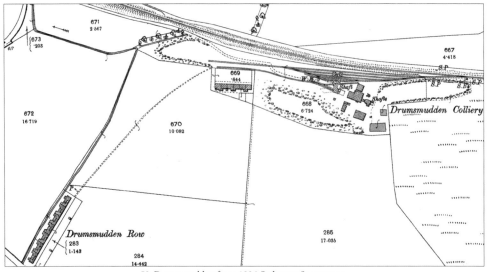

58. Drumsmudden from 1896 Ordnance Survey map
Reproduced by permission of the National Library of Scotland

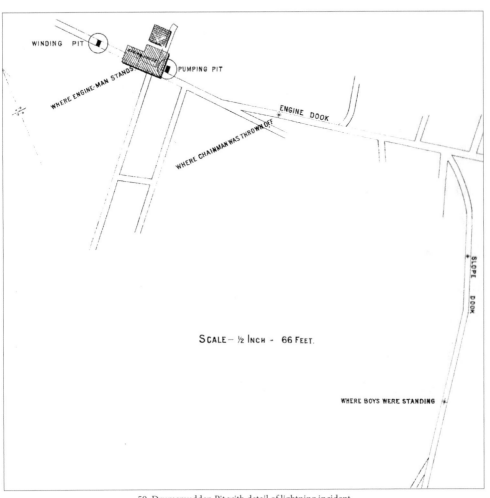

WINDING PIT

WHERE ENGINE-MAN STANDS

PUMPING PIT

ENGINE DOOK

WHERE CHAINMAN WAS THROWN OFF

SLOPE DOOK

SCALE – ½ INCH – 66 FEET.

WHERE BOYS WERE STANDING

59. Drumsmudden Pit with detail of lightning incident

21

Ellerslie

★

According to local tradition, Sir William Wallace was born at Ellerslie in Ayrshire, and not Elderslie in Renfrewshire. The basis for the Renfrewshire claim is apparently only due to the fact that the local community bears the name. The claim for Ellerslie in Ayrshire is based on the facts that Wallace's family were the proprietors of the estate of Riccarton Castle, located nearby.

To many Ayrshire residents, however, although we are keen to claim Wallace as one of our own folk, few have any idea where Ellerslie was. It wasn't until recent years, when the claim of Wallace as an Ayrshireman was promoted, that the knowledge that there was an Ellerslie in the shire became better known. To most, however, its whereabouts is still a mystery.

The Ellerslie that Wallace was born at was probably a farm or country residence, part of the extensive Wallace lands around Kilmarnock. It was located somewhere to the west of the town, virtually on the boundary with Kilmaurs parish. The name is not shown on Pont's map of 1654, but there is a symbol indicating that there may have been a tower house in the vicinity.

The name survived in local parlance, however, and in the early 1800s, when Annandale Colliery was established by the Cuninghames, the miners' rows erected to house the workers were known as Ellerslie. These date from before 1856 and are located in Kilmaurs parish, at the eastern extremity of Annandale farmlands. Annandale Colliery Pit Number 1 was established on the north side of the old Annandale Road, and a mineral siding was laid into it from the main Kilmarnock-Troon line. Squeezed into the gusset formed by the railway and a minor stream, a second coal pit was established, but this was not very large.

Between the two pits the village of Ellerslie was established. North of the Annandale Road a row of ten houses was built, originally with gardens located between the houses and the road. Alongside the road was a row of buildings, and to its side was a railway shed, a siding leading into it. The stream headed south towards the River Irvine, gradually coming closer to the railway, forming a long triangle of land. On this were two other rows of houses, formed of two terraces. The northern one had ten houses in it. The southern row also had ten houses. Both of these rows had gardens to the west, backing onto the railway siding. In the gap between the two sets of gardens was a well, source of water for the community.

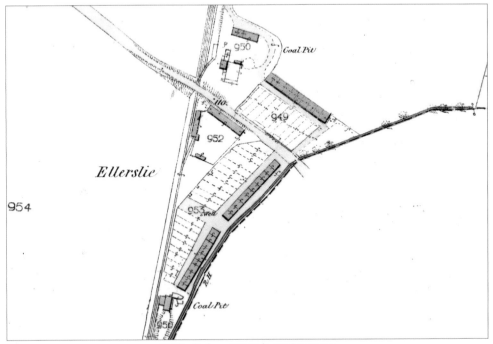

60. Ellerslie from 1860 Ordnance Survey map
Reproduced by permission of the National Library of Scotland

The houses at Ellerslie remained occupied until around 1900, when they started to be emptied. In 1895 the second coal pit was gone, as was the railway shed. Within a few years the three rows of ten houses were removed, the northernmost standing in ruins, the southern two totally cleared. By this time Annandale Pit Number 4 had been sunk, occupying the site of the older second pit. Only the four houses on the south side of the road remained. In 1900, of the 34 houses which at one time existed in the village, there were eleven unoccupied. The village remained the property of the representatives of W. C. S. Cuninghame.

At the outbreak of the First World War all of the houses in Ellerslie had gone. The site was redeveloped and new railway sidings were formed. By this time, it wasn't coal that was being worked, but a new brick works was erected. This was located north of the original Ellerslie village, the old rows and gardens being obliterated with new sheds, cranes, and railway sidings.

The whole site from the Irvine Road south to the Dundonald Road has gradually been redeveloped by an expanding Kilmarnock. New housing estates have been erected on Springhill farm to the south of Ellerslie. The site of the village is currently occupied by a small engineering firm's premises.

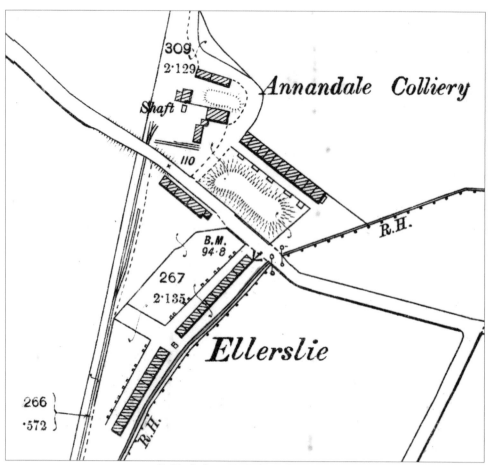

61. Ellerslie from 1896 Ordnance Survey map
Reproduced by permission of the National Library of Scotland

22

Fardalehill

*

In 2015-16 a new housing estate of large private houses was built on the western side of Kilmarnock, just off the Irvine road. Built by Bellway Homes, the estate comprised 96 homes in the first phase. The development was named Fardalehill. To most people, the name is thought to come from a farm on the Old Irvine Road. The farm, as is the new housing estate, is located in Kilmaurs parish, but both are more readily associated with the ever-expanding town. South of the farm, located by the side of the minor road that links the old and new Irvine roads, there used to be a small community known as Fardalehill, home to numerous miners.

Fardalehill Row occupied the eastern side of the Fardalehill Road. There were four blocks of houses, the northernmost comprising two larger properties. South of this was a row of six miners' homes, with sizeable gardens to the rear. Immediately south again was a row of four houses, again with large gardens to the rear. A final block of four houses made up the southern end of the row.

The houses existed prior to 1856, being shown on the Ordnance Survey map of that time. The spelling used then was Fardlehill. The villagers had access to water from either a pump, located at the southern end of the row, or else from a well, positioned at the end of the gardens, there being a path between the row of six and the row of four leading to it. At a later date, certainly by 1908, a water main was led into Fardalehill, and the residents had access to water taps in the street.

In 1887 a survey of the population of the district found that Fardalehill and Ellerslie had a joint population of around 450. Of this, Fardalehill probably had a slightly larger majority, perhaps around 250 people.

By 1900 Fardalehill was the property of Lord Howard de Walden. In the old rows there were a few houses occupied by agricultural workers – Andrew Hannah, ploughman; Hugh Smellie, ploughman, and James Stead, labourer – but the rows were owned by the trustees of W. C. S. Cuninghame. At the time the houses were let to miners – though numbers 5-8 were empty, awaiting demolition. By 1913 the houses were the property of the Caprington Coal

Company Ltd. Some of the older houses had been pulled down, and when the housing inspectors visited on 26 November 1913 there were only ten houses surviving – the middle row of four being demolished. These were very old, being built of stone. Each house had two apartments. The kitchens measured 12 feet by 10½ feet; the bedroom 10 feet by 9 feet.

The village had to share two dry closets. At the time these had the luxury of doors. However, the villagers had neither wash-houses nor coal-houses, and they needed to store their coal beneath the bed. With no wash-houses, the womenfolk were forced into doing their washing on the kitchen floor. Luckily, there was a supply of gravitation water.

The floors in the houses were laid with brick tiles, but to save the cost of constructing the buildings, the areas beneath the beds were unfinished, comprising of hardened clay. The rent payable for each house was 1s. 7½d. per week.

Being built in a mining area, the cottages at Fardalehill were susceptible to subsidence. In 1913 it was noted that one of the houses had its gable-end shored up with timbers. In other residences, a number of walls had large cracks in them.

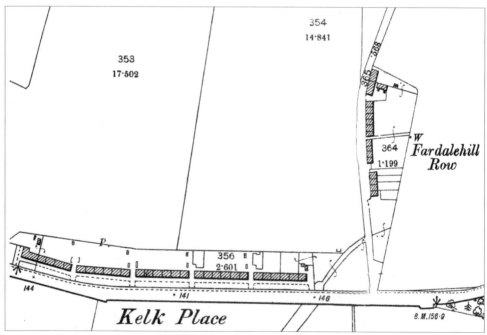

62. Fardalehill from 1896 Ordnance Survey map
Reproduced by permission of the National Library of Scotland

Adjoining Fardalehill, by the side of the Irvine Road, was a long row of houses known as Kelk Place. These houses, which numbered 30 in total, built in five blocks of six homes, were probably built to rehouse miners from the old Fardalehill cottages, for they were originally of a superior standard to the old cottages. They were erected from brick sometime after 1860, appearing in the Post Office Directory of 1868. In 1875 a report on mining homes noted that these houses were more like a true cottage than a miners' row, and that the houses had hedged gardens to the front, filled with flowers. The residents paid 6s. per month for a large kitchen with a stone floor and two small bedrooms. However, as time passed, and the mines in the vicinity were closed, the houses fell into dilapidation, the owners, Caprington Coal Company, being very lax in their maintenance. Again, the houses suffered from subsidence, there being many cracks and rents in the walls.

Kelk Place houses were four apartments in size, with kitchens 18 feet by 12 feet. These did not contain beds, unlike most other miners' cottages. One of the rooms measured 10 feet by 9 feet, but the other two were small, only being 9 feet by 6 feet, reached in a line from the kitchen.

Kelk Place had no wash-houses, the residents being expected to do their washing in their homes. The residents shared two dry closets per six families, one of which had a door, the other did without. Small ash pits were provided, as were wooden coal bunkers. Each house had a garden to the rear, and in front of the houses were small plots. The residents paid 1s. 10½d. per week for their homes.

The name Kelk Place probably comes from George Kelk, who was the factor to the Duke of Portland in the first half of the nineteenth century. Kelk was born around 1783 in Sutton-cum-Lound, a village near Nottingham. During his time factoring on the Portland estates around Kilmarnock he lived at Braehead House in Kilmarnock.

The houses of Fardalehill and Kelk Place were demolished prior to 1937, the site of both rows being left as small parcels of ground. The last buildings to survive were the two cottages at the northern end of Fardalehill Row, but these were eventually removed. Ayr County Council had decided in 1932 to demolish all of the old miners' rows in Kilmaurs parish and rehouse the residents in new council houses at Crosshouse. Thus, around a dozen rows in the parish were cleared, and by 1940 the village of Crosshouse increased in population to around 1,800 with the erection of 300 houses.

23

Fergushill

★

Fergushill was located in the parish of Kilwinning, a couple of miles east of the burgh. The village was positioned at a cross road, adjacent to North Fergushill farm, which survives. At one time a minor railway passed across the roadway at the crossroads, and one row of houses was built facing directly onto the line. This row had ten houses in it, facing over the rails onto the roadway leading to Broomhill farm. This was known as Thatched Row, for obvious reasons, the roof remaining as such as late as 1913, when the inspectors came to look at the village. All of the houses in this row were single-apartment, not having coal houses or washing houses. For the benefit of the residents of the ten houses, where 38 folk lived, there were just two earth closets. The residents paid one shilling per week in rent.

The second row was built alongside the minor road linking Sevenacres with Benslie, heading towards North Fergushill farm. This row also had ten houses in it, though the furthest away house, nearest the farm, was larger, with a projection facing onto the road. This second row of houses had gardens to the rear, and at one corner of the garden area was a public well, from where the residents were able to draw water. This row was known as Front Row.

On the opposite branch road forming the crossroads from the first row was a short row of three buildings, larger than the miners' rows. The building at the end, adjoining the cross roads, was latterly a smithy, where repair work for the mines was carried out. Next to it was a store and office for the coal company, resulting in the row being named Office Row.

The first three rows at Fergushill probably date from around 1835, soon after Archibald Finnie acquired the mining rights in the area from the Earl of Eglinton.

Separated from the village a bit, but associated with Fergushill, was High Row. This was located alongside the road, next to the main railway line at Windyhall. This row had nine houses in it, plus a tenth building which was used for the original Fergushill School. On the opposite side of the railway, down nearer the Lugton Water, was a row of five houses known as Viaduct Row. High

Row was demolished before 1895, when only the former school building and a couple of homes survived. They were still in existence in 1931, David Donaldson, a miner, having knocked two houses into one. Viaduct Row survived longer, being abandoned in the early 1900s. In 1909 there were only three houses occupied – one in the middle had been demolished and others had been knocked into one larger house.

Mining at Fergushill may have started around 1704, for in that year Bailie Gray of Irvine and his partners were noted as having a coal works there. In 1721 the works were sold to Provost William MacTaggart of Irvine. He was a very forward-looking coalmaster, for in 1719 he had gone to London to purchase a Newcomen steam pump to draw water from the Auchenharvie pits at Stevenston, the second in Scotland. In 1725 MacTaggart laid a waggonway to the pits at Fergushill, the second of these in Scotland. In 1799 Fergushill House, which stood near to South Fergushill farm, was sold to the 12th Earl of Eglinton and it was noted that 'the colliers were sold with the land'.

Mining in the area expanded as the nineteenth century passed, the Eglinton family developing their mineral resources considerably, resulting in more mineworkers being required. At Fergushill new rows of houses were built to accommodate them, the *New Statistical Account* of 1842 noting that 'a village containing upwards of 200 people has sprung up within the last few years'. Front Row had a further terrace added in line with it, facing the road, built of brick. This had five houses in it, their gardens to the rear. In 1913 Front Row had three of the double-apartment houses empty, but the remaining twelve homes had a population of 63. This was spread rather unevenly, for in 1913 the inspectors discovered one of the houses had thirteen folk living in it, and the room of the house only measured 9 feet by 6 feet 3 inches.

Adjoining the Office Row, lining the roadway heading north-eastwards, four additional terraces were erected, named Wellington Row. These terraces had six houses in each, with gardens to the rear and wash-houses at the foot of the gardens. In 1913 130 folk lived in the houses, sometimes up to thirteen per house. The houses had two apartments within them, the walls of brick and the roof of slate. The inspectors noted that there were 'no coalhouses, no washing houses, except wooden erections, which make the place hideous.… The front is unpaved, with open syvor, and a muddier frontage it would be impossible to find.'

Behind the second row, parallel with it, was a long row of sixteen houses. This was known as Galston Row, though the inspectors noted that there were only ten houses in it, perhaps the houses being rebuilt at one time, as they had two apartments in each. Three of the houses were empty, meaning that the remaining seven homes had a resident population of 33. The rent was one shilling and threepence per week.

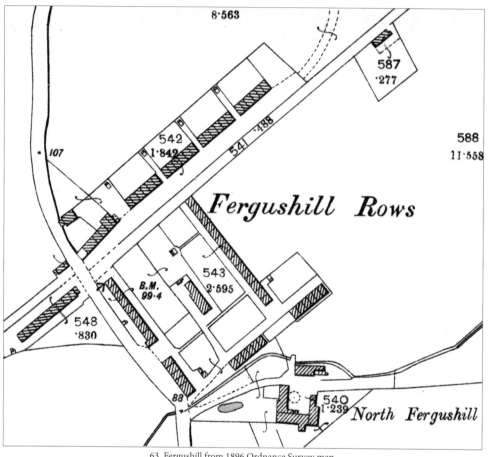

63. Fergushill from 1896 Ordnance Survey map
Reproduced by permission of the National Library of Scotland

At right angles to the parallel row were two other rows, located near to North Fergushill farm, which were built perpendicular to the main road through the village. This row had two terraces, each of six houses.

In the centre of the largish square formed by the rows was a large building which served as Fergushill Co-operative Society's bake house and store. The society sold groceries and other requirements to the residents, and with their delivery vans were able to sell farther afield, in other nearby mining communities.

There were a number of different pits around Fergushill, some only lasting for a few years, others much longer. One of the mines produced shale from which oil was extracted. This sideline operated from 1864 until at least 1873, the shale producing between 13-14 gallons of oil per ton. This oil had to be sent in tanks to either Glasgow or Bathgate for refining. Death was common, such as when Andrew Allardyce was killed in Fergushill Number 22 (the Diamond Pit), in August 1913, aged 47. The number of pits at Fergushill was considerable, that numbered 29 opening in 1886. Much of the coal was transported by rail to Ardrossan, from where it was exported to Ireland. The company even had its own 515-ton vessel, the SS *Archibald Finnie*, which came into service in 1893. Unfortunately it collided with another vessel one month after it was launched, whereupon it sank off Ballyhalbert, Northern Ireland.

The population of Fergushill was around 200 in 1841, rising to 412 in 1891 and starting to drop again, being 363 in 1913.

To the north-east of the village were the remains of Fergushill Tile Works. The old cottage occupied by the manager long survived the business, and the hole in the ground from where the clay was extracted soon filled in to become a lochan. The tile works were established in 1831 and the drainage tiles produced were used primarily on the Eglinton estate, though others were sold elsewhere. The business was busy for a decade or so, but soon it was stockpiling so many tiles that it was eventually closed in 1855, the materials being sold off.

From the early 1800s the Fergushill collieries and the village were owned by Messrs Archibald Finnie & Son. Finnie expanded the coal mines soon after he had acquired them, and it is known that he added the rows at nearby Benslie in 1841 to house an increasing workforce, expanding them again in 1857. Finnie was keen on the promotion of railways, being a member of the committee that proposed the Glasgow, Paisley, Kilmarnock and Ayr Railway.

Archibald Finnie was born in Kilmarnock on 1 March 1873, the son of a local businessman. He played an active part in the politics and church in the town, and served as Provost of Kilmarnock from 1837-40. He was a member of Kilmarnock High Kirk, and a Life Governor of the British and Foreign Bible Society. He died in 1843 and was succeed in the business by his son, also known

64. Fergushill Co-operative delivery van

as Archibald. He similarly played an active part in local politics, serving as Kilmarnock's provost from 1858-61. He was noted as being philanthropic towards his miners, but this was perhaps only to keep them on good terms. He awarded prizes for the best kept houses in the rows, and paid for the erection of Fergushill Church and the new Fergushill School. He built a miners' institute in Springside and founded a savings bank in the rows, offering a higher rate of interest than that offered by the regular banks. However, when the miners went on strike in 1861 he came down hard. He evicted the strikers from their homes and arranged a pact with neighbouring landlords so that they could not find accommodation with them. To break the strike, or at least allow the pits to continue working, he brought mineworkers from Cornwall to the area, paying them less than the wages the striking miners were getting at the time. Finnie died in 1876 and was succeeded by his son, Archibald Finnie IV. He was in the midst of negotiating a new lease for the coal at Fergushill with the Earl of Eglinton when he died in 1883, aged 32. The business was then taken over by the Finnie sisters – Jean, Mary Ann, Helena, and Margaret.

In 1858 a new school building was erected at Fergushill, a little to the south of the village, on the opposite side of the road from North Fergushill. The school was funded by the Earl of Eglinton and Messrs Archibald Finnie & Sons, the latter controlling its operation. In 1872, when the Education (Scotland) Act came into force, the school was passed over from the coal company to Kilwinning Parish School Board. At one time 307 pupils were educated within its stone walls. The school remained open until the mining communities in the district were being cleared away, closing in 1950.

Fergushill School was also used by locals as a place of worship, known as Fergushill Mission. This was originally run from Kilwinning Abbey Church, but it was later transferred to Mansfield Church in Kilwinning. On Saturday 19 October 1878 the foundation stone of a new church building was laid by Rev William Lee Kerr, minister of the Abbey Church. The new church was erected at Benslie, in a more central location to serve the nearby villages of Sourlie, Doura and Benslie, in addition to Fergushill. As well as those who belonged to the established church, in 1870 it was reckoned by Father Thomas Keane of Irvine that there were 80 Roman Catholics living in the community.

65. Fergushill School

As with many mining communities and industrial areas, temperance was promoted heavily in the Victorian and Edwardian periods. At Fergushill the Noble Resolve Tent of the International Order of Rechabites was opened on 18 October 1904. A group for youngsters, the Lugton Glen Juvenile Tent, was formed in 1906. By 1913 the membership stood at 18 state members, 25 order members and 6 members' wives, plus 29 juveniles.

The inspectors in 1913 were not very complimentary regarding the houses at Fergushill, and concluded with the comment that 'the whole village is an eyesore.' When the rows at Fergushill were closed many of the residents moved to Dirrans in Kilwinning, a new council estate erected in the 1930s. Others were rehoused in the new council houses at Girdle Toll, Irvine. By 1939 all of the houses at Fergushill were empty and some became the property of the local farmer, James Howie of North Fergushill. The houses at Viaduct Row were empty too.

24

Garrallan

★

Garrallan House is a fairly imposing small country house, located to the south-west of Cumnock. It was for many years owned by the Douglas family, but in 1819 the heiress married Hamilton Boswell of Knockroon, from when the estate became the property of the Douglas Boswells. It remained their property until they sold it soon after 1920 to the Stevenson family, the Boswells having purchased the ancestral seat of Auchinleck House. The Douglas Boswells were keen on developing the minerals on their estate, and thus a number of coal mines, freestone quarries and clay pits were sunk over the years. To accommodate the workers, miners' houses were erected before 1855. A second row was added after 1875, when new mines were sunk.

In 1913 James Brown of the Ayrshire Miners' Union visited the Garrallan Rows to see for himself the conditions endured by the mineworkers' families. He noted that there were 22 houses, four of which were two apartment homes, the other eighteen being single-apartment. They were leased by the Carriden Coal Company from the Boswells of Garrallan. Residents at this time paid a rent of two shillings and one penny for the two-apartment houses, one shilling and eleven pence for the single-apartment homes. The single-apartment houses were located back to back from each other, though Brown did note that one of these single-apartment houses had been halved again, to form two small rooms, occupied by two tenants.

In the double-apartment houses the kitchens measured 14 feet by 12 feet, the main room 12 feet by 12 feet. The single-apartment houses had one room measuring 15 feet by 13 feet.

The Garrallan Row was located by the side of the Skares Road, which linked Cumnock with the mining village of Skares. The houses were situated on the north side of the road, between the Changue Burn and the larger Rose Burn. The houses faced onto the road, and to their north were gardens. Beyond the gardens was the Ayr and Cumnock railway line.

Hart's Row had two houses in it, occupied by Robert Ballantyne, colliery engineer, and William Gillespie, miner, in 1914. Changuebank Row was occupied by miners, colliers, pitheadmen and others.

The Roseburn Row had six houses in it, again the property of the Boswells but leased to the Carriden Coal Company. This row was located to the west of the Rose Burn, the houses occupying a thin stretch of ground between Woodhead Road and the burn itself. The adjoining gardens were tiny, even by miners' row standards. In 1914 the occupants were David MacCrindle, Francis MacFedries, John MacCrindle, William Moyles and George Young, colliers, and William Walker, pitheadman. This row of houses was also known as Roseburn Cottages. They were probably the oldest of the rows at Garrallan, appearing, as they do, on the 1857 Ordnance Survey map. Across Woodhead Road from

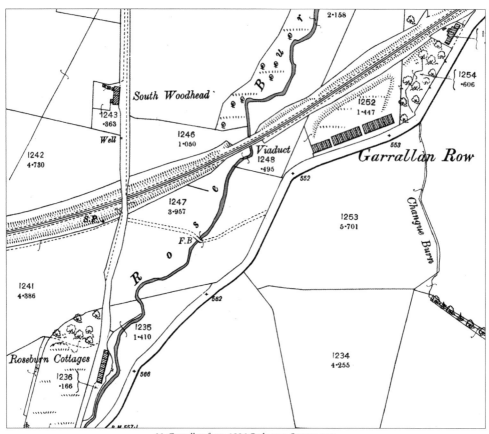

66. Garrallan from 1896 Ordnance Survey map
Reproduced by permission of the National Library of Scotland

Roseburn Cottages was an old quarry, the cottages perhaps being houses occupied by quarrymen prior to the sinking of the coal pits.

The houses at Garrallan were described as being in 'a shameful state of repair. We saw in one house a pail placed in bed to catch the water which was coming in from the roof…. All of them were very damp. We saw in another house the roof discoloured and the paper hanging in shreds from the walls.' One of the residents told Brown, 'Ane has nae heart to clean them, for your work is never seen.'

Inside the houses the floors were covered with bricks, which were badly broken. In the double-apartment houses the bedroom had a wooden floor. The houses at Garrallan had six dry closets between them, but the condition these were in was such that no self-respecting adult would use them. There were no wash-houses or coal houses, the residents keeping their coal beneath their beds. Water was obtained from a pipe that came from field drains.

The Garrallan Colliery was sunk by the Carriden Coal Company in 1907 and a second pit followed in 1910, the first coal being raised in June 1911. An older coal mine had existed on the estate, for William Hastie was killed in the pit by 'bad air' on 11 September 1849. The company was renamed the Garrallan Coal Company Ltd in 1917 but it was sold in 1925 to the Banknock Coal Company, and thence in 1927 to the Mount Vernon Coal Company. This company closed the pit in the same year. The pit was reopened at a later date, finally closing in 1960.

Although many of the Garrallan residents were disheartened regarding their homes, they were keen to improve their lot, and in 1897 a branch of the Lugar Temperance Society was established. The Rev Alexander MacDonald, of the United Presbyterian Church in Cumnock, often made his way to Garrallan to hold mission services. The parish minister did likewise. In 1876 Matthew Smith held evening classes in music, and there was a quadrille band, magic lantern entertainment shows, dancing classes and a branch of the Ancient Free Gardeners.

In addition to the row at Garrallan, there were a number of other cottages, mostly located at either Woodhead, to the north, or else at Garrallan Smithy, which was located to the south of Garrallan House. William MacCaa (1852-1929) was the smith at Garrallan for 53 years. In addition to the blacksmith's workshop being located at Garrallan Smithy, in 1855 there was a small post office.

Woodhead was almost a separate community of its own. There were a number of cottages built alongside a minor roadway that linked the main Ayr-Cumnock road with the Skares Road. Owned by the Marquis of Bute, by 1914 there were only three houses in occupation, home to labourers, William MacMurdo, Robert MacGill and Robert Black.

Garrallan Public School building still survives, having been abandoned for many years. Prior to the education act of 1872 there had been a small school in the area, which could accommodate 28 pupils, but to which 48 attended. The new school was erected in 1876 (to plans by James Ingram) to educate the children of the district, but it needed to be extended in 1886, in 1900 the roll being 228. James Wilson (1850-1927) served as headmaster at the school from when it opened for the next 38 years. In 1921 Skares and Garrallan schools shared the same headmaster. It was later used as a special school, but was finally closed in 1972. The building is being restored and the schoolmaster's house stands in front. Apart from Garrallan House which predated the community, this is now the only indication that at one time there was a small community in existence here.

25

Gasswater

★

My grandmother, Mary Love, was a member of the church women's guild in Cumnock. One day the guild was heading off to the borders on a bus trip, which took them up the A70, Muirkirk road, from Cumnock. Just beyond Cronberry, my grandmother pointed out to a fellow member in the bus the spot where she had been born. The woman looked out the window, and exclaimed, 'Oh, Mary, I didn't know you were born in a field!' She wasn't of course, she was born in the lost village of Gasswater, of which nothing remains, and which has been gone for decades.

My gran was born at Gasswater on 25 November 1911, the daughter (and one of eight children) of John Kerr Park and his wife, Isabella Bain Hamilton. John was a colliery engine-man, and he had moved to Gasswater from Muirkirk, following the work, much like most other men of his time employed in the mines. Fairly soon after my grandmother was born, and within the year, the family moved into 37B Store Row at nearby Cronberry, seen by the family as being superior to the old rows they had left behind. Gasswater was, even then, on its last legs and being abandoned.

Gasswater village was strung out alongside the Muirkirk road, and owed its origin to the local coal mines. There was also an extensive lime quarry and limekilns nearby, which also employed a number of men. The community dated from the eighteenth century, for a 'water machine for drying the coalwork' was installed in 1769.

The lime works at Gasswater were established in the mid-eighteenth century, converting limestone into lime. On Armstrong's map of Ayrshire, published in 1775, 'Limeheugh' is indicated, implying that the quarrying for limestone was underway at that time. In a narrow glen formed by a small stream, east of the Muirkirk road, a series of limekilns were constructed, their remains long surviving, until surface coal mining destroyed their remnants in the twenty-first century. A number of bell pits were sunk to supply coal for the works, and the remains of these were long visible on the moor – little bings and mounds of grass-grown debris appearing to rise from the rough moors of Dalfad and Welltrees.

On Friday 21 October 1831 two men died in a coal pit near to the Gasswater Limeworks. The men were brothers of the name Baird, sons of a local farmer. They had gone to the mouth of the pit that was being sunk at the time, and which had reached 5 fathoms (30 feet) in depth. One of the lads persuaded the other to lower him to the bottom, but when he got there he fell down, asphyxiated by the gas. The brother on the surface raised the alarm, and a man surnamed Murdoch came to his aid. He was lowered down the pit, but also collapsed due to the gas. A second helper, David Macleod went down the pit, and he, too, collapsed. James Davidson then made an attempt at a rescue, but as he neared the bottom he felt the gas and called out to be hauled back up. He tried again, but had to be hauled back up by a rope that he had tied around his body. A fire was lit and lowered into the pit, but the smoke made it difficult to see. However, it caused one of the asphyxiated men to moan. Those on the surface turned the windlass and discovered David MacLeod hanging onto it by one hand. He managed to recover sufficiently to be able to walk back to Auchinleck that night. The two men who were left in the pit died, the man named Baird and that named Murdoch, the latter leaving a wife and young family.

67. Gasswater

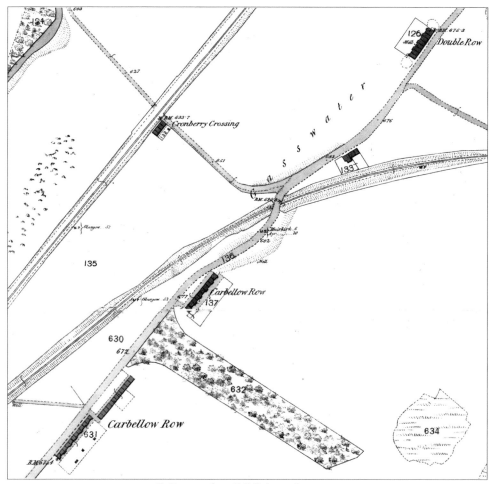

68. Gasswater from 1860 Ordnance Survey map
Reproduced by permission of the National Library of Scotland

At Gasswater a sizeable population continued to grow as new rows were erected. In 1851 the Census lists some of the houses which existed at that time: Red Row of sixteen houses; High Row; Roadend Row; High Gilhaugh; Low Gilhaugh; Stables; Railway Row of four houses; Plantation Row of ten houses; Brick Row of 24 houses; Quarry Row of nineteen houses; and Store Row.

Four rows existed at Gasswater in 1860 - Brick Row (24 houses), Stone Row (fourteen houses), Baxter's Row (three houses) and School Row (four houses), and at the Gasswater Limeworks were another dozen, divided into two rows (the Stone and Stable Rows).

In addition to the main community of Gasswater, often referred to as Low Gasswater, there were also two rows of houses at Upper, or High Gasswater. These were the houses of Gilhaugh, arranged in two rows. The lower row was located on the western side of the roadway that led into the Gasswater Limeworks. This row had six houses, the front doors facing onto the roadway, with gardens to the rear, stretching back to the burn. On the opposite side of the burn were the two Dalfad coal pits, one of which was disused by 1856, the other still operating into the new century. The High Gasswater Row was still occupied in 1908.

The upper row, High Gilhaugh, was located a few hundred yards farther up the roadway, nearer to the limekilns in Gilhaugh. There were eight houses here, the gardens located to the rear, rising to the branch line that made its way into the limeworks. Around fifty yards or so further on were the first pair of limekilns in the glen, still operational in 1856. By 1895 the houses at Upper Gilhaugh had been abandoned, and the limekilns were by then disused.

A school existed at Gasswater for a time, John Cooper being teacher there in 1859. In 1878 the Auchinleck Parish School Board conducted its own census in the area to find out the need for future schooling. At Gasswater it found the population to be 308, of which 67 children were aged between 5-13. It is said that the first adherents of the Baptist Church in the district came to Gasswater in 1875 to find work. James Fleming had arrived from Kilmarnock and he was to hold services in William Arthur's house. They met to worship as a group, and within a few years were numerous enough to build a church in Cumnock.

There was little time for leisure at Gasswater. There are few records of any groups or associations in existence from the community, other than the Gasswater Quoiting Club, which existed in 1903, playing in Cumnock & District League. Quoiting was a very popular sport amongst miners, and tournaments or challenges attracted large audiences at the rinks which were formed on clay beds. Prize money was offered by the challenger, and side bets took place amongst the supporters of each. The quoits themselves were flat circular metal hoops, often with a handle-shape cut out on one side of the hole. Weighing from eight to twelve pounds, they were thrown across the pitch at a pin stuck into the ground, the nearest thrower winning. The distance was often up to 22 yards.

Some of the mines remained active even although the ironworks at Lugar was closed, such as Gasswater (closed 1861). A new mine was sunk at Cronberry Moor in 1922 by William Baird & Co. Ltd. The shaft, which was 45 fathoms in depth, was built of concrete and corrugated iron sheets, instead of timber, as a fire precaution. Hugh Murray was appointed as the first manager in 1923, remaining there for five years. Some of the houses at Gasswater were occupied again, whilst newer houses were being built at Cronberry. At Cronberry Moor pit James Mair, of Gasswater, was killed on 2 February 1924, aged 48, when there was a considerable fall of stone from the roof.

The elongated and dispersed community of Gasswater was also owned by Baird. Here were two stone rows and two brick rows, the population in 1913 being 97, living in 34 houses, though a number of houses were empty. Water was obtained from a trough 300 yards distant from one row, or else from a pump 200 yards distant from the other three. The closets had no doors and so were not used by the adult population. The community had begun to decline at the turn of the century. Carbello Pit closed in 1906, and many of the smaller mines were by then abandoned. Houses still occupied were in the Brick, Stone, Baxter's, and School rows, the six houses of the Stable Row closed by 1910. By 1920 around half of the other rows had been vacated and by 1930 only the three houses in Baxter's Row were still occupied.

The Hedworth Barium Company Ltd began development work and mining at their Gasswater Mine in 1917, extracting the mineral both by open cast and by forming an adit level 81 feet below the shaft collar height of 1,054.73 feet above sea level. This mine lasted only until 1921 by which time 7,976 tons of barium sulphate had been removed. A second company, the Wrentnall Baryta Company Ltd, resumed mining operations in 1923, installing new electrical plant for treating barytes. In September 1923 F. Floyd was appointed as manager.

In 1924 twelve new four-apartment houses plus one double storey five-apartment house was built at Gasswater for the employees in the barytes mines. This was located in a new position, nearer to the Gass Water itself. The houses stood near the depot where the barytes stone was received at the end of an aerial haulage way. The Cairnhill Pit, a coal mine sunk in 1956, was later to be built here.

Wrentnall excavated in the region of 300,000 tons of barytes during their 24 years of ownership, at which time it was the United Kingdom's largest producer. ln 1942 there were 42 men employed in the barytes mines, some of whom were housed in the eight 'Wrentnall Cottages' and one wooden house at Gasswater village. The pit manager lived at Wrentnall House, 10 Barrhill

Terrace, Cumnock, and latterly at 31 Auchinleck Road. The house in Barrhill Terrace was erected in 1924 at a cost of around £750. In addition to the Gasswater mine, Wrentnall developed three associated mines, all operated as one unit, the Central, South and Burnside pits, the latter, furthest east, sunk in 1931. It proved to be unproductive, but was redeveloped in May 1956. Wrentnall Baryta continued the work until 1947 when the company was taken over by Anglo-Austral Mines Ltd. The barytes mines were closed in 1965 and Cairnhill pit in 1976. The site was cleared away, and the last of the houses named Gasswater were to be demolished too. The site of the houses, and of Cairnhill Pit, has been obliterated by the arrival of the open cast mine, settling ponds now occupying their rough location.

Today, anyone wishing to find relics of Gasswater will need to look hard for clues to its existence. The two Carbellow Rows on the west side of the plantation are marked by a series of hawthorn trees, which actually grow in what was the interior of the houses. On the ground, poking through the grass, can be found some old bricks, stone, quarry tiles and pieces of concrete. Of the third row, which was located on the opposite side of the road from the Muirkirk 6 milestone, nothing remains, the last of the buildings removed when the road was realigned.

The four houses which existed at Cronberry Crossing have had their roofs removed, the southern wall demolished and the four windows that faced the railway bricked up. A corrugated iron roof formed a shelter for cattle, but even this has been abandoned and the roof is mostly missing and the walls starting to crumble. The blonde sandstone walls survive on three sides, as do four windows that faced the railway. Inside, four fireplaces survive on the two gable ends, indicating the fires that formerly existed in the room and kitchen.

The Double Row has a few stones protruding from the grass at the roadside, the farmer using the foundation as a useful platform and ramp down into two fields. The school row is gone, apart from two or three hawthorn bushes that formerly formed part of the garden hedge.

Of Upper Gasswater, all has been obliterated from the landscape. The huge Dalfad open cast coal works has ripped the surface of the countryside to reveal the coal beds below. The two rows at Upper Gasswater are totally gone, though the site of the upper row is still visible on the ground, next to a dilapidated fish hatchery. Farther east, beyond the old race course that can just be made out on the ground, the stony foundations of the Stable Row poke through the grass.

26

Glenbuck

*

The furthest east one can be on a public road in Ayrshire is on the A70, Edinburgh and Lanark road, where it leaves the county at the old toll cottage at Glenbuck Loch. Local lore claims that the cottage is actually located in two counties, having been built exactly on the boundary when tolls were exacted on passing carts and other vehicles. Glenbuck Loch is an attractive sheet of water, nestling across the boundary line between two steep hills – Hareshaw Hill to the north and Bell Knowe to the south. At the dam a minor road strikes north, signposted Glenbuck. This leads to the site of the former village of that name – access to which is blocked by a locked gate – and to the former estate policies of Glenbuck House.

The village of Glenbuck will probably be remembered much longer than it might be, if it were not for one thing – the legendary football manager, Bill Shankly, was born there. Shankly was to rise through the ranks of football to become one of the longest-serving and most respected of football managers ever. He made his name at Liverpool Football Club, and to this day fans of the team make a pilgrimage to the site of the old village to pay their respects. At the roadway into the old community, which has been totally obliterated by opencast coal workings, stands a memorial stone, commemorating the fact that Shankly was born there. The stone, erected in 1997, contains the inscription:

Seldom in the history of sport can a village the size of Glenbuck have produced so many who reached the pinnacle of achievement in their chosen sport. This monument is dedicated to their memory and to the memory of one man in particular, Bill Shankly, the Legend, the Genius, the Man. Born – Glenbuck, Ayrshire, 2nd September 1913. Died – Liverpool, 29th September 1981. From Annfield with love. Thanks Shanks. Bill Shankly's achievements: Liverpool F. C. 1959-1974. League Champions 1963/64, 1965/6, 1972/73. Runners Up 1968/69, 1973/74. Second Division Champions 1961/62. F. A. Cup Winners 1964/65, 1973/74. Finalists 1970/71. U.E.F.A. Cup Winners 1972/73. European

Cup Winners Cup Finalists 1965/66. Semi-Finalists 1970/71. European Cup Semi-Finalists 1964/65. This plaque was laid on April 27th 1997 by Scottish Coal, Liverpool Away Supporters' Club, Network 5.

Bill Shankly was born at 2 Auchenstilloch Cottages, in Glenbuck, the son of John Shankly, who was employed in the mines. Bill was the youngest of five boys and five girls. The cottage was tiny, and as with many miners, they were able to knock a hole through the wall to create a larger dwelling. Shankly was brought up in a footballing household, his elder brothers being accomplished players. Alec was to play for Ayr United and Clyde; James for Portsmouth, Sheffield United and Carlisle; John for Portsmouth, Blackpool and Alloa; and Robert for Alloa, Tunbridge Wells and Falkirk. Bill wished to play for Glenbuck Cherrypickers, but this team had folded before he was old enough. His first signing was with Cronberry Eglinton F. C., playing from 1931 until 1932. In December that year Shankly signed for Carlisle United, on a wage of £4 per week, before moving to Preston North End in 1933. He was to gain a Football Association Cup Winner's medal with Preston in 1938. His skill on the field was recognised by the Scottish national side, and he was capped five times before the outbreak of war put his career on hold. In 1942 Bill played with Liverpool in a guest appearance against Everton. After the war, Shankly returned to Preston, where he was player and captain. In 1949 he was appointed as manager at Carlisle, moving quickly from team to team thereafter – from Carlisle to Grimsby, Workington, and Huddersfield, before being appointed as Liverpool manager on 1 December 1959.

Liverpool was languishing in the second division at that time, but their fortunes were about to change, guided by a man who lived and breathed football. Within a few years they had moved up to the second division, winning it in 1962. Back in the first division they only took two years to win it, after which they became a mighty force in English football. In 1973 Shankly's Liverpool won the EUFA cup, beating favourites Borussia Monchengladbach. He announced his retirement on 12 July 1974. He died in Liverpool on 29 September 1981.

Bill Shankly never forgot Glenbuck. He was to write in his memoirs that, 'Life was not easy in the village when we were growing up. No disrespect to Glenbuck, but you could have been as far away from civilization in Outer Mongolia. The winters were cold and bitter with four months of snow.'

In addition to the memorial at Glenbuck, a statue of Shankly was unveiled at Annfield on Thursday 4 December 1997. The statue was sculpted by Tom Murphy, depicting Bill with his arms outstretched, greeting his adoring fans. With his Liverpool scarf around his neck, he is cheering on the team he made his own. As the statue was being crafted, various folk who knew Bill added their comments, from his tailor, who advised on buttons, to his wife, who added a piece of clay to the work.

Bill Shankly is remembered for many amusing footballing quotes, the most famous being the time when he said that, 'Some people believe football is a matter of life and death, I am very disappointed with that attitude. I can assure you it is much, much more important than that.' He also said, 'If you are first you are first – if you are second, you are nothing.' Others were, 'The trouble with referees is that they know the rules, but they don't know the game,' and 'Football is a simple game based on the giving and taking of passes, of controlling the ball and of making yourself available to receive a pass. It's terribly simple.'

The name, Glenbuck Cherrypickers, was originally a nickname, but the team grew to like it and it eventually became its official title. How the name came about is not known now – there are stories of some of the lads marching along the street as though they were in the 11th Hussars, also nicknamed Cherrypickers; or of the team meeting outside the village shop, run by Milliken, where a basket of cherries were on display. When the team broke up and returned home, the basket was empty. Or could it be a nickname given to the team from those outwith the area, describing them as cherrypickers – folk who picked the stones from the coal in the pit.

In any case, Glenbuck Athletic Football Club was formed in 1888 and was to show their skills early on by winning the Ayrshire Junior Cup in season 1888-89. Proving that this was no fluke, the club won the trophy the following year, and again in 1890-91. In 1906 three cups fell to their skills – the Ayrshire Charity Cup, the Cumnock Cup and the Mauchline Cup.

The team was to produce fifty players who went on to have professional footballing careers. Indeed, Rev M. H. Faulds wrote that, 'It can be safely claimed that no village of similar size in all Scotland has a record to equal that of Glenbuck. Altogether, the Glenbuck story is a remarkable page in football history.' Seven sons of the glen were to be capped for Scotland – Bill Shankly (13 times), John Crosbie (twice), Alec Brown (twice), Tommy Brown (twice), Robert Shankly (once), George Halley (once) and William Muir (once). Alec

Brown is claimed to have almost single-handedly won the F. A. Cup for Tottenham Hotspur in 1901, scoring four goals against Sheffield in the semi-final and the solitary goal against Southampton in the final. Another notable footballer from the village was Robert Blyth, better known as 'Reindeer', an uncle of Bill Shankly. Local tales claim that he could run 100 yards in eleven seconds wearing his football boots. Another soccer family was the Knox's. There were five sons, Hugh, Alec, Tom, William and Peter. In addition to playing in various teams, they often entered five-a-side competitions, where they excelled. In fact, in one single year they won 40 of the 41 tournaments that they had entered.

Glenbuck as a village dates back to the mid-eighteenth century. The wild countryside of Muirkirk parish was prospected for its possible minerals, and in 1795 an English-based company, led by John Rumney of Workington, took a lease on the lands of East Glenbuck farm. In the valley of the Stottencleugh Burn an ironworks was established, located at the east end of what was to become the village. The works were in operation by late 1796, and produced iron from the ironstone mined in the hills thereabouts.

Glenbuck ironworks produce was widely distributed initially, with iron being exported as far as Ireland. The company also found some lasting fame in

69. Glenbuck from the south-east

the fact that it manufactured the rails used in what was to be Scotland's first railway, the line from Kilmarnock to Troon. This was laid in 1810 by the Duke of Portland as a means of quickly transporting coals from his Kilmarnock area collieries to the harbour, from where it was exported to Ireland and elsewhere.

The order for iron rails was considerable. In 1810 it was noted that the contract was for 70,000 cast iron rails, an order worth around £20,000. Other notable orders that are known of include cast iron water pipes for the Belfast and Dublin water committees.

Being isolated and remote from any nearby centre of population, houses were built for the workers. Perhaps the oldest was a row of six houses, built in a single terrace, overlooking the ironworks from the hillside above. This was known as Stair Row.

As with almost every ironworks in Scotland, apart from the Carron works at Stenhousemuir, the ironworks at Glenbuck found themselves in difficulties during the Napoleonic Wars. The company was to go bankrupt in 1813. The works appear to have still remained fairly extant for decades thereafter, for on 23 May 1845 an advertisement appeared in the *Glasgow Herald* offering the works for sale, informing prospective purchasers that the furnace could 'be relit at little expense.' Despite the manufacture of iron in Scotland being a growing industry, the works were not to be sold. Some old stonework associated with the works remained behind the Jubilee Rows for many years.

The village went into decline once more, and it wasn't until a new, larger ironworks was established at Muirkirk that the demand for coal and ironstone grew again. Dozens of mines and pits were created across the parish, and many of these were to be found in the Glenbuck area. By 1856, when the Ordnance Survey passed through, making their maps, the village was well established. The old row of six houses still survived near the ruins of the old ironworks. Near it, but to the west, were three other houses, and in a building that may have originally been part of the ironworks was a school. It is known that the schoolmaster in the early 1800s was Thomas Clyde, as he was a creditor of the ironworks when it closed. Unfortunately, so, too, were many of the residents of Glenbuck, who had been issued with promissory tickets in lieu of wages by the company.

To the west, almost a separate community, was the rest of Glenbuck, in 1856 consisting of four rows of houses, built on either side of the road that crossed the Stottencleugh Burn Bridge Number One. At the eastern side was a block of three houses, built in a bend of the stream, at angles to the road. On the west side of the bridge, on the south side of the road, was a row of three or four homes.

On the north side of the road, heading west from the bridge, was a row of seven small cottages. Immediately west of this was another row of six houses. These houses all had their own garden ground. In addition to the rows mentioned, there were a couple of solitary houses in the valley, some of which may have been shepherd's cottages or managers' homes.

70. Glenbuck Main Street

The old pits at Glenbuck were comparatively small, but successfully excavated coal for many years. One of them was known as The Davy Pit (its name has been spelled variously at Davy, Davey, and Davie), its old chimney standing long after the pit had closed in 1906, until it was deemed unsafe and was demolished in 1915. The Davy Pit was operated by the Cairntable Gas Coal Company Limited. Around this time a new colliery was being sunk at Glenbuck by Burnbank Coal Company.

Death in the pits was all-too common, and many miners were to lose their lives underground. Among those who died were the following selection. Thomas Haugh, an engineman, was killed on Sunday 16 June 1884 when his head was crushed by the connecting rod of the water engine wheels. Haugh had been cleaning them at the time. An unmarried man, he was only twenty years of age. On Friday 17 June 1887, at the Davy Pit, a fall of stone from the pit roof killed John Dunbar and injured three others – two of whom were his sons. A fall of stone from Galawhistle Pit on 17 October 1894 killed Thomas Davidson, a Glenbuck miner. A large lump of coal fell on William Reid in the same pit on 15 April 1899, killing him instantaneously. In Grasshill Pit, Archibald Allison was killed when he was struck by a hutch on 20 July 1922. He was only eighteen years of age and lived with his parents in Glenbuck's Grasshill Row.

By 1895 Glenbuck had grown considerably. A new large coal mine, Grasshill Number 2 pit, had been established at the west end of the village, and to house the workers a new row had been built between the pit and the western community. Grasshill Row contained 33 two-apartment houses built in a single terrace. Five coal-houses existed for the use of the families, and small allotments were located between the road and the houses. The second row of houses on the north side of the road, west of Stottencleugh Bridge, had been demolished.

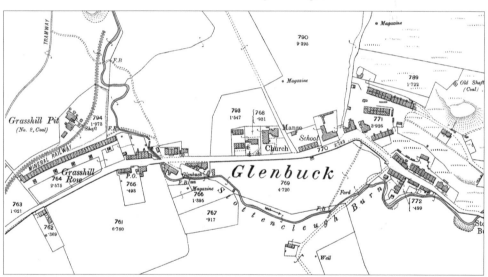

71. Glenbuck from 1896 Ordnance Survey map
Reproduced by permission of the National Library of Scotland

When the housing inspectors visited Glenbuck in 1913 they only looked at Grasshill Row. At the time three of the houses were empty, but the remaining thirty houses had a population of 123 living in them. The rent payable to the owners, William Baird & Company, was 7s. per lunar month. For this the residents shared a dry-closet per four homes. These were rather unusual in that they had sparred gates which could be locked, but which inside had seating for two persons! The houses themselves had two rooms, the kitchen having a floor space of 15 feet by 12 feet, the room 12 feet by 9 feet. The floors were made of wood and a gravitational water supply was had from Hareshaw Hill.

Although the Grasshill Row was newer than many of the houses at Glenbuck, they suffered from large cracks in the walls. These were blamed on the mossy land the insufficient foundations were laid in, plus the vibrations caused by the engines passing along the railway sidings at the coalpit, located immediately behind.

East of the bridge, on the north side of the road, were four houses in a block, plus some additional buildings. On the south side, in an angle of a field, were another four or five homes. Here also was the Glenbuck Inn, or the Royal Arms Inn as it was later to be known. It was placed on the market in 1925 and was acquired by John Wilson of the Empire Bar, Muirkirk. In 1951 the license was transferred to Alexander V. Hazle of Glenbuck.

72. Glenbuck with church (left) school (centre) and Jubilee Row in bottom right

The two halves of Glenbuck had by 1900 been joined to form one community, with houses and other facilities erected in the gap between. In the centre a stone-built church was opened on 16 July 1882, designed by the Ayrshire architect, Robert Ingram. To its side was a substantial manse, and around both were extensive grounds. The church was served by four ministers over its lifetime. On the front wall of the church building was a large stone with an inscription commemorating the local Covenanting martyrs. The church was closed in May 1954. The building stood for many years, but was demolished in late 1994. The Covenanter stone was saved at the time of demolition and relocated to Muirkirk churchyard.

In addition to the parish church, there was a hall associated with the Brethren in the village. This was established in 1887 by the keen members of Lesmahagow assembly who seem to have spent much of their time in other communities, spreading the word. The assembly at Glenbuck continued to exist until 1954.

73. Glenbuck with church (right) and the football field in foreground

Just to the west of the church was a large house, occupied by the village schoolmaster. To the west of the schoolhouse was a small pair of rows, four homes in each. This was known as Auchinstilloch Row, but to the locals was better known as the Monkey Row. The cottages were placed on the market in 1923 but didn't sell. They were subsequently sold privately.

East of the church was a row of six houses, built facing directly onto the road. This was known as Spireslack Row and was built by William Baird & Company. The houses were small single-storey structures, and by 1914 they had been reconfigured into three pairs, to allow for greater space.

Between this row and the old row of three houses at Eastern Glenbuck was a new school, erected in 1876. A substantial building, two large gables faced the main road, with hipped gables to the east and west. With the increasing population in Glenbuck, the old school was deemed insufficient for the number of children in attendance. Whilst a new school was being built, the children were educated in a byre at West Glenbuck farm. During the winter of 1875-6 it was so cold that schooling had to be abandoned for a few months.

The new school was opened on Monday 13 March 1876. A total of 106 children enrolled but were immediately given a week's holiday, whilst the painters completed work inside. The only teacher employed at the time was W. S. Baikie. He had a number of struggles to contend with, for when payment was due to the school board, many pupils failed to turn up. Similarly, when a new text book was introduced in 1878, those families who couldn't afford it kept their children at home. A parent who was called to Cumnock J. P. Court that year for not paying the fees was sent to jail because he was unable to afford them.

In 1881 the school was extended, and attendance increased to 220 the following year. The closure of Lady Pit resulted in families moving away, and the school roll fell to 140. New pits being sunk brought back the population, and in 1889 the roll had increased to 220. By 1900 the roll was in the region of 300, perhaps its highest. In 1921 the pupils were delighted at the introduction of flushing toilets. Declining with Glenbuck itself, the roll fell to 42 in 1939 and to 33 in 1947. The school was closed for good in August 1951.

North of the original row of six houses were two rows of homes, built on the hillside. The front row had sixteen houses in it, built back to back with each other. This row was two storeys in height, the homes accessed from the northern side. Most of the houses were occupied by colliers, but by 1914 two of the houses were empty.

Behind this row was a second row, comprising of two terraces of houses almost joined to each other, but separated by a narrow close. The western bock was a twin of the front row, with twelve houses. The row to the east had eight houses in it, all double-storey. These houses were known as New Terrace, but by 1914 all of them were empty and uninhabitable.

In the glen, where once the ironworks was located, a street of houses was formed, the buildings facing each other. Six houses were built onto the north-western end of the old school, which was converted into two houses. This became known as Old School Row. Double-storey in height, the buildings were covered with hipped roofs and the upstairs flats were accessed from external stairs to the rear.

South-east of the old school was a new row of nine houses, and next to it was a block of two larger homes. This row, which had single storey dwellings, was known as the Jubilee Row. The pair of houses was known as Rowanbank. In 1914 here lived Robert Anderson, collier, in the first house, with Constable George Forsyth in the police house next door.

On the opposite side of the street, an L-shaped block of ten homes occupied a meander of the burn, and east of this were two blocks of two houses. This was known as the Office Row. The houses were single storey in height, the houses in the close being rather small, only having a front door and window facing the lane. On the hillside above the old ironworks was a pair of houses, with small gardens to their rear. These cottages were known as Braehead.

In 1929 two new blocks of council houses were erected at Glenbuck and in November 1930 were let to the first tenants. As with many old mining communities, the name of the street was rather uninspiring – they were called 'Council Houses'! One of the families that moved into the new homes were the Shanklys, who were given the keys to number 5. The welcome addition of a bath and running hot water was to be a boon that they never experienced in their old home.

74. Glenbuck – Grasshill Row

The Glenbuck Co-operative Society was established in 1887 and had a store in the village. The society had a bit of trouble in getting started, for the mine-owners weren't keen on the proposals, preferring that the residents spent their little money in the company store. At length, the farmer at West Glenbuck, James Callan, agreed that if the tenant of his cottage was to leave, the society could have it for a shop. This took place, and on 7 May 1887 it opened for business. At first there were only fourteen members, but this quickly grew to 140 at its peak. At a meeting in 1953 it was agreed to close the society, merging the stock with that of Muirkirk Co-op. The shop at Glenbuck was then closed, and villagers had to buy their provisions from a mobile shop that came from Muirkirk.

Other commercial properties in the village included Messrs Bain & Sons, who operated a fruit shop at the building known as The Castle. Bain's premises were destroyed by fire in 1960. The post office in Glenbuck was run by the Muir family for 68 years. Mrs Muir had taken over the job of postmistress in 1894 and served until 1912. Mrs John Muir followed until 1946, and Mrs David Muir until 1960. After this the postmistress was Mrs Anderson, whose husband owned a small mine near Ponesk.

Glenbuck had a poor supply of water for many years, despite being in an area of high rainfall and with the Stottencleugh Burn passing right through it. Up to 1909 water was drawn from local wells, one of which was located at the end of the Office Row. In that year James Young of Muirkirk was given the contract to create a new supply of water from Hareshaw Hill, piped into water valves.

The local landowner at Glenbuck for many years was Charles Howatson. He was born in 1832 at Cronberry farm. He always claimed that farming, sheep-breeding and Covenanting were unusually strong in his pedigree. He worked for Bairds and when that company (as the Eglinton Iron Company) acquired Muirkirk Ironworks in 1856 he was appointed as manager at the age of 23. He retired from the business in 1870. In 1859 he was married to Wilhelmina Fletcher, whose ancestors were Airds of Crossflatt. He inherited this Muirkirk farm on her death. In 1865 he acquired Dornal estate and in 1872 bought Glenbuck estate, previously owned by Col. Dickson of the Cumberland Iron Company. Howatson bought a pen of ewe hogs that were to take first place at Ayr in 1864. He went on to breed numerous successful rams and in 1909 was paid a record price of £250 for St Columba at Lanark market. He gained some fame from breeding top blackface sheep, resulting in them producing a heavier fleece. His sheep were to win top prizes at various agricultural shows, especially the Royal Highland Show, where he won consecutively for many years. In 1880 he erected Glenbuck House. Charles Howatson died in 1918 and is buried in Auchinleck kirkyard. He was succeeded by his only son, Captain Charles Nile Howatson, who died in 1924.

Glenbuck House was designed by the Ayr architect, John Murdoch, in the neo-baronial style that was in vogue at the time. Around the house Howatson planted woodlands, and the immediate policies were decorated with ornate gates and stonework. The house was demolished in 1948. Today, visitors can walk through the former policies towards the bird hide on Glenbuck Loch. In spring the woods are awash with snowdrops and daffodils. Old iron fences line the roads and the stone walls that survive here and there hint at lost glories.

A new Public Hall had been erected west of the houses next to the schoolhouse. This served the community until the Second World War. The hall was closed with a declining population, but in 1948 it was taken over by Replin Company who established a textile finishing factory there. In 1953 the final meeting of a church group in Glenbuck Public Hall finished and it was expected the wooden building would be demolished soon after. However, the building went up in flames early on Monday 19 October, destroying everything.

As with most mining villages, there were plenty of organisations to entertain the residents. Amongst those in existence at Glenbuck were the Glenbuck Yearly Friendly Society (a temperance organisation), as well as the Priesthill Tent of the Order of Rechabiltes, founded on 23 October 1897. In 1903 the John Brown Tent was opened for juvenile members – it was named in honour of the famous local Covenanting martyr, John Brown of Priesthill, who was martyred on the other side of the hill from the village. In 1913 there were 79 state members, 76 order members and 90 juvenile members.

A murder committed at Glenbuck in 1908 brought some national newspaper attention. Thomas Bone, Junior (aged 28), was charged with the murder of his wife, who was nineteen years of age. He was taken to Glasgow High Court, where he was found guilty. He was sentenced to hang at Ayr prison on 29 May 1908. However, the day before he was due to be executed he received a reprieve from the Secretary of State for Scotland, his sentence being commuted to one of life imprisonment. Bone was sent to Perth jail to carry out his sentence, but on 13 November 1912, whilst the warder had a fifteen-minute break from watching him, he took a bedsheet, tied it around his neck, and hung himself from a hook on the wall. When the warder returned and found him, his body was still warm, but he couldn't be revived.

It wasn't just great football players that Glenbuck produced. The village was also noted for its famous quoiters. Tom Bone (1868-1916) was the top quoit player in the county, especially at 21 yards. He was born in Glenbuck and lived there all of his days. He started playing as a youth, and at the age of 20 became renowned beyond his village for his skill. It was said that he could throw a quoit from 21 yards and land it around a watch. In 1888 he played the noted quoiter of the period, James MacMurdo, at Cumnock, beating him by 61-42. He won the Scottish Championship in 1889 for the first time, and in 1908 won the British Championship, beating the English champion, James Hood of Liverpool. Locally, the annual competition was played for the Ballochmyle silver quoit, and Bone won this fourteen times. He was to sustain an eye injury at the pit, affecting his play thereafter. He died on 15 November 1916, having never married. A new quoiting green was opened at Glenbuck on 30 April 1904. The first game played thereon was against Muirkirk, the home team winning 76-63.

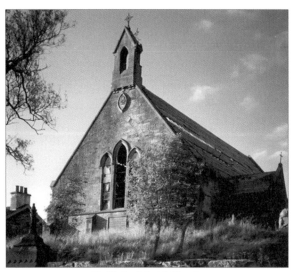
75. Glenbuck Parish Church

The closure of Grasshill pits was the start of the decline at Glenbuck. The pits, which employed around 200 men, around 150 of which lived in Glenbuck, were first closed in May 1932, but after a period of five months were re-opened in October. The pits closed again in 1933 and were never to re-open. In 1935 most of Office Row was demolished, as was the whole of Old School Row, totalling sixteen houses.

The annual Glenbuck Old Folks' Re-Union started in 1924 and ran for many years. Speakers were invited to the village to tell of their reminiscences, the first speaker being John Rodger, headmaster of the school from 1889-1927.

In 2005 there were plans to create a new village at Glenbuck. Scottish Coal Company Ltd applied for planning permission to develop Glenbuck farm into a series of new low-impact houses and crofts. These were to be located on the site of the village, on what had been an open cast coal mine. However, these proposals never materialised.

The visitor to Glenbuck today can find little of the former community surviving. Low walls indicating Rowanbank can be seen at the roadside. Behind this the stonework of the former ironworks can be seen, built into the hillside, the arched opening the only real distinctive feature. A few walls of the manse garden remain, as do a number of mature trees that formerly grew in the church grounds. Further west, slight remains of walls can be seen to the rear of the former post office. The only substantial ruins remaining are those of Spireslack farm, located slightly to the north, the roof crumbling and the roughcast scaling from the sandstone house. From the front door one can look south over where once a thriving community existed, nowadays blighted by the remains of an open cast coal mine.

27

Glengyron

★

The story of the Glengyron Ghost is one that is still sometimes mentioned in the Cumnock area. Many years ago, some of the houses in the miners' row were gaining an unenviable reputation for being haunted. A number of strange sounds were being heard, especially in late evening and early night-time, which could never be satisfactorily explained. The strange goings-on were the talk of the row, and at some point word spread farther afield, so much so that a national newspaper came to find out more.

It turned out, however, that there were no supernatural beings frequenting the houses after all. Apparently one of the families in the row had a young son, named William MacDonald, who was often sent to bed earlier than he would like. To amuse himself, he discovered that he could open the hatch into the loft of his house and climb into the roof-space. The houses at Glengyron were all joined together, with no spaces, and thus young William was able to crawl along the whole length of the row from his own house. One day he had the idea of 'haunting' some of the other residents. He got a reel of thread and he laid it across the rafters from various houses to the hatch at his own home. On the end of the threads he tied various odds and ends, so that he was able to lie back in bed and pull the various ends to cause things to move in the loft. If the residents of the house below were quiet enough they could hear the strange noises coming from above, but if they opened the hatch to the loft they were unable to see anything which could have caused it.

The haunting at Glengyron lasted for some time, before young William was eventually discovered. He was later to run his own paint and wallpaper shop in Cumnock, and serve as a Justice of the Peace. But there were still folk who knew him as the 'Glengyron Ghost'!

The long row of houses at Glengyron was located to the south of the Ayr and Edinburgh railway, about a mile and a half west of Cumnock New Station. The row, as mentioned, consisted of one long line of houses, 44 in number. On the south side of the houses was a narrow footpath, whereas to the north was a wider pathway, with seven wash-houses, evenly spaced along the length of the row. North of the wash-houses were gardens, in the space between the wash-houses and the railway. Two water pumps supplied drinking water to the residents, sourced from Cumnock's gravitation water scheme since 1880. However, the height of the row above sea level (around 530 feet) meant that the head of water was only 90 feet or so, resulting in a low-pressure supply, often struggling to cope in summer months. Every three homes had to share one dry-closet.

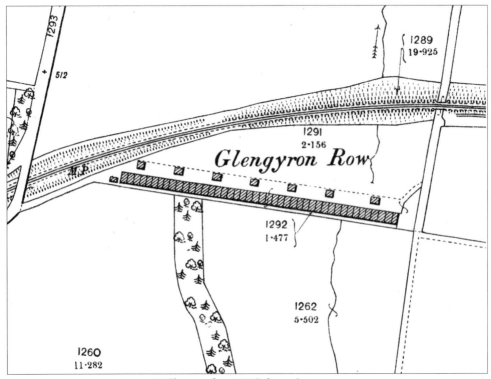

76. Glengyron from 1896 Ordnance Survey map
Reproduced by permission of the National Library of Scotland

By 1914 a couple of houses at Glengyron had been re-jigged, to form two larger houses and two smaller houses. Originally, all of the homes had two apartments, whereas the remodelling resulted in two houses of three apartments and two of one.

The standard size of the kitchen at Glengyron was 15 feet by 12 feet. The room measured 10 feet by 9 feet. For this residents paid a rent of £4 16s. per year. The three apartment houses had a rent of £7 per year, the one apartment homes paying £2 12s.

Most of the men living at Glengyron worked at the nearby Glengyron Coal Pit, which was located at the end of the field to the east of the row. Investigations into the possibility of coal mining at Glengyron were made between 1780 and 1786 by the Earl of Dumfries. For a short time there were some shallow workings in the area. Glengyron Pit, located by the side of the railway, was sunk in 1865 by the Eglinton Iron Company, later to become William Baird & Co., who also owned the row of houses. The pit operated for almost forty years, employing 120 men. The mine manager for many years was Hunter Bowie, who was also in charge of the pits at Knockterra and Hindsward close by. He did not live in one of the cottages in the rows, instead being resident in Greenmilll House in Cumnock, a property of the Marquis of Bute. The pit was closed in 1909, the last hutch of coal being raised on 6 April that year. Work on dismantling had, in fact, started the month before.

At least one of the residents of Glengyron was killed in the Garrallan Colliery nearby. Andrew MacMeekin lost his life in an accident on 8 August 1911.

In the late nineteenth century, house number five in the row was used as a reading and recreation room. In the late nineteenth century and into the next one, Rev Alexander MacDonald of Cumnock's West United Free Church held mission services at Glengyron.

By 1914 house number one was used as the village store, operated by Lugar Ironworks Co-operative Society. Although long gone, the existence of the store is recalled in the name of the field on Changue farm that runs between the steading and the site of the co-operative – Store Park. At the time the houses were in a bad state of repair, two of the houses in 1914 being empty. Those that were still occupied were in a poor condition – the floors comprised of brick tiles, many of which were broken. One house at least had a leak in the roof, and the resident had to catch the drips in a basin. Another resident had a boarded up window that had remained thus for a year, despite repeated requests to have it repaired.

Today, nothing remains to indicate that the long row of houses once existed, the land having reverted to agricultural use.

28

Glenlogan

✷

The village of Glenlogan was located on a minor road to the south-east of Sorn, on an elevated position on the edge of Airds Moss, south of the River Ayr. The houses were erected prior to 1856 by the Eglinton Iron Company to house men who worked in the various ironstone pits in the area. The properties were actually owned by the local estate, Glenlogan, owned at that time by the Ranken family. In 1845 blackband ironstone was discovered in the vicinity for the first time, after which the stone was worked in order to supply Lugar Ironworks, established in 1846 by John Wilson of Dundyvan and James and Colin Dunlop.

There were four rows of houses at Glenlogan, though these rows were all of different sizes. The first row was located alongside the main road. There were ten houses in this row, and each had a small garden plot to the rear. In front of the row, halfway along it, was a wash house. Immediately behind was the second row, built parallel to the first row. This row also had ten houses in it, but at the western end was an additional building, perhaps a wash-house.

The third row was built at a shallow angle to the first two rows. Again it had ten houses, some of which had gardens on the north side. The fourth row was the smallest. It was parallel to the third row. There were only four houses in this row, with gardens to the north. Between rows three and four was a water pump, installed around 1900, and the only one in the community.

In 1881 the census enumerators discovered that Glenlogan had a population of 122 residents. The rent in 1900 was £2 10s. 0d. per house, every resident being charged the same figure.

The Eglinton Coal Company operated the Glenlogan Pits in 1865. On Saturday 1 April 1865 a rock fall in Glenlogan Number 10 pit killed three young men. The victims, John Brown, William Wallace and Edward Pillin, who were all aged between sixteen and eighteen years, were engaged in a process named 'brushing' when a fall of debris landed on them. They were killed instantly. Two other miners, Patrick Marley and John Wallace, made a lucky escape.

In 1900 the front row at Glenlogan had six empty houses, the other four occupied by a widow (Mrs Heggarty), two miners (John Robertson and William

Harley) and another man, James Callendar, described as a 'residenter'. The second row had six empty houses, the four occupied houses being home to miners (William Hardy, Andrew Curran, David MacVickers and Robert Fowler). The third row had five empty houses, the other five occupied by miners James MacEwing, Archibald Black, John Kyle and William Reynolds, and all of the houses in the fourth row were occupied by miners (John Kyle, William Reynolds, William Davidson, Hugh Reynolds, John Bell and William Baxter).

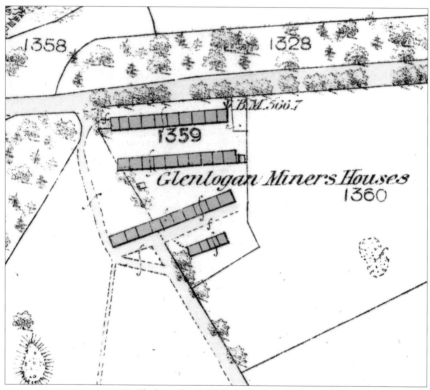

77. Glenlogan from 1860 Ordnance Survey map
Reproduced by permission of the National Library of Scotland

In February 1914 the Ayr County Council Sanitary Authority visited the rows at Glenlogan and condemned them as being unsuitable for habitation. However, the First World War commenced and the occupants had to remain for another four years. The houses at Glenlogan were gradually emptied before 1919, the last occupant of the houses being Mr Todd. The houses were demolished around 1921. Today only grass-grown mounds can be found where at once a community existed.

29

Grievehill

★

Grievehill was a remote community perched high on the moorland between Nithsdale and the valley of the Glenmuir. It was in New Cumnock parish, just short of Old Cumnock parish, and the houses were located 1,127 feet above sea level, making them extremely windy and cold in the winter. In one or two accounts the name is spelled Greavehill.

The presence of coal may have been known about for a number of years, but in 1788 Captain Maxwell, owner of the lands, began to work the coal. Its presence attracted others, and in 1792 a coal agent, Mr Robertson, arrived and established that there were plentiful seams near the surface. Lord James Stirling, the Lord Provost of Edinburgh, sent some men to negotiate with Captain Maxwell, purchasing the lands. During subsequent digging, a nine-foot seam was discovered, and they had prospects of finding a twelve-foot seam. Thomas Honeyman acquired the lands, but, within a few years the lands were sold to Sir Charles Stuart Menteth, owner of Closeburn Castle.

Sir Charles came from an ancient landed family, but he was keen to extend the family estates and increase their prosperity. He acquired Mansfield and planned the coal and limestone works on it. Other coalmasters in New Cumnock parish sold their coal locally and north into the county, so Sir Charles decided to head the other way – taking his coal south to Dumfriesshire. He built a haul route from Grievehill around the side of Craigdullyeart Hill, through the Ellergoffe pass and down to Kirkconnel. At nearby Sanquhar he established a coal yard, where Dumfriesshire customers could purchase the coal.

On making a route up past Hall of Mansfield and Watstonburn farms, the roadway to Grievehill turned towards Millstone Knowe. As the years passed, the hillside here was disfigured by numerous small pit shafts and levels, probably too many to list, and the old Ordnance Survey maps of 1857 show innumerable pit hollows, former mines and existing works.

The first houses reached at Grievehill were located to the left, on the north side of the road. They had gardens to the west of them. Beyond, the next building was on the right, and following this was a row of cottages, formed into a terrace. To the south of these houses were extensive gardens, though tilling the soil would have been difficult, the uplands having either thin soil or peat. Across the road from the last house in the terrace was another building, its purpose now unknown.

It is thought that the community at Grievehill was established by Sir Charles. The presence of coal and limestone in abundance was the attraction for him, and he is noted as being the person who invented the three-draw kiln.

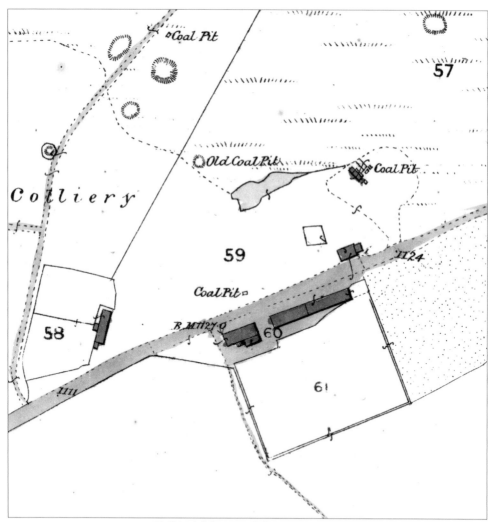

78. Grievehill from 1860 Ordnance Survey map
Reproduced by permission of the National Library of Scotland

Lime was worked in quarries as well as mines across the southern side of the estate, alongside Mansfield Road and Craigdullyeart Hill, whereas coal was easily obtained higher up, where the seams were just below the surface. Indeed, some of the first coal wrought was done by opencast means, the coal virtually being under the sods. At Grievehill he established a number of small mines, some of which were little more than adits into the hillside. Another seam gained the nickname Noah's Ark, from its U-shaped profile. The colliers employed lived in houses that were built at Grievehill, at the end of the roadway from Mansfield Road up past the lime kilns at Hall of Mansfield.

In 1841, when the Census was taken of the population of the country, the enumerators visited Grievehill and found sixteen families living in the cottages. Two of them were unoccupied, indicating that there were eighteen houses here at one time. The sixteen heads of household were John Callan, Thomas Gracie, Robert Person, William Hendrie, John Kerr, Alexander Dempster, William Hannay, Joseph Duncan, Alexander Hyslop, William Shields, William MacMurdo, William Mitchell, William Hardie, John Mitchell, John Gair and Robert Trotter. Many of these surnames survive in the district today. Of the sixteen heads of the house, twelve were employed as miners. Joseph Duncan was a blacksmith, William Shields was a mason, and William MacMurdo and Robert Trotter were agricultural labourers.

The houses at Grievehill were not big, probably comparable in size to most other miners' rows of the early nineteenth century, and like most of these communities they were home to sizeable families. At the time of the 1841 Census, John Kerr's house was home to nine residents. James Duncan's house was occupied by eight folk and John Callan's by seven. In total, the sixteen houses had a resident population of 82.

The mines manager at Mansfield Colliery was Robert Kerr (1803-1864). He had become the manager of the colliery sometime before 1851. He was born in Sanquhar in 1803, the son of James Kerr, a coal agent, and Mary Milligan. He lived in Kirkconnel for some years, where his six children were born, before going to Grievehill. He lived at Mansfield Cottage for most of this time, although the John Kerr listed as a resident of Grievehill in 1841 may have been one of his sons. He was a coal salesman, and a second son, Robert Kerr, is noted as the engine-keeper there.

Sir Charles Stuart Menteth sold the coalworks at Grievehill in 1858 to a company owned by Robert Kerr and James Gray. Gray (1823-1904) was the owner of the Pathhead Colliery, located nearer to New Cumnock, whereas Kerr was manager at Mansfield. The partnership was dissolved in 1864, when Kerr died at the aged of 62. Gray continued working the Pathhead and Mansfield mines alone until he died in 1904, aged 81.

By 1861 there were still around half a dozen families living at Grievehill, but it was in decline. Within another decade the cottages were abandoned and they fell into disrepair. Today they have gone completely, the modern Grievehill open cast coal mine having obliterated the site of the houses, working the rich seams that existed near the surface.

30

Hagsthorn

★

The countryside separating Dalry and Kilbirnie is covered with numerous small pit bings – relics of a time when almost every field in the area had a small mine working the coal or ironstone seams with which the area abounded. A look at the map of the area shows dozens of old spoil heaps, nowadays beginning to blend in with the rolling Ayrshire countryside – grass grown and in some cases covered with trees.

These bings belonged to the coal and ironstone mines that operated in the early nineteenth century. The mines had names like Lintseedridge, Mossend and Swinlees.

The miners who worked in the pits had to live somewhere, and one of the communities that was established for them was known as Hagsthorn. This was located on the south-eastern side of the road from Dalry to Kilbirnie, just within the Kilbirnie parish boundary. About half a mile to the south west were the rows of Borestone, mentioned earlier in this book. At one time the boundary was more obvious than it is today, for it was marked by a shelterbelt of trees separating Lintseedridge and Mossend farms. On the right hand side of the road, heading from Dalry, the first row of houses was positioned facing onto the road. This had twelve houses in it, though the last two houses had been at some point converted into one dwelling. Behind the row was an open area, and beyond this were the garden plots for each of the houses.

At the end of the first row was another building, set back more from the road, and divided into two. Only a narrow gap separated the corners of the two gables.

A further roadside row followed, this one having eight houses in it. Again a couple of houses had been joined to form one larger home, and the first two houses were of a different size to the rest of those in the row. Parallel with this row was a further row of houses, all of which were a different size.

Finally, at the Kilbirnie end of the community, was a fourth row, again positioned facing onto the roadside. This row also comprised of six houses, with gardens located to the rear.

The houses at Hagsthorn appear to have been erected sometime between 1860 and 1890. They were positioned on a low ridge, so that to the front of the rows, the land dropped down to the Pitcon Burn, whereas to the rear the land fell away to the meadows alongside the River Garnock. The Pitcon Burn was sometimes used as a source of water, but a public well was located a few hundred yards along the Kilbirnie road, located at the roadside.

Most of the residents at Hagsthorn were Roman Catholics. It is said that when the trains filled with Irish workers and their families arrived at Dalry station, the local minister and priest were there to greet them. Protestants were guided by the minister to the mining communities at Barkip (known also as The Den), Carsehead or the Peesweep Rows. The Catholics were sent by the priest to either Borestone or Hagsthorn.

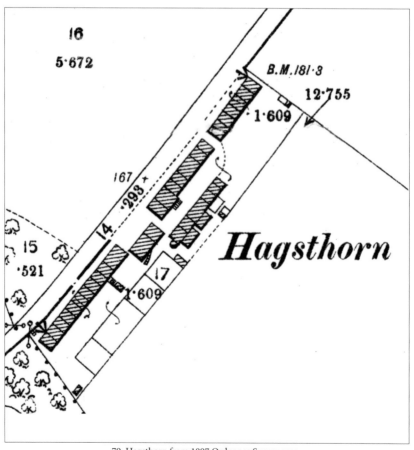

79. Hagsthorn from 1897 Ordnance Survey map
Reproduced by permission of the National Library of Scotland

The houses at Hagsthorn have all been demolished and the site totally cleared. Today, the area occupied by the houses and gardens forms a long, narrow field by the roadside, and the passer-by has little to let them know that once many families lived there. The name survives to some extent, however, for in Kilbirnie one of the streets bears the name Hagthorne Avenue, though why the spelling was changed is unknown.

31

Kerse

*

The village of Kerse was never a large one. It probably only ever grew to have around 22 houses in it, used as homes by workers from the ironstone pits that littered the hillside above. It was sometimes known as Kerse Square, the houses there being an example of a colliery square. The village was located by the side of the road that linked Patna with Drongan, just one and a half miles north of the former. What made Kerse slightly more important than a few of the other miners' rows that existed in the district, was the fact that it had a store and school, so the name was better known.

The village was owned in its entirety by the Dalmellington Iron Company, and most of the residents were employed by the firm. The original Kerse pits were opened by the Summerlee Iron Company of Coatbridge around 1856. Located high on the moor above Kerse itself, they lay on Dunston Hill. To reach them, a steep incline of 1 in 11 was laid with rails, and ropes and pulleys were used to haul the wagons back up to the mines. This little branch line came from a junction near to Smithston farm.

Kerse Store was established as a branch shop of the Dalmellington Ironworks Co-operative Society, which was based at Waterside in the Doon valley. A tiny shop, it was located in what may originally have been another house. The door and window of the shop matched the houses in the row, and the only real thing that identified the shop was a wooden sign affixed to the gutter at the bottom of the roof, announcing 'Kerse Store'.

Although Kerse itself was a small community, the store had a good trade in making deliveries to houses in nearby mining communities, where no such facility existed. Thus men and boys travelled on bicycles to places such as Tongue Bridge Row, Cairntable and Hollybush with provisions. Often the deliveries were on tick, and workers at the ironstone mines would have to pay off their debts to the store whenever they received their wages.

At the north end of the village was the old school, originally established by the Dalmellington Iron Company, but in 1872 taken over by Dalrymple School Board. Around 1870 the roll was 165, but 35 pupils regularly failed to attend. In

1879 the roll was 131. To teach the children there were a schoolmaster and three pupil teachers. Pupils attended this school from much of the east end of Dalrymple parish, in which Kerse was located. A visit from His Majesty's Inspectorate found the school to be in a deplorable condition. They found the building to be suffering from damp, and there was evidence of rats. In fact, things were sometimes so bad that the rats were discovered to have eaten the children's lunches.

80. Kerse with store in centre and school in the trees

In March 1914 a new school was opened at Kerse to replace the old one. This was built further up the hill from Kerse itself, on an elevated position between Kerse and Tongue Bridge Row. Although located in a more rural location, it was better positioned for the pupils from other rows who also attended. The new school was designed by the Ayr architect, Alexander Caldwell Thomson.

The new school was far superior to the old one. The pupils could now enjoy five classrooms, a domestic classroom, laundry, science laboratory, a woodwork room and a central hall, where assemblies and other group activities could take place. The first headmaster at the school was Alexander Lyle, who remained until 1922, living in the adjoining schoolhouse. Heads who followed were David Wilson (1922-49), and Miss I. Haines, who became Mrs Reid (1949-62). The roll in 1951 was 72. The school was closed on 29 June 1962, the roll having plummeted with the demolition of local miners' houses. The building, which still survives, was used for a time as an outdoor centre, a factory for Timpo Toys, and then SYEO Fashions.

In 1928 Kerse still had eighteen houses occupied, three of which were actually made up from two smaller houses being joined together. The residents worked in the pits, such as Quintin Blane, collier; James Blane, miner; Robert Logan, miner; Ivie MacCrorie, collier; George MacTimpany, collier; and William Douglan, collier. Other occupations represented at the time were storeman (Joseph Howatson).

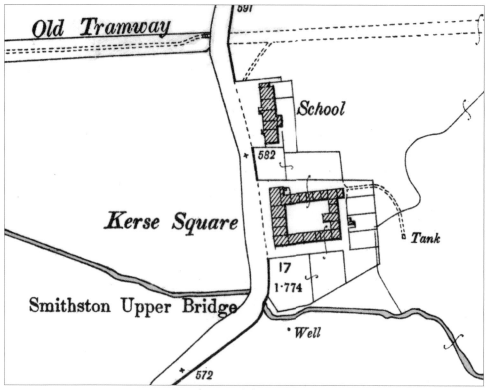

81. Kerse from 1896 Ordnance Survey map
Reproduced by permission of the National Library of Scotland

The village of Kerse survived until the 1930s. By this time the houses were unfit for habitation, and the county council erected new homes at Polnessan, on the main Ayr to Dalmellington road, to rehouse the inhabitants. Polnessan was built in the early 1930s, the houses being described as model homes. Kerse was abandoned and the rows demolished. The site of the community remained as grassy fields for many decades, but in recent times a couple of large bungalows have been erected on the site.

32

Kersland

★

Across Ayrshire, and in many ironstone mining areas, the manufacture of bricks became a subsidiary industry. In a lot of cases spoil heaps cast up from the extraction of ironstone and coal could be converted into common bricks, and a number of companies saw this as an opportunity of making money from a different source. At Dalry, the Kersland Brick Works were established on the site of the old Kersland Ironstone Pit, which had been disused from at least 1895. The old bing, which was a considerable feature on the landscape, was gradually reduced as the bricks were being made, small tramways having been laid across the heap to transport the raw material to the new kilns.

As said, the brickwork was built on the site of the old ironstone pit, which had been sunk sometime before 1855. At that time the pit had a couple of surface buildings indicated on detailed maps – an engine house and another building housing a boiler. A small mineral railway entered the pit grounds, branching from the main line. Forty years later, the bing was much larger, but the mineworkers had gone. Their homes, Kersland Row, were still there, but they were not to last too long thereafter, for the maps of 1909 show the houses as roofless and abandoned.

Kersland was located at West Kersland farm, located on the east side of the River Garnock, a few miles from Dalry. It was only half a mile away from the other lost village of Carsehead. The village consisted of three rows of houses, one of which was located at the farm, and which had five houses in it. Located by the side of the road, these houses were irregular in size, indicating an old age, perhaps being farm-workers' houses that had been adapted for miners.

The two main rows at Kersland, erected to house the pit-workers, were located to the south-west of West Kersland, built at the corner of what would have once been a field, but which was now the corner of the ground on which the pit sat. The shorter row, known as East Kirkland Row, was located alongside the old road through the farm steading, and contained six houses. The front doors faced directly onto the public road. To the rear, or west, was a roughly surfaced area, and beyond this were small garden plots.

The longer row, West Kirkland Row, was built at right angles to the first row, facing onto a minor trackway that led from West Kersland to the railway bridge, and thence by a track to a ford across the River Garnock. This row had eleven or twelve houses in it, again facing onto the road, but with a yard and gardens to the rear. The rows were the property of William Baird & Company.

In March 1879 there was a disaster at the rows. At the time some of the miners responsible for shot firing rocks and coal on the face kept their own gunpowder in their homes. In a number of cases, against company rules, the miners prepared the flask with powder and a fuse beforehand, to save time when they were underground. Naturally, this was a dangerous practice and one Saturday afternoon one of these flasks blew up, totally demolishing three of the houses in the rows. The *Ardrossan & Saltcoats Herald* tells the story:

> The houses are principally occupied by miners in the employment of Messrs Baird & Co., and several just now are unoccupied. The explosion occurred in the large row in a house about the centre, occupied by a contractor named William Marshall. Marshall, it seems, in his blasting operations, uses a considerable quantity of gunpowder and it appears he had just stocked himself the previous night with two barrels, each containing 25 lb, and when the accident occurred there were upwards of 30 lb of powder in the house.
>
> Marshall had opened a 25 lb keg on Saturday morning and taken a quantity away with him. The remainder was left behind and Mrs Marshall, as is custom, was engaged on Saturday on filling the remainder of the keg into a flask for her husband's use when the unfortunate occurrence took place.
>
> She states that when in the act of filling the flask, her little girl came alongside with a lighted straw and perceiving the danger she grasped at the child when it is supposed part of the burnt straw fell amongst the gunpowder. This instantly ignited and caused an explosion which was heard some distance away and which has been most disastrous in effect.
>
> The Marshall's house and also the one alongside, occupied by Robert Kerr, miner, having been entirely demolished, the roofs of both houses having been entirely blown off. How the inmates escaped it is impossible to understand and what is even more remarkable, the

broken keg of powder was afterwards found uninjured. The neighbours who were thrown into a state of great alarm on perceiving the nature of the accident were not long in getting the flames subdued and rescuing the inmates.

Peter Drain, who lives next door to the Marshalls, and whose home has been rendered uninhabitable, states that he was putting on his boots at the time, and he immediately ran out. Amongst the first persons he saw was Mrs Marshall who managed to run out from amongst the falling debris. The gable of Drain's house was rent and several pieces of furniture were broken. The man Kerr who lives in the other house next to where the explosion occurred and whose house is entirely wrecked, was luckily away from home.

The persons injured are as follows: Mrs Marshall – burned on hands and face – Agnes Marshall (3) – daughter of Mrs Marshall, was seriously burned on arms, face and body, and recovery is doubtful; Anthony Marshall (7) – slightly burned on head; John Marshall (11) – not burned, but hurt by falling stones, etc., and the tips of several fingers cut off by flying debris; Thomas Wardrop (2), son of John Wardrop, miner, badly burned on face and hands and lies in a critical state; Ann MacDonald (6), daughter of Andrew MacDonald, miner, burned about neck and face; John Jones, an infant, carried by the girl MacDonald, was found buried in the debris, but strange to say escaped with very few injuries apart from being slightly burned on the face.

Doctor Sloan of Dalry was in attendance and ministered to those who were severely burned. The poor people have almost lost everything in the shape of furniture, for what is saved is very much damaged. Marshall, along with his family, were accommodated by the neighbours, and as it happened there were one or two empty houses in the row, into which the occupants of the wrecked houses were removed.

Marshall states that he has been in the habit of using powder of this quantity for years, and has invariably a stock of it at his home, but that he had just made arrangements whereby in future he would keep it away from his dwelling place. He appears ignorant of the law regulating the storing of explosives which only allows a maximum of 30 lbs to be kept. Superintendent MacCracken of the Dalry Constabulary along with several constables went to the scene of the disaster and immediately after the accident the powder that was left over was removed to a place of safety at Highfield.

West Kersland farm appears to have been given up as a working farm in the late 1800s, for by 1895 there is only one building remaining, no doubt the former farmhouse, probably converted into another mineworker's house. By 1909 it, too, was roofless, as were most of the rows. In 1900 the houses were still the property of William Baird, but of the eighteen houses, five were empty. The principal occupation of the tenants remaining were seven miners, one labourer, one runner, one charfiller, one widow, one drawer and one driver. Soon after, these houses were emptied. The walls stood for some time thereafter, the gardens overgrown and turning wild, and anything that remained crumbling away. Today, only the remnants of the old bing survive, the site of the pit, brickworks and houses being reclaimed by nature.

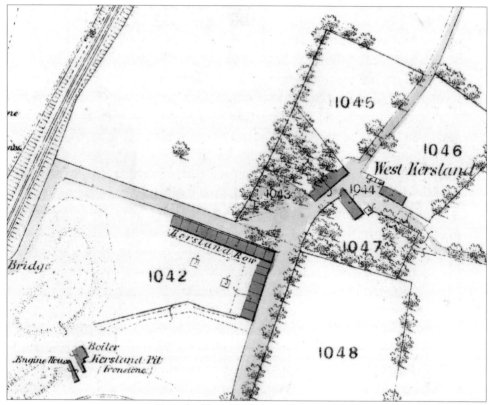

82. Kersland from 1858 Ordnance Survey map
Reproduced by permission of the National Library of Scotland

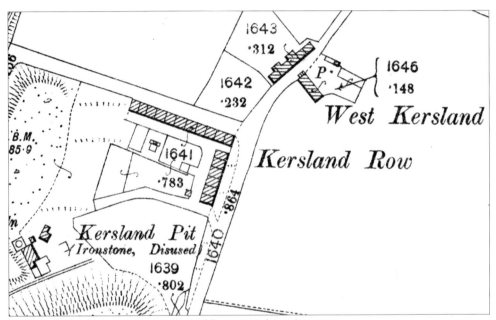

83. Kersland from 1897 Ordnance Survey map
Reproduced by permission of the National Library of Scotland

33

Knockshoggle

*

Like Drumsmudden, Knockshoggle is one of those guid auld Scots names that could almost be made up. And yet it was at one time the name of a small Ayrshire village, practically hidden from the outside world in a sheltered holm by the side of the River Ayr. As the crow flies, Knockshoggle was located just over one mile to the east of Annbank, but on the opposite side of the river. It was positioned to the east of the Enterkine Viaduct, erected in 1872 as part of the Ayr to Cumnock line. Some accounts name the village simply as Knockshoggle, others use Knockshoggle Holm or Knockshoggleholm. The old Ordnance Survey maps spell the name Knockshogle Holm, with one 'g'. There can still be seen a few ruins associated with the old houses that stood here, but the name has almost been forgotten, other than for Knockshoggle farm, which still sits above the holm.

The village was probably created to house miners in the late eighteenth century. Certainly, there are records of births in the village from 1812, when Elizabeth MacGhie was born to John MacGhie and his wife, Agnes Steven. It was noted that coal had been wrought at Knockshoggle, and this no doubt explains the existence of the old village. The natural hone stone rock which was quarried at Stair also existed at Knockshoggle and was quarried here for a time. Locally, the stone was known as clay-slates, and it was dug out, cut to shape, and sold around the country for the purpose of sharpening knives and other fine blades. The business of mining the hone stone here appears to have died out when the works at Milton, near Stair, took off, producing hones in larger quantities.

In 1841, when the *New Statistical Account* of Coylton parish was compiled, Knockshoggle had a population of 109. The Ordnance Survey map of 1857 depicts a selection of houses, basically arranged around a small square field that extended to around two acres. Even then, there were around four cottages in ruins, their thatched roofs removed and the walls left to crumble. When the surveyors for the Ordnance Board visited in 1860 they noted that there were, 'six or seven cottage houses on the south bank of the Water of Ayr, partly in ruin and partly thatched.'

Compiled in 1846, the *Topographical Dictionary of Scotland* states that the village had 102 inhabitants. It continues, describing the community as comprising 'a group of cottages, chiefly inhabited by persons engaged in agriculture.'

The 1851 Census states that the village had 68 residents, living in sixteen cottages. Most of these were employed in mining. In one cottage, occupied by the Lindsay family, there were ten residents – John Lindsay (aged 46), his wife Margaret and their five sons – James, Hugh, Alexander, Robert and Thomas. Thomas was just ten months old, Robert was eight years old and attended school. The older brothers James (15) and twins Hugh and Alexander (13) worked in the mines. The cottage was also home to three step-children, Alexander Galloway, James and Susan, Alexander Galloway being employed as a coal miner, even at the age of eleven years!

In the house next door, the Paterson family resided. Whether or not there was a school in the village is unlikely, but in 1851 James Paterson, then aged 53, was listed as a teacher of English, reading, writing and arithmetic. Three of his sons were miners (aged from eleven to seventeen) and in this instance twelve people occupied the cottage.

The next cottage was noted as being uninhabited. Next again was home to the family of Susan Clark, a widow, and her two sons, again coal miners, a lodger and his two children. James Martin, listed as a pauper, his wife and son lived next door, and in the next cottage was another miner, William Wilson, and his family, nine in all. The following two cottages were unoccupied.

William MacGown lived in the next cottage. He was a shoemaker who had come over to Scotland from Ireland. Next door was Jane Ferguson and her three children. She was listed as a hand sewer, her children as paupers. No doubt Jane tried to make some form of income from repairing and making clothing. Her husband may have died young. Next door an old couple lived, John Kennedy, aged 75, and his wife, Ann, also 75. He was a retired miner. Edward MacNeill, a miner, lived next door with wife and two daughters. Margaret Murdoch and her two young children occupied the next cottage – she was a seamstress. William Jackson, aged 65, lived in the next cottage. He was a house thatcher who had been born in Lanarkshire.

In the next cottage lived Mary Brawly, a washerwoman and outdoor labourer, with her two sons. Her elder sister lived with her. The last cottage was occupied by Archibald Kennedy, a coal miner, his wife and two sons. Many of the residents were born in other mining areas, no doubt moving to find work as older mines were worked out and new pits were sunk. In addition to those who came from Ireland, the adults were born in the parishes of Coylton, Dailly, Tarbolton, Auchinleck and Sorn in Ayrshire, or else in Lanarkshire, Kirkcudbrightshire and Renfrewshire.

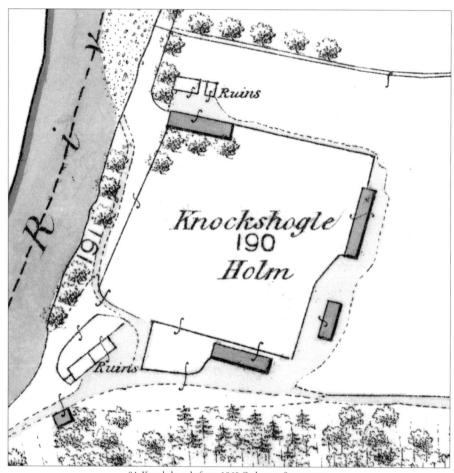

84. Knockshoggle from 1860 Ordnance Survey map
Reproduced by permission of the National Library of Scotland

With the loss of local industry, and with the residents expecting a better standard of living, Knockshoggle was gradually abandoned. At one time there were only eight cottages still lived in, the rest having fallen into ruins. Some of the eight cottages were still thatched. By 1895 only one cottage remained in occupation, positioned next to the river. There lived James Smith, collier, and his family. When he moved out, the village was no more, and the site of it is gradually returning to nature.

In the middle section of Coylton kirkyard there is a memorial stone commemorating John Stewart, who died at Knockshoggle Holm on 23 November 1909 aged 61. His wife, Margaret Campbell survived him, and died in Tarbolton in 1918. Another stone in the kirkyard commemorates many members of the Campbell family. James Campbell, who erected the stone in memory of his extended family, died at Knockshoggle Holm on 17 September 1845, aged 78. His father had been the tenant farmer in Knockshoggle farm itself, dying in 1786. The Campbell family were to move to Coylton, where James Campbell was married to Margaret Dickie, daughter of David Dickie, landlord at the village pub. The family ran what became the Finlayson Arms Inn in the village for a good number of years.

Another family from Knockshoggle Holm was the Wilsons. Alexander Wilson appears to have arrived at the community sometime around 1820 with his new wife, Elizabeth Ferguson. He worked in the local mines and he and his wife had a number of children, all born in the village. Alexander Ferguson Wilson was born in 1833 and was married in 1854. He emigrated to Utah in the United States in 1879, taking his family with him. The family continued to work in the coalmines in America, but a number of them were to be killed in mining accidents.

34

Knowehead

★

Knowehead was a small village in the parish of Galston. Today there is virtually no indication of it ever having existed.

The village was created sometime in the early 1800s. Located to the west of Knowehead farm, it was positioned just north of a minor burn that flowed into the Cessnock Water. A coal pit shown on the 1857 Ordnance Survey map was probably the reason for the village's existence. This pit was fairly small, but a tramway from the Galston Branch of the Glasgow and South Western Railway swung around the knoll on which Knowehead farm sits, serving this pit and others on Holmes estate.

The miners' houses were located on the opposite side of the railway from both the farm and pit. The first row was located on a north-south axis. There were fourteen houses in the row.

At the southern end of the first row was a second, striking off at an angle, overlooking the minor burn. This had fourteen small houses in it. In front of the houses was a single wash-house to serve all of the occupants.

To the west of the second row was a line of buildings, which probably predated the village. This was Burnfoot, perhaps itself a small farm at one time. It was later to become incorporated in Knowehead farm. At the north end of the north row was a larger building, its purpose now unknown.

At the end of the second row, by the side of the small stream, was a quarry, probably initially used to win stone with which to build the houses. By 1895 this quarry was no longer worked, but at the foot of it was a well, from where the villagers drew their water.

Writing in 1875, Archibald Adamson in *Rambles Round Kilmarnock*, described Knowehead as a 'quaint village, with the smoke curling from the cottage chimneys'.

Life in the village could be harsh. Although each cottage had a coal fire, it was difficult to keep the house warm. During a prolonged spell of severe weather in February 1895 one of the residents, the elderly Mrs White, was to succumb to the freezing cold. She was described as being old and infirm, living alone and struggling to look after herself. A neighbour had helped her into bed at ten o' clock one evening, but the following morning she was discovered outside, her lifeless body lying on the ground a short distance from her home. She was lightly clad and it is thought that she had got up during the night and had wandered outside and was overcome by the intense cold.

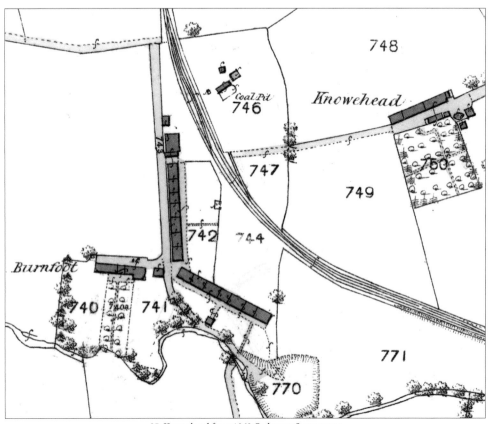

85. Knowehead from 1860 Ordnance Survey map
Reproduced by permission of the National Library of Scotland

The sad tale of Mrs White prompted someone to write to the *Irvine Valley Weekly Supplement and Advertiser* newspaper a week after she was found dead:

An old woman, Mrs White, who lived alone, was found frozen to death at Holmes Row last week. She had been in such a state of body and mind for a considerable time past as rendered her incapable of looking properly after herself; so some one is morally responsible for her death.

Did neither the Minister of the Parish, the Inspector of the Poor, nor the Sanitary Inspector know of her condition? She was very, very much in want of attention from all these three officials. The public ought to know if none of the three thought it his duty to look after the poor old woman.

Sympathy

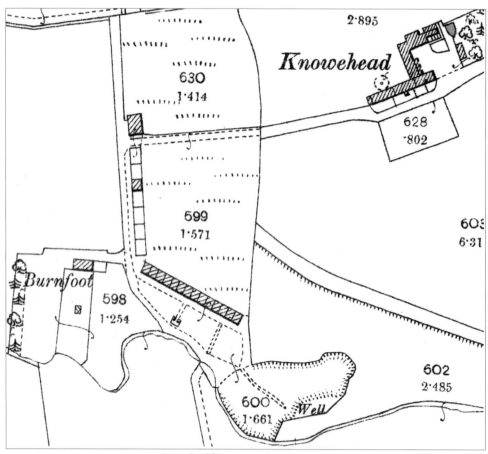

86. Knowehead from 1896 Ordnance Survey map
Reproduced by permission of the National Library of Scotland

Apart from the issues raised, it is interesting to note that the writer referred to Knowehead as 'Holmes Row'. Holmes House was located further east, on an elevated stretch of countryside. It was a rather fine Tudor-style building, owned for many years by the Fairlie family.

The coal pit at Knowehead was closed and all evidence of it was cleared away by 1895. The demand for housing in the district had reduced, and the first row of houses had fallen into disrepair. Indeed, most of the houses had lost their roofs, leaving just the walls standing. Only one of the houses, part-way down the row, still had a roof at this time.

Some of the names of the families who lived at Knowehead can be recalled. One of these was the Quigley family, John Quigley living there in 1851. This family was later to move to Glasgow where they adopted the surname Tweedie for some reason. Robert Reid (born in 1840 in Riccarton parish) was a coalminer who lived at Knowehead. According to the 1871 census he lived there with his wife, Margaret Gibson, and six others in the tiny house. By 1881 he had moved back to Riccarton. Some of the small cottages were joined together to allow the larger families to live in them. For example, in 1881 James Graham (c.1839-1895) lived at number 19/20 with nine others.

35

Lethanhill

✶

The first houses to be built at Lethanhill, high on the moor above the Doon valley, was to become known as the Peewit Row. Ten houses were constructed on a fairly level stretch of the hillside, around 1849, when the Burnfoot pits were sunk. A couple of years later the 1851 Census enumerators arrived and made the first real record of who lived in the community. The surnames of the first ten families to occupy the houses were Gibb, Hope, Davidson, Higarty, Dally, Wilson, Frew, Hunter, MacMillan and MacBurnie. There were a few other families in the rows who lived with the main tenants, plus a number of lodgers. In total there were 72 folk living in the ten houses.

Some work has been done to find out where these folk came from, and it was discovered that only one family was local, being born in Dalmellington parish. The others came from Lanarkshire, Ireland, Wigtownshire, Renfrewshire, Fife, Midlothian and elsewhere in Ayrshire.

The Peewit Row was built on a north-west-south-east axis. On the south-west side of the row were the gardens, each looked after by the occupier of the house, the thin moorland soil coaxed into producing some sort of return, even if it was only potatoes.

The second row of houses to be erected at Lethanhill was the Whaup Row. Although built in a parallel fashion to the Peewit Row, the Whaup Row was located 500 yards further up the hill. It was around this row that the bulk of the village of Lethanhill was to be built.

The Whaup Row had 22 houses in it, again all of one apartment. The walls were built of stone, quarried at Dunaskin. The kitchen measured 18 feet by 10½ feet, the scullery 9 feet by 6 feet. As time passed, many of the houses were joined to form larger units. In 1914 the rent for a single-apartment house was 1s. 9d., whereas a double-apartment was 3s. 6d. The conditions were poor, and in 1913 the inspectors who visited found one woman standing outside in the rain doing her washing. There were no closets, wash-houses or ash pits. A few had wooden closets. Each house in this row had a brick coalhouse, which made it appear to be a much superior place compared with the other rows. By 1861, when the second set of Census enumerators visited Lethanhill, the population had risen to 203, living in the two rows.

In the mid-1860s a new track was laid from Burnfoot, near Patna in the valley below, straight up the hillside towards Lethanhill. This allowed easier access to the village, but its steepness was to remain a problem. A secondary problem was the fact that at the foot of the hill were gates which were kept locked by the iron company. Thus, only those with permission could take carts or other wheeled vehicles up to the village. A house near to the gate acted as a gatehouse, the occupant paid to keep the key and only allow authorised vehicles through, in addition to ambulances or hearses. If any family was moving house from Lethanhill to another community, they had to ask permission from the ironworks company to allow their goods to be transported this way. Permission was usually granted, but only if any outstanding debts to the company were settled.

The new road had been vital in transporting materials for building more rows of houses. These were erected near to the Whaup Row, making a sizeable community there. By 1871 there were 190 houses, with a total population of 1,421 residents. Each house appeared to have a family in residence, plus a goodly number of lodgers.

The next phase of building saw the construction of the Step Row, the Low Row, the Diamond Row, School Row, Stone Row, Store Row, White Brick Row and Briggate Row. The Stone, Store and Whaup Row were positioned round an open area of ground that became known as the Square, the unofficial village centre.

The Step Row had 24 houses in it. It was built alongside the line of the boundary between Burnfoot and Drumgrange farms, though the line of the dike had gone. The row gained its name from the fact that, unlike most of the other rows at Lethanhill, it was built up the line of the hillside, and there were five 'steps' in the line of the roof.

The houses in the Low Row were arranged in three terraces. The first, that nearest the roadway into the village, had 21 two-apartment houses in it. The front doors were facing south-west, towards the lonely Peewit Row. In front of the houses was a narrow pathway, and alongside it ran the mineral siding that headed east to the coal mines of Corbie Craigs and Drumgrange. The Low Row was built of bricks. In each house the kitchen measured 17 feet by 11½ feet. The main room was 9 feet square, and the scullery measured around 8 feet by 7 feet.

For this amount of room space, the tenants paid a rent of 2s. 3d. per week. Water was obtained from a gravitational supply, which often froze in winter. In the scullery was a boiler which could produce hot water. Other facilities were sparse. There was no ash pit for the whole row, and neither was there a coal house. If the call of nature came, the residents had to either use a pan in the house, or else head out into the moor. Only one wooden outbuilding serviced as a toilet, shared by the whole row.

87. Lethanhill Low Row

The second terrace in the Low Row was located immediately to the east of the first row. This row had houses the same shape as the first row, but there were 24 of them. The houses were very damp, the main source of water ingress apparently being through the bottom of the front doors, which bore the brunt of the storms making their way across the moors in front of the houses. To the rear were gardens, stretching backward from the homes. The residents, as with most of the occupants of miners' rows, had to keep their supply of coal in their sculleries. The ashes gathered from the foot of the grates were scattered about the houses to the front and rear, building up over the years. These were seen as helping to reduce the muddy pathways on either side of the row, but in fact did little to help. The third terrace in the Low Row had a further twenty houses, again brick-built and facing the mineral line.

Just beyond the third Low Row terrace was the Briggate Row. It faced a branch line from the railway that passed in front of the Low Row. This branch was little more than a siding, constructed to allow deliveries to be made to the village store. The Briggate Row had twenty houses in it, all single apartment, apart from where two houses were joined to form one larger dwelling. A water pump was located at the west end of the row, at the side of the gardens, which had a gravitational water supply fed to it. The residents complained that the supply was poor, and that they had to share the pump with the residents of the White Brick Row. The tenants in the Briggate row paid 1s. 9d. a week in rent in 1914.

The White Brick Row was built lengthways to the north-west of the Briggate Row. Originally there were 26 single-apartment houses in this row, but as with many houses in the community, a number had been joined to form one larger house. Most houses had a front door facing the rough pathway in front of the terrace, and to its side a single window. The roof was a single length of tiles, at every second house pierced with a chimney stack on the apex. The rent was the same as the houses in the Briggate Row, unless it was a double house, for which the rent was 3s. 6d.

88. Lethanhill School and Church

On the opposite side of the store's railway siding was the Old School Row, its back to the White Brick Row. The front faced to the south-west, generally in a downhill direction, over the allotments each house was supplied with. This row had 24 houses in it, divided into two terraces of eighteen and six houses. In style, the houses were the same as the Low Row. As expected from the name of the row, this was where the original school for the children of Lethanhill had been.

At the north-west end of the Old School Row was the Diamond Row. There were only four houses in this row, generally of the same style as the Old School Row.

Across the Square from the Whaup Row was the Stone Row. This was named from the buildings having been erected with stone quarried at Dunaskin. There were sixteen two apartment houses in this row, the houses having kitchens measuring 17 feet by 11 feet. The rooms were 9 feet square, and the sculleries were 9½ feet by 8 feet. Rent payable for houses of this size was 2s. 3d. per week in 1914. As with the rest of the village, there was basically no ash-pit, coal house, wash-house or closet for any house. Only in a few cases did the residents have their own self-built timber closet.

The new village attracted the attentions of a reporter from the *Glasgow Herald*, who published his article on 28 January 1875. He noted that 'whatever may have been the condition of miners' houses in Ayrshire a few years ago', those in Lethanhill, 'were well constructed, commodious and cheap.' He complained about the condition of sanitation in the village, and the lack of means of disposal for waster. Water was obtainable from either springs on the hillside, or else from a pump which raised water from the old Number 9 pit. It was noted that this water, when added to broth or porridge, turned it black!

At the first Lethanhill and Burnfoothill re-union, which took place in Patna in 1965, the speaker, William Murphie, recalled what the village was like:

> I must say without reservation or qualification or equivocation that the 'Hill as a village was unattractive, forbidding, yes, and ugly. The drab, barrack-like uniformity of the miners' rows, planned with no eye to beauty but seemingly to conform to the alignment of the railway tracks that intersected them, presented a picture of unrelieved depression and deadness. The immediate prospect back or front was horrible, open middens and sewers, with the odd pit bing here and there. Situated as it was 900 feet above sea level and refreshed by winds austere and pure, our village should have had a clean bill of health. Yet, enteric fever was not unknown, and enteric is engendered by foul water. It should never have been, and yet the 'Hill reared hardy, tough youngsters – we're not called the 'Hill Arabs for nothing! Nonetheless, the spirit of the 'Hill folks transcended their harsh, cruel, frustrating, physical environment and in time there evolved some attempt at self-expression, cultural and even aesthetic, social recreation and fun and games.

The ironworks company established a store in the village which sold provisions to the villagers. The store received its goods at around four o'clock in the afternoon, and from then until seven at night locals could be seen queuing to buy bread and other necessities. Around 1878 the store was extended with the addition of a beer shop, where beer and ale could be bought. A number of other small shops were run from their houses by various villagers over the years, often widows. One of the longest-lasting was Mrs Nugent's, located in the Low Row. She sold sweets, cigarettes and tubs of hot peas. She also had the novelty of a fruit machine in her premises, operated by tokens which had to be bought from her, and then spent again in the shop.

The first school at Lethanhill was located in a house at the end of what became known as the Old School Row. Run by the ironworks company, scholars' parents were charged 2d. per week for their education. The growing population, and the introduction of compulsory education for children aged 5 to 13 in 1872, meant that the school couldn't cope with the numbers of children in the village, so a new school was opened opposite the eastern end of the Step Row. A single-storey structure, it had slate roofs and various chimneys from fireplaces in each classroom. In 1872 the roll was around 290, but only about 210 attended. In 1879 the roll was 212, taught by a school mistress and four pupil teachers, three of which were female. Headmasters included David Vallance, David B. MacLean, Frank Ferguson, James Parker MacAulay and George J. Donohoe.

In 1901 the national school leaving age was raised to 14, resulting in the building becoming too small once more. In 1912 a new extension was added to the side of the school, containing three classrooms, plus teaching facilities for woodwork, domestic science, science and art. Again this was to be too small, so in January 1928 a new school was opened. This was built about 150 yards to the north-west of the old school, behind the church. The school had accommodation for 300 pupils, the roll in 1950 being 195. By 1951 the roll had dropped to 140. The school outlasted the village, however, for Patna Junior Secondary couldn't cope with the numbers, and many children were bused daily up and down the hill. It was eventually closed in 1959, the pupils transferring to the new Patna Junior Secondary School, which had just opened.

When the 1928 school was opened, the older part of the original school was leased to the locals who converted it into a village hall. A committee was formed to run this.

Although most children who passed through the doors of Lethanhill school had little to look forward to when they passed out, other than a life in the mines, or as miners' wives, a few did manage to achieve greater things. John Hastings Millar was born in the rows in 1921. He left Lethanhill school and attended Dalmellington Higher Grade school for a time, followed by Ayr Academy. He then studied at the University of Glasgow and Trinity College, graduating as a minister in 1948. He was to serve at Glasgow Greyfriars Church before returning to Ayrshire to be minister at Crichton West Parish Church in Cumnock for many years.

89. Lethanhill from south-west

Robert Murphie and his wife had three children who were to become teachers – William, Ruby and Nancy. William (born in 1895) was able to move up through the ranks of the profession, ending up as rector, or head teacher, of Fort William Academy.

In the nineteenth and twentieth century emigration was promoted amongst the mining communities across Scotland and beyond. Canada was keen to get workers into the dominion, and Australia and New Zealand made a similar call. One who headed for New Zealand was John Kirk, who lived at 68 White Brick Row. His youngest son, George Kirk, was only six weeks old at the time. It was 1868 and life in the mines was difficult. John's grandson, Norman Kirk, was born in New Zealand in 1923. Life didn't appear to have become any better for his family, for his father was often unemployed, and Norman Kirk started work clearing gutters at the age of twelve. He worked on the railways but ill-health meant that he had to move to the ferries. In his spare time, he taught himself politics and soon was serving in the Ferry-Workers' Union. In 1948 he moved to Kaiapoi to work for the Firestone Tyre Company. In the town he rebuilt the local Labour Party and it became so respected that it won the local elections in 1953. At 30 years of age, Kirk was to be the youngest mayor in New Zealand.

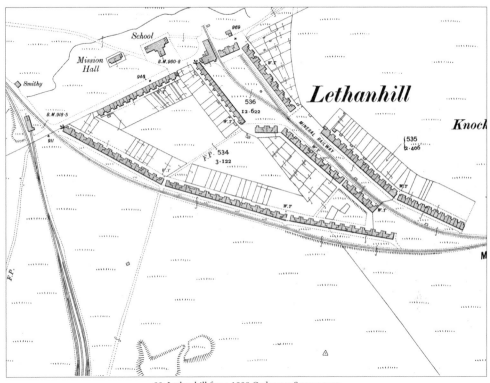

90. Lethanhill from 1909 Ordnance Survey map
Reproduced by permission of the National Library of Scotland

Kirk's political goals did not stop there. He was to be elected as Leader of the Opposition in the New Zealand parliament. At the general election in 1972 he led the Labour party to a landslide victory and he became the country's prime minister. But Kirk's health was never great, and he died on 31 August 1974 after only 21 months in office, suffering a heart attack. He was 51 years of age. His contribution to New Zealand politics was regarded as being considerable, however, the Auckland Star reported that 'the [Labour] party owed its win more than anything else to the personality of its leader – eloquent in speech, devastating in criticism, a humanitarian with wide horizons, a man of the people writ large.' Kirk introduced laws that established the Queen as monarch of New Zealand, removed compulsory military service and improved social care. President Gerald Ford of the United States wrote that, 'Mr Kirk was an eminent leader internationally as well as at home and a valued friend of the United States. Norman Kirk's humanity, sense of justice and zeal in pursuit of peace will inspire people everywhere long after his passing.'

Although it was a few generations back, Kirk had a longing to visit the home of his ancestors. In 1968 he made a pilgrimage to the Doon valley, carrying a copy of his grandfather's birth certificate. Arriving in Dalmellington, he was to meet up with some distant cousins.

91. Lethanhill War Memorial

At Lethanhill the war memorial was erected in July 1920. A twelve-foot tall obelisk, it was sculpted by Kennedy of Ayr. On it are the names of sixteen men who paid the ultimate price for defending their country in the First World War. When peace resumed after the Second World War, a further three names were added to the side. The main front of the white granite obelisk reads: Erected by public subscription and dedicated by the inhabitants of Lethanhill and Burnfoothill to the revered memory of their glorious dead who in making the supreme sacrifice during the Great War 1914-1918 nobly sustained freedom's cause.

Not listed on the memorial, but one who played an important part in the war, was Nurse Agnes Park. She lived in Lethanhill but served with a French company at the front. When the Allied forces left one of their positions she decided to stay, treating the wounded. When relief medical staff arrived she still refused to leave, remaining to treat every last wounded soldier. For her services she was to be presented with the Croix de Guerre for her devotion to duty and bravery in the field. When she returned to Lethanhill she was treated as a hero, and they presented her with a gold watch.

In 1921 a new road giving access to Lethanhill and Burnfoothill was built from Downieston, near Patna, across the hillside. Campaigns for a new road commenced in 1919, when local councillor, William Park, added his support to a 3,000-name petition. Ayr County Council agreed to build the road so long as the locals subscribed £150 towards the cost. This was quickly forthcoming, and the road was constructed by Peter Campbell of Cumnock at a cost of £4,065 12s. 8d.

Another improvement in living conditions occurred in 1926 when electricity was supplied to the village for the first time. Electric bulbs, wirelesses and other domestic appliances could be used, and another novelty was the introduction of street lights amongst the rows. Originally, the ironworks company installed just one socket in each house, with the rule that only a wireless may be allowed to be plugged into it. As expected, this rule was flouted, for the convenience of electric kettles and other appliances was too great an attraction.

The minister from Waterside visited Lethanhill and held services in the school up until the 1880s, when the lease of a house became vacant. This building, at 165 Step Row, was converted into a Mission Hall, James Baillie being listed as the lessee. He was Irish by birth and served as superintendent of the Sunday School. The first communion service held at Lethanhill took place in 1896. The church at Lethanhill was erected in 1903 and was opened in October 1904 by the Very Rev Thomas Martin DD, Convenor of the Home Mission Committee. A simple structure, it was erected from timber and sheeted with corrugated iron. The building fund had aimed for £299, the cost of building the church, but it raised £464, allowing an iron railing to be erected around it. Major donations of £50 came from the Dalmellington Iron Company, the Home Mission donated £51 10s. and £6 7s. came from overseas supporters. A management committee was formed to run the church, comprising the parish minister (Rev George Hendrie at the time), his assistant (Rev James Dalgetty), and eight villagers. These were James Baillie, James Gibson, John Gillespie, James Hampson, William Moore, Gilbert Park, John Robertson and David Wightman.

In 1936 Lethanhill and Waterside churches were erected into a quoad sacra parish of its own, separated from Dalmellington. The church marked its independence by erecting a new belfry. In April 1938 the new brick-built belfry with its bell was dedicated at a service conducted by Rev Hendrie, who had been minister of the church for over forty years. Others who took part in the service included Rev Thomas Calvert, the minister at the time, and Revs Ninian Wright and Alex Philp, ministers at Dalmellington. The new belfry was designed by Messrs J. B. Wilson, Son, and Honeyman, architects, Glasgow. The bell had previously been located in the belfry of St Valley Parish Church, Dalrymple, which had closed. The building had been purchased by Lieutenant Commander Bethell, and he presented the bell to Lethanhill. A church hall was opened in November 1936. With the population moving out, the last service at Lethanhill was held on Sunday 22 February 1953.

The church was closed in 1947 and the building was put up for sale. It was purchased by the Benquhat Silver Band. Being a timber and corrugated iron structure, it was easily dismantled and transported in sections to Dalmellington where it was rebuilt by the side of the Muck Water as a rehearsal room.

As with all mining communities, death was never too far away. Not everyone was to suffer in the pits. On 29 December 1907 a boy aged thirteen years, the son of Henry Graham, was playing on the ice on a pool in a former open-cast pit. When he fell through the ice he was drowned in the freezing water. At least two other deaths occurred on the mineral lines which passed very close to the houses. These were youths, and both were knocked down by passing coal or ironstone wagons.

Similarly, mining accidents were a frequent event in the calendar of the community. One could never tell when they were likely to take place, and the womenfolk often worried all of the time that their husbands were working in the bowels of the earth. When a fall of rock buried a miner in Pennyvenie pit on 18 November 1932, Thomas Ballantyne, a fellow miner, who lived at 175 Lethanhill, tried to attempt a rescue but he, too, was injured. He was to receive an honorary certificate and £10 from the Carnegie Hero Fund in February 1933.

Lethanhill Thistle was the local football team, playing at juvenile level. The football field was located in front of the first block of houses in the Low Row. Never the best playing surface, the field was tended as best they could by the players and supporters. Archie Ballantyne and Tom Ravie were regarded as the team's two best players. Jimmy Weir also played for Thistle, but signed for Ayr Football Club, and then Celtic, playing left-back from 1904 until 1910, winning two Scottish Cup medals and the league championship six times.

The population of Lethanhill began to decline in the late 1800s. In 1890 there were 93 houses that were unoccupied, the population at the Census of 1891 being 736. However, in 1899 the Dalmellington Iron Company sank a new coalmine to the north of the village, known as the Houldsworth Pit. Miners flocked back to Lethanhill, resulting in all of the houses being occupied and the population rising once more.

The first houses to be demolished at Lethanhill were the first that had been erected – the Peewit Row. In the early 1900s, as folk moved out of the houses, they were shut up until only one remained in occupation. However, around the same time the slag bing at Waterside was becoming so large that there was no room for more tipping. It was decided to dig a new channel and redirect the River Doon, allowing more room for the dump. A group of Irish navvies carried out this task, and for the time they worked on the job they lived in the old houses. Once they moved on, the houses were demolished.

Clearing Lethanhill began in 1947, the first residents moving into newly-erected council houses in Patna. A list for priority housing was compiled, so that married couples and sub-tenants were given new homes firstly. By 1951 the Diamond, Peesweep and Whaup rows were totally empty, and the remainder of the rows only had around ten to fifteen percent occupancy. The period of evacuation lasted seven years, the last to move out doing so in 1954. Accounts vary as to who this was – either James Stevenson, who moved out on 31 August 1954, or Robert Bryce, who had to be moved under protest to Patna at the age of 79.

Only the schoolhouse remained occupied, the head teacher still in residence. Appointed in 1950, George J. Donohoe was forced to remain in residence as his contract included the tenancy as part of his wages. When the school closed in 1959, with the opening of a new larger school at Patna, he was forced to remain for years thereafter, travelling down and up the hill each school day. The house is still occupied, the last building in Lethanhill.

The school building remained until 1959, and the newer half of the building was used as a shed by the farmer up until 1983, before it, too, was flattened.

In August 1965 the first 'Hill Reunion took place at Patna Primary School, with over 400 former residents turning up to hear William Murphie reminisce about his time in the village. The re-unions continued for many years thereafter.

It is still possible to make one's way to Lethanhill. The 'new' road built in 1921 leaves the main Doon valley road just to the north of Patna, at the railway bridge. It crosses through a couple of fields before striking quickly uphill. It appears to climb in levels, soon passing the old Schoolhouse. Another level or two brings one to the war memorial, virtually the only remnant of the village of Lethanhill. The foundations of the old school and church can just be made out on the ground, but to find the footings of the rows themselves one has to venture into the plantation of pine trees which occupies the site of the old village. Soon, one will see the remains of brick walls, stone foundations and various bits and pieces that once formed parts of miners' homes.

92. Lethanhill – remains of old house

A large block of concrete, which was formerly part of one of the buildings, lies at an angle on the side of the roadway up past the Step Row, heading towards the transmitter on the hillside. On it are painted the words, '1851-1954 Long Live The Hill'. In the immediate vicinity are the ruins of the old store, and over the fence can be seen an almost complete wall with a window, the last major relic of the Whaup Row. If one takes a wander through the pine plantation,

210

which occupies the full site of Lethanhill, one can find more remnants. Foundations of the Stone Row protrude through the woodland floor, and the White Brick Row has more remains. There, one can see the large creamy-coloured bricks that gave the row its name, as well as the stone rear walls, and stone slabs that formed the sides of many fireplaces. The easternmost gable of the row survives to over 8 feet in height.

93. Lethanhill – memorial stone

Of the Briggate and Old School rows, there is little to be seen. Similarly, the Low Row has more or less completely gone, but here and there can be found some brick foundations and remnants of fireplaces. At one location the iron bars that supported the sink in the scullery still stand proud from the ground. The remains of the Step Row survive in the stone foundations. Here and there, through the whole forest plantation, one can come across brick-built closets, eerily standing amongst the trees. One of the last facilities to be added to the houses, they appear to be one of the last structures to succumb to the ravages of time.

To the south-west, one can see the brick base of the old drumhead at the top of the incline down to Waterside. The site of the Peewit Row is gone, the surface here having been dug away and refilled when the Burnfoothill area was worked as a surface coal mine.

36

Loudounkirk

★

Loudounkirk was, like Alton, another of the small estate villages associated with Loudoun Castle. The community comprised of a row of cottages along the north side of the road which makes its way along the right bank of the River Irvine on the opposite side of the river from Galston. Today, only the old kirkyard of Loudoun Kirk survives, in which stand the ruins of the ancient church.

The original village probably only had eleven or twelve cottages, all of them single storey. There were two main rows, the easternmost comprising four homes. As with the rest of the village, the roofs were thatched, although the cottage at the western end was unusual in that it boasted a slate roof. The cottage at the eastern end was different too, in that it occupied a trapezoidal-shaped plan. The eastern gable, with its chimney, was built at an angle to the road. This came about as it followed the north-south line of the field boundary, the side of the cottage abutting the Galtscroft Plantation.

The western row appears to have had six houses, again all butted end to end. The houses were white-washed, thatched and had roses and other plants growing up the front walls, which faced directly onto the road. Between the two rows was a gap, giving access to gardens and orchards to the rear, running down to the Alton Burn. In front of the cottage walls was an area set aside for walking, the base of which was cobbled. A stone-lined gutter marked the edge of the roadway.

On the opposite side of the street was a large thatched cottage, facing the western end of the rows. To either side of it were small allotments and gardens used by the villagers. This cottage was demolished before 1895.

The folk of Loudounkirk had to walk across a footbridge over the Alton Burn to a well on the opposite side from where they could draw their water.

Most of the residents of Loudounkirk worked for the Earls of Loudoun at Loudoun Castle. The cottages were occupied by foresters, gamekeepers, gardeners, labourers and stable hands. Many of the womenfolk were employed as maids and kitchen staff in the castle itself.

94. Loudounkirk from north-east

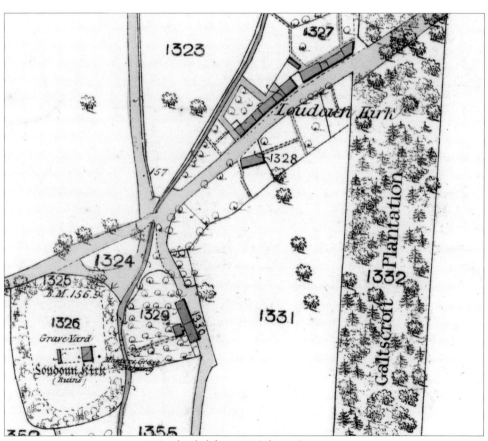

95. Loudounkirk from 1860 Ordnance Survey map
Reproduced by permission of the National Library of Scotland

In later years, when a number of new coal mines had been sunk in the district, the houses at Loudounkirk were occupied by miners. In 1900 the community was the property of the trustees of Lord Donington, widower of the 10th Countess of Loudoun. There were eight homes in the village, but four of these were joined to form two larger dwellings. These were numbers 5/6 (occupied by James Macintyre, collier) and 7/8 (let to James MacHoull, collier). The other houses were occupied by Thomas Houston (collier), William Wilson (roadsman), Henry Trgambole (collier), and Samuel Graham (collier).

Loudounkirk, because of its quaint thatched roofs and tidy appearance, often attracted artists and photographers. It is recorded that the feu duty payable for one particular cottage at Loudounkirk was 3s. 4d., plus two fat hens.

After the First World War families began to expect more of their homes. Thatch was seen as being old-fashioned and troublesome, and the cottages were hard to keep warm. Loudoun estate was also in some decline, and gradually the residents were found new homes. In the 1930s the village was more-or-less cleared, the two rows flattened. Only the cottage near to the kirkyard gates survived which was occupied by the parish beadle. At the end of the Second World War this, too, was finally abandoned.

96. Loudounkirk from south-west

Prior to the outbreak of the Second World War, the houses at Loudounkirk were the property of Robert Auld, of Laigh Hapton, Darvel. There were only four houses in the community still occupied, number 1 being let to Albert Collins, engineman; number 2 to Michael Flynn, miner, and number 5 to John Malcom. Another cottage, presumably across the road, was let to William Macintyre. Within a few years they, too, had been abandoned, and today the site of the village is overgrown with bushes and shrubs.

97. Loudoun Kirk

37

Meadowside

★

There is one solitary standing structure remaining of Meadowside, a simple little water meter house, sitting by the side of the road between Auchinleck and Catrine, just west of the Sorn turn-off. All around it is open farmland, often ploughed as though there was never a community beneath the turf. However, when the plough has turned a furrow over the site of the row of houses that stood here, the soil appears a different colour – more brown and loamy than the reddish soil of the surrounding fields.

To locals, the name Meadowside has virtually disappeared too, though some still refer to the vicinity by the village's nick-name – 'The Dundy' or 'Dandy Raw'. The Sorn turn off is often referred to as the Dundy corner, and bus-drivers often have to learn this, for the Kilmarnock to Cumnock bus passes this way, and folk often ask to be let off there.

It is said that the row of houses at Meadowside became known as the Dandy Raw from it being occupied by the better class of miners – the managers and oversmen, hence their more 'dandy' clothes. The lower class of collier was housed in another nearby row, usually referred to as 'The Poverty', for reasons that can easily be surmised. The row may also have gained its upper class epithet from the fact that water was introduced to the row as early as 1878, when piped water was laid in to the community at the same time as the villages of Sorn and Catrine.

Meadowside comprised of a single row of brick-built homes, twenty in total, alongside the road. They were erected in 1873-4 by Messrs Gilmour, Wood and Anderson, a coal company based in Auchinleck, to house their miners. The firm had obtained a lease of the mineral rights on Gilmilnscroft estate, at the time the property of Margaret Gray Farquhar. Mines were sunk to the south of Gilmilnscroft House itself, on the western extremity of Airds Moss. The row was later owned by the Gauchalland Coal Company, which started in Galston and latterly was based at Troon. The proprietor was Adam Wood, who was also the Troon harbour master.

98. Meadowside from north-west

In 1882 one of the houses (Number 7) became vacant and William Hastie, manager of Gilmilnscroft Collieries, reckoned that it could provide a much-needed location for meetings of a variety of types. Thus, the Meadowside Hall was opened, used for religious services on a Sunday, as well as meetings on other days during the week. The Sunday services were conducted by various local ministers. Initially, Rev Dr Rankine of Sorn held a meeting in Sorn manse, to which he invited the Revs Aeneas Gordon and James Copland of Catrine, as well as Mr Hastie. It was agreed that the ministers would each hold a service at the village once a month, thus providing religious services all year round. Previously services were held by Rev Matthew C. Thorburn, assistant minister to Rev Dr Rankine, in kitchens at Meadowside, much to the annoyance of the 'guid wives'. The harmonium was introduced at services in 1906, resulting in increased attendance.

A Sunday school was soon established, and a good number of teachers were willing to assist in educating the children. It was quite significant that the local landowner's daughters, Gertrude Farquhar and her sister, Lady Fitzroy, took part in these services.

The reading and recreation room was added in 1884, being opened by Rev R. Menzies Fergusson, and the books were the gift of Sir Walter and Lady Mary Farquhar of Gilmilnscroft. The Reading Room was given a wooden floor in

1909 and the hall was renovated in 1921. Here also the annual soiree of Meadowside was held, the first one taking place in 1908.

In 1899 the houses at Meadowside were occupied by George Campbell, labourer; Andrew Clark, collier; James Niven, pitheadman; Richard Folley, collier; James Logie, fireman; Jean Moore; James Black, miner; Andrew Clark, collier, James Dunlop, gatekeeper; Samuel MacCutcheon, labourer; James Pooley, miner; John Logie, miner; John Hodge, collier; David Gibb, collier; William Ramage, bottomer, Hugh Gray, collier; George Robertson, collier, Andrew Dunlop, roadman; and William Pooley, collier.

In the Great War the village lost a couple of sons - Private David Black, of the Seaforth Highlanders, was killed in action on 4 November 1914 and Private James Randall, of the 5th Battalion, Royal Scots Fusiliers, was killed on 30 December 1915, aged 22. Another serving son, Sergeant James Steven, of the Royals Scots Fusiliers, was awarded the Military Medal for his part in the Battle of Augi, near Jaffa, and was fêted at his home at Meadowside when he returned from the front in July 1918.

The rent payable for the main Meadowside houses was £5 4s. 0d. per annum in 1900, the Hillend huts, which were located nearby, being £3 9s. 4d. When the Gilmilnscroft Mines closed in 1925 the houses were proposed to be demolished, but they were still occupied until 1937 and were demolished before 1939, when only a strip of ground survived, owned by Mrs Norah Farquhar Oliver.

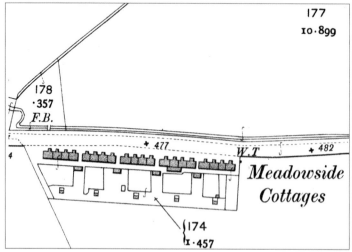

99. Meadowside from 1909 Ordnance Survey map
Reproduced by permission of the National Library of Scotland

38

Montgarswood Bridgend

*

Half way between Mauchline and Sorn was a small village known variously as Bridgend of Montgarswood, Montgarswood Bridgend, or simply Bridgend. The houses were located on either side of the road, the present B741, where it makes a sharp bend to the east of East Montgarswood farm, dropping to Bridgend Bridge over the Burn o' Need. This bridge was erected in 1768 but has been widened and rebuilt since. According to the *Catrine and Sorn Almanac* of 1882, Bridgend had a population of 76.

This village was created sometime between 1766, when the new turnpike road was created, and 1787. It was established by the laird of East Montgarswood as a weaving community, but it never grew to be any more than thirteen houses, no doubt the larger and more prosperous milling village of Catrine attracting the weavers. According to Adam Brown Todd, the weavers at Bridgend produced everyday goods, including 'blankets, druggets, and such like fabrics for the farmers' wives of the district.' An old plan of East Montgarswood farm, dated 25 September 1823, notes that there was the 'site of old mill' on the Mill Holm, downstream from the community.

Many of these houses were also occupied by workers at Bridgend Tile Works. This was located on the southern side of the Mauchline road, east of the Burn o' Need. The buildings formed a large 'U' shape, and the clay pit used for making the tiles was located east of the works. The works were in existence by the time of the 1857 Six Inch Ordnance Survey map, and date from sometime after 1825, the year in which the Duke of Portland is reckoned to have introduced tile drainage as a method of improving land to Ayrshire. The works disappeared early in the twentieth century.

Other residents may have worked at the flagstone quarry, located to the west of the clachan, which was marked as disused on the Ordnance Survey map of the time.

At one time an 'adventure school', or unofficial school run by a teacher, existed at Montgarswood Bridgend, for Covenanting historian and poet, Adam Brown Todd, attended it around 1832, when it was run by a former stonemason,

James Begg. In his *Reminiscences of a Long Life*, Todd wrote: 'But old James Begg was not a mason of the Hugh Miller stamp, though fully as orthodox Christian as he, for, on the Saturdays, when the Shorter Catechism was always gone over from beginning to end, the children repeating question about, when, at the end, any of them would start off and repeat the creed, whenever they came to the words "the holy Catholic Church," Mr Begg dashed the book against the wall – he not being able to see in the word "Catholic" aught else than the Roman Catholic Church, or faith, which he dreaded and hated most heartily'.

100. Montgarswood Bridgend from north

A former resident of Bridgend was to gain some fame for a time as 'The Railway Poet'. William Aitken, the son of a shoemaker, was born in Sorn on 26 March 1851, which happened to be the village's 'Wee Race Day'. Whilst still a youth he moved with his family to Montgarswood Bridgend. At the age of eight he started working in the fields and at the age of ten he was apprenticed as a shoemaker under James Baird at Bridgend. He had little formal education, only attending school when he could. On the first Monday in May 1871 he started work as a signalman at Kilmacolm for the Glasgow and South Western Railway Company. He was later employed as a district officer at Kilmarnock and Glasgow for the same company. Aitken later became an Inspector on the Glasgow and South Western Railway.

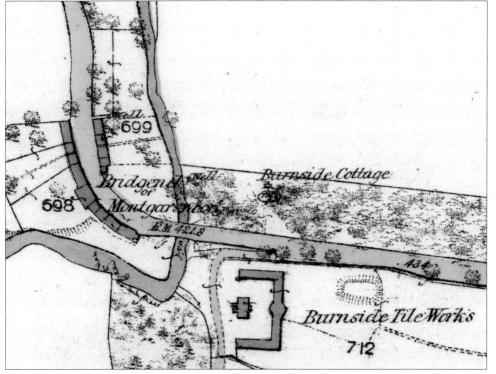

101. Montgarswood Bridgend from 1860 Ordnance Survey map
Reproduced by permission of the National Library of Scotland

At an early age William Aitken had started writing poems, and he sent these to various local newspapers. His poems are shrewd observations on human life and character, and many of his more popular works were accounts of incidents and events in the life of the railway. As such he became known as the 'Railway Poet' or the 'Laureate of the Line'. His first book of poems was entitled *Rhymes and Readings*, published in 1880, with a preface by Rev Dr Rankine. *Lays of the Line* was published in 1882. In 1893 a third book of his poems was published, entitled *Echoes of the Iron Road*. In 1913 he published another work, entitled *Songs of the South-West*.

Aitken was a devout man, and for a time was active in the Railway Mission at Greenock, which he founded in 1885 under the name of the Railwaymen's Christian Association. He was a member of the Congregational Church in Greenock and was superintendent of the Sunday School. He composed an address entitled 'I'm jist a boy', which became a popular recitation piece at Band of Hope and Sunday school recitals.

Aitken died at Greenock on 27 October 1931 aged 80 years. His body was returned to Sorn, where it was buried in the kirkyard. A gravestone over it reads:

William Aitken, Ex-Inspector G&SWRy. Born at Sorn 26th March 1851, died at Greenock 27th Oct 1931. Jean McClymont Richmond, wife of the above William Aitken, died at Greenock 30th April 1934 in her 83rd year.

Although established as a weaving community, by 1900 Bridgend seems to have had more than its fair share of shoemakers, four houses being occupied by them – James Baird, another James Baird, James Cunninghame and James Johnstone. Three of the houses were empty or in ruins. In 1903 the remaining houses were noted as being damp and past their best, the others being roofless and beginning to decay. And yet by 1940 seven remained in occupation, only number 7 being empty and condemned. The occupied cottages had Loudon MacAuslan, David Purdie, James MacGregor, Henry Kilmurray (pedlar), James Cummings, Mrs Smith and William Murdoch (labourer) as tenants. The houses were owned by the trustees of the late John Kerr, apart from Number 1, which was owned by James Wilson, joiner, of Auchmillan, and Number 8, which was owned by Sorn estate.

102. Montgarswood Bridgend from south

222

One of the cottages at Bridgend appears to have been a small shop, for in 1919 it was noted that the houses in the hamlet were all occupied, but that the shop was empty. After the Second World War was over, and when peace resumed, the houses were demolished and the residents were re-housed in Catrine.

39

Mosshouse

*

The road from the A70, Cumnock to Muirkirk road, leading into the former mining community of Cronberry, leaves the main road half a mile east of Lugar. A few hundred yards along the minor road, it rises up on an embankment before dropping down once more. This was to allow it to cross a railway bridge over the Ayr and Muirkirk branch of the railway, which has long gone, and even the bridge has been removed. The road continues along, turning right and goes past a cottage named Mosshouse, before passing the site of the Cronberry viaduct, which was on the Auchinleck to Muirkirk branch of the railway – the viaduct was removed in 2008. The road crosses the Mosshouse Bridge and then a turn can be made to the right into Cronberry. The present Cronberry village comprises of former miners' houses, built to rehouse many of the occupants of the old miners' rows that formed a much larger village, before it was decided to relocate the residents in Logan, near Cumnock.

Halfway between the two former railway bridges, on the right hand side of the road, was a farm named Mosshouse. This was part of Auchinleck estate and in 1875 was tenanted by John Pearson. On the left hand side, nearer the main road, was a small village which bore the name Mosshouse Square. This community predated Cronberry and it was in decline by the time the new rows at Cronberry were erected.

Mosshouse Square formed a large open U shape, the open side facing south-eastwards, towards the main road. There were around 24 houses in the community, facing an open courtyard. Most of the houses were of different sizes, or at least the Ordnance Survey map of 1857 would lead one to think this.

In the centre of the long side of the U was a narrow pend through the buildings, which led to a washhouse, perhaps the only one in the community. The path from the pend continued to Mosshouse farm, no doubt used by the residents to walk to the farm to buy milk.

On the opposite side of the road from Mosshouse Square was Mosshouse Pit. This had a small railway siding leading to it, and the pit bing was located to the north-west of the pit head. Mosshouse was used to mine ironstone, and being the nearest pit to Mosshouse Square itself, would perhaps imply that most of the men living there were ironstone miners. At the time, which would be in the early nineteenth century, ironstone miners regarded themselves as superior to colliers, mainly because they had what was a slightly cleaner job. However, it wasn't too long before the ironstone seams became either worked out or unproductive, and the stone miners had to join the colliers.

There was a second Mosshouse Pit near to Carbello farm, also working ironstone. In one of these pits John Cameron lost his life on Saturday 17 December 1859. He was placing a hutch onto the cage when he slipped on the frosty ground. He plummeted 360 feet down the shaft, his body being severely mangled by the fall.

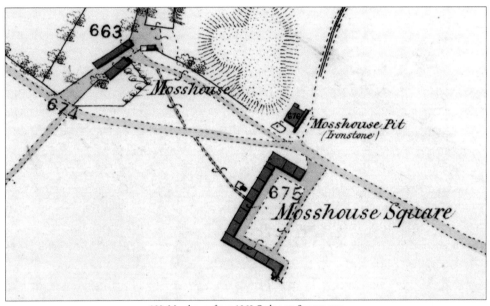

103. Mosshouse from 1860 Ordnance Survey map
Reproduced by permission of the National Library of Scotland

Mosshouse was abandoned sometime before 1895, for the Ordnance Survey map of that date doesn't even give a hint that there was once a village there, and within a few years even Mosshouse farm itself was gone. Today, the old bings give the sole evidence of the existence of Mosshouse Pit. Only the cottage called Mosshouse survives to retain the name, in addition to Mosshouse Bridge.

40

Neiphill

★

Heading out of Kilmarnock, along Dundonald Road, one comes to Mount House, a considerable country house erected in the second half of the eighteenth century and for many years owned by the Duke of Portland's family. By the mid-nineteenth century it was occupied by Alexander Guthrie, a local coalmaster. His Georgian mansion with gardens and policies around it was in stark contrast to the colliers' homes which stood nearby.

Almost immediately to the west of Mount House's gardens, on the western side of Kilmarnock, was the small clachan of Neiphill. The name was sometimes spelled Neephill, or Neipshill. This comprised of a row of houses on the west side of the minor road that linked Dundonald Road with Springhill farm. The row had four houses at the southern end of the community, with a further five houses or so immediately to the north. Behind the houses were large gardens stretching to the west. The houses had access to a well for water – this was located in the garden of the southernmost cottage.

At the north end of the row was a small fenced in plot, in which was located a small school building. This is shown on the Ordnance Survey map of 1856. By the early 1900s the school must have been closed and the map refers to it as a Sunday School. Adjoining the school playground was a lane striking west, to a further row of cottages, known as Coalhall. At the western end of Coalhall was a mineral siding, making its way to the Annandale pit. No doubt most of the residents of Neiphill were employed in the local pits.

Certainly one of them did, for John Park was killed in March 1867 at the age of 22 years whilst working in Grange Number 1 pit. This was located near to Grange farm, which was just off the western end of Kilmarnock's Portland Road. A newspaper report tells of the mystery surrounding his death:

Shocking death of a miner. Early on Monday morning the miners employed at No. 1 Grange Pit, Kilmarnock, on going down to their work found the body of a man lying at the bottom of the shaft shockingly mutilated. The remains were immediately conveyed to town, where they were identified as those of John Park, a miner, 22 years of age, residing with his father at Neiphill, in this vicinity. It is believed that the man had wandered off his road. As the entrance to the pit (which is 85 fathoms deep) was barred in the usual way, it is not known how the unfortunate man came to fall down the shaft, there being no reason to believe that he committed suicide.

By 1900 Neiphill was the property of J. & M. Craig and there were twelve houses in the village, all being occupied. Craig also owned other properties in the vicinity – two houses at Low Thirdpart, six at High Thirdpart and sixteen houses in Kiln Row, all of which have disappeared, like Neiphill. The firm of J. & M. Craig was established in 1831 and ran the Dean, Hillhead and Perceton fireclay works in Kilmarnock. They produced sanitary ware for many years, the business being taken over by Shanks of Barrhead in 1918.

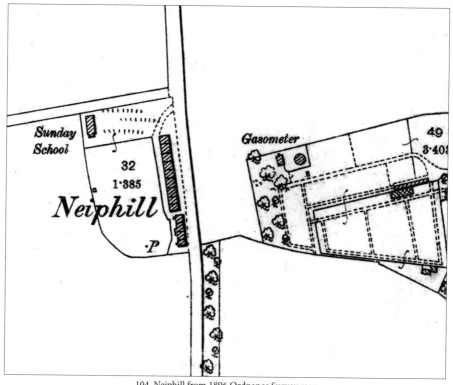

104. Neiphill from 1896 Ordnance Survey map
Reproduced by permission of the National Library of Scotland

By 1937, when the next large-scale survey for maps was made, Neiphill was in severe decline. There were only four cottages still roofed, located at the northern end of the larger terrace. The southern four houses were gone, as were some of the houses in the large row. The school building was also demolished, and the row of houses at Coalhall was also gone. The last cottage at Neiphill was probably abandoned in the early 1950s.

The site of Neiphill is currently a plot of rough ground immediately to the south of the Premier Inn, located by the side of the Moorfield Roundabout. The roundabout basically occupies the piece of ground that separated Neiphill from Coalhall, the latter row of houses being located west of the present roundabout.

41

Old Rome

✱

The name Old Rome is something of an enigma. How did this little roadside village obtain its name? Was it thought that the village appeared to be older than the ancient city of Rome itself, or did the name come from some other source? In fact, is there, or was there ever, a New Rome in the area? It seems not, hinting that the name is derived from something else. The *Statistical Account*, written in 1792, names it as Rumford, and Thomson's *Atlas of Scotland*, published in 1832, has it as Romford. Blaeu's map of 1654 may give the best possible derivation, for thereon it is called Old Room. Room is an old Scots word that describes a piece of land for which a certain rent was payable to the landowner and often sub-divided.

On the road from Kilmarnock to Troon, now the A759, the village of Gatehead is passed through. Here the road has to cross the railway line by means of a level crossing, followed by the River Irvine, over the Romeford Bridge. Immediately once the river is crossed, one enters what had been Old Rome village. Most of the houses were arranged along the east side of the roadway, there being none on the west. The fields there were part of Fairlie House's policies, so the houses were located farther away from the laird's house.

Immediately south of the bridge was a row of cottages, the first of which appears, from the maps, to have been larger than the rest. It may have had some other use in the past. Adjoining it in a single row were five other homes. At the gable end of the last cottage a minor road strikes east, passing Old Rome farm itself, which still exists, on the right, and the buildings that formed the old distillery. This, in itself, made Old Rome fairly unique in Ayrshire.

On the south side of this minor road, which led to the gates of Caprington Castle, was a second row of homes, probably originally five in number, but by 1857 at least one of these was in ruins. A small field created a gap between the houses, followed by a short row of three houses, positioned perpendicularly to the main road. These looked over a small courtyard, towards the gable of the next row of houses.

This next row comprised of eight houses, all joined together. A narrow lane between two gables separated it from the next line of homes. This was the largest continous line of houses at Old Rome. Eleven houses of different sizes were linked together along the roadside. Perhaps the cottages were originally all of a muchness, but as the years passed two may have been knocked into one, or else they had been built at different times, the farthest south, and probably newer houses, being slightly larger than the northern ones.

Parallel with this row, in the field to its east, was another line of houses, much smaller in size, and regularly built. There were ten houses here. As with most homes of the time, occupation of the dwellings was cramped. One resident, Peter Quigley (1824-1881), lived in one of the cottages with his wife and five children – he had lost at least one other child in infancy.

The village of Old Rome was probably created to house workers in a coal mine that had been established here in the late eighteenth century. The *Statistical Account* refers to the 'village, named Rumford, has of late years started up close by Fairlie Bridge. It contains at present 74 inhabitants.' Certainly, the 1841 census lists 68 men who worked as miners living there, dropping to 44 by 1851. A good number of the colliers were of Irish birth.

The pit referred to was located immediately south of Old Rome farm, east of the perpendicular row. The mine had been abandoned by 1857, when the first detailed maps of the area had been made. A couple of old buildings still stood at the spot, however.

Perhaps the pit was closed much earlier, for in May 1843 there was a collection taken at Dundonald Parish Church which was to be distributed amongst the unemployed colliers. Similarly, the previous year, the minister was allowed £2 from the parish funds to assist the folk of the village, for at that time it suffered badly from unemployment and fever had struck many households.

In the first years of the 1840s the charity had been in the opposite direction, for a collection was made at the collieries of Oldrome (as it was written) as well as Shewalton. There were mission stations of the church at both locations in the 1830s.

Coal from Old Rome colliery was in the main sold locally, but it is known that some was exported to Ireland. In the early 1800s there were proposals to construct a branch railway line into the pithead, to ease export of the coal, but this line was never built. Perhaps the difficulty in digging cuttings and building embankments, as well as crossing the River Irvine, prevented its creation due to cost. In any case, the opening of a new railway station at Gatehead may have resulted in the requirement for a line of its own becoming less of a need.

The *New Statistical Account*, written in 1841, described the pit as it was at that time:

> The depth of the shaft is 37 fathoms [222 feet], and cuts through four different seams in the following order:
> At the bottom of the shaft is a seam of blind or charred coal, 3 feet 4 inches in thickness; 13 fathoms above, there is one of common coal, of the same thickness; 8 fathoms above that, one of 6 feet; and 2½ fathoms higher still is one of 2 feet 8 inches.

The population of the village was at one time quite considerable. In the 1841 census there were 261 residents. Ten years later, the census return had shown that the population had fallen to 204. Thirty years after, in 1881, the village appears to be on its last legs, for the population was by now just 34.

With a fall in miners' wages in the mid-1800s strikes became common. The Lanarkshire miners started them and they quickly spread to Ayrshire. On Wednesday 14 September 1842 about 600 miners gathered outside the pits at Gatehead at two o'clock in the morning, preventing the miners there from working. After this, they moved on to Old Rome, where they apparently met in the gardens behind the rows. The leaders of the strikers addressed the crowds, 'urging them to insist upon the increased wages, and reduction in weight of out-put of coal, from the masters,' according to a report in the *Kilmarnock Journal*.

The mine owners had different thoughts. The Ayrshire Yeomanry was called out, and it seems to have prevented any riots or damage to the pithead. The local *Journal* couldn't believe that 'any operatives connected with the county' would get involved in such activity, obviously blaming the Lanarkshire men for stirring up trouble.

A number of miners from Old Rome became registered as paupers with Dundonald Parochial Board. The board dealt with them how it could, but one of the more unusual responses was to help the paupers to emigrate and thus set up a new life elsewhere. In the minute book of 1852 there is this example:

The committee having considered the application of Edward Laurie, collier, latterly residing in Old Rome, authorised the Assistant Inspector to take Laurie to Glasgow and to purchase for him such things as he indispensably requires so that he might be entitled to sail for America and the parish relieved from the necessity of maintaining him as a pauper.

One of the more obscure links Old Rome has in history is its association with Robert Burns. In the 1775 Register of Baptisms and Marriages for Dundonald parish, the following entry is found:

James Allan in Old Rome and Jean Brown in Irvine, after having their purposes of marriage three several Sabbaths proclaimed in this Congregation, were married at Old Rome on the 21st April 1775 by Mr Walker.

James was the eldest son of John Allan, who worked on Fairlie estate. James' new wife was a half-sister of Agnes Brown, who was to marry William Burnes, who also worked on Fairlie estate for Alexander Fairlie of that Ilk from 1750-1752. William and Agnes were later to move to Alloway, where the famous Scots bard was born in 1759.

James Allan's third son, Alexander Allan (1780-1854), started off in life as a shoemaker but headed for the sea and was to establish what became known as the Allan Line in shipping. At one time this was the largest private shipping company in the world.

Originally, the Allans lived on a cottage on Fairlie estate, but in 1789, on the death of James, they moved into a cottage in Old Rome village. It is said that James left his wife £20 when he died. She managed to bring up their seven children and was remarried to Adam Baird in 1805. Both of them died within weeks of each other in 1821, her husband from a broken heart at the loss of his wife. Jean's will left the same £20 her first husband had left, to be divided between their children. Alexander Allan, however, having started to make his fortune, did not take his share.

It was to the Fairlie estate cottage that Burns himself visited on more than one occasion, including on the night of 30 July 1786, when he escaped the wrath of James Armour. The poet wrote of his predicament to his friend, John Richmond:

Old Rome Foord, 30th July 1786

My Dear Richmond,
My hour is now come. – You and I will never meet in Britain more. I
have orders within three weeks at farthest to repair aboard the Nancy,
Captain Smith, from Clyde, to Jamaica, and to call at Antigua. This,
except to our friend Smith, whom God long preserve, is a secret about
Mauchlin. Would you believe it? Armour has got a warrant to throw me
in jail till I find security for an enormous sum. This they keep an entire
secret, but I got it by a channel they little dream of, and I am wandering
from one friend's house to another, and like a true son of the Gospel,
'have no where to lay my head'. I know you will pour an execration on
her head, but spare the poor, ill-advised Girl for my sake: tho', may all
the Furies that rend the injured, enraged Lover's bosom, await the old
Harridan, her Mother, until her latest hour! May Hell string the arm of
Death to throw the fatal dart, and all the winds of warring elements
rouse the infernal flames to welcome her approach! For Heaven's sake
burn this letter, and never show it to a living creature. I write it in a
moment of rage, reflecting on my miserable situation, exil'd, abandon'd,
forlorn.
I can write no more – let me hear from you by the return of Connel. I
will write you ere I go.
I am, Dear Sir, yours here & hereafter
Robt Burns

Burns prepared to emigrate to the West Indies, on board the Nancy, a ship that
by chance was later to be captained by his cousin, Alexander Brown, by which
time it was renamed the Bell. As he waited at Old Rome until his passage was
ready, he checked the proof copies of his poems, about to be printed in
Kilmarnock. With their subsequent success, he cancelled plans to emigrate and
instead managed to persuade Armour to allow him to take the hand of his
daughter in marriage.

The Romeford Bridge appears to have been erected soon after the turnpike
act which established the road here in 1774. Its name confirms that there was
an old ford across the Irvine at this point, known as the Rome Ford. The river

forms an ancient boundary, for not only is it the northern edge of Dundonald parish, it is also the dividing boundary between the ancient Ayrshire divisions of Cunninghame (to the north) and Kyle, in which Old Rome is located. On later maps its name appears to have become known as Old Rome Bridge.

How the village got its supply of water is not known, perhaps the proximity of the River Irvine explains this. However, there was a well by the side of the river to the east of the old distillery which may have been used, at least part of the time.

The Old Rome Distillery was located by the side of the River Irvine, within the village of Old Rome. The distillery was founded in 1812 by James Fraser. When his tenure of the building expired in 1821 it passed to others, but it seems to have struggled to be profitable for most of its existence.

In 1820 the Old Rome Distillery Co. placed an advertisement in the *Air Advertiser*, in which they 'Beg to inform the public we have recently employed an experienced distiller from Inverness who has recently been employed in making Ferintosh of the first quality and, as the malt is prepared in the same way and the still is small, the public may rely upon getting a quality of spirit which for flavour and wholesomeness was never surpassed by legal or illicit distillation, and is made entirely from malt.'

In 1825 John Ramage took over the distillery, keeping it going for just one year. In 1826 the Old Rome Distillery Co. was founded, only to go bankrupt within the same year. It was owned by White & Wilson. James Forrester took over in 1827, his tenure lasting only for two years.

In July 1829 Old Rome Distillery was offered for let, and when it changed hands it was converted into a brewery. This, too, was a short-lived venture. It had been acquired by James Mill, but the business went bankrupt once more, in 1840. According to the 1841 Census, there was one distiller living at Old Rome village at that time, Jane Mill, aged 55, and one spirit dealer. By 1851, there were no distillers or spirit dealers listed.

A new school was erected at the southern extremity of the village in the early 1800s to supply education to the children. In 1842 an advertisement was placed in the *Ayr Observer* looking for a schoolmaster to take up the post. His salary was to be £2. In 1844 the roll was over 90 pupils. In 1868 the schoolmaster here was listed as being Gilbert Buchanan. The school was later to become the Free Church School with financial support from the laird of Fairlie.

Old Rome farm was occupied by the Todd family for much of the life of Old Rome village. In 1852 the tenant was James Todd, whereas by 1900 it was John Todd. The farm was part of Caprington estate, the property of the Cunninghame family.

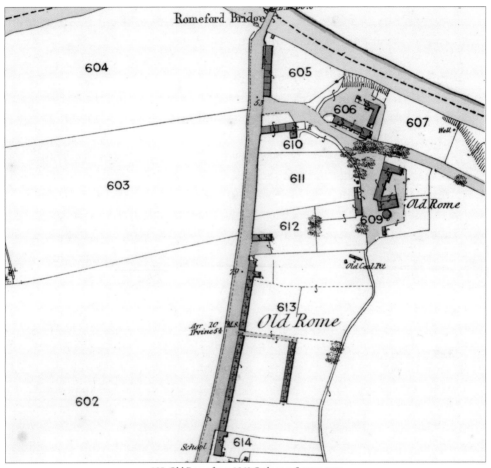

105. Old Rome from 1860 Ordnance Survey map
Reproduced by permission of the National Library of Scotland

A later mine was established in the vicinity, but much of the village had been demolished by this time. Fairlie Colliery was sunk in the early 1800s, and was still operational in 1899. A property of William Cathcart Smith Cunninghame of Caprington, the mine was located to the south of Old Rome, near to Templeton farm.

With the demolition of the rows of houses (they were cleared away by the time of the 1895 Ordnance Survey map), only four houses remained, probably formed from the old distillery buildings. In 1899 these were occupied by Robert Wilson, ploughman; Hugh Cunningham, miner; and William MacTaggart, ploughman. The fourth house was empty. A further four houses in the area were occupied by John Wyllie, engineman; George Parker, miner; William Fraser, miner; and James MacCrindle, miner.

Peter Quigley moved from Old Rome to Knowehead, near Galston, another of Ayrshire's lost villages, no doubt following the work available in the pits. In 1875, when Archibald Adamson was writing his *Rambles Round Kilmarnock*, the village was almost dead. He wrote:

> Beyond, on the brow of a steep brae, where the road swoops down and crosses a fine bridge that has recently been erected over the Irvine in place of the old structure, I passed Old Rome, a row of ruined cottages of mean appearance that were at one time occupied by a colony of colliers, who left the place when the pits in the neighbourhood became 'worked out'.

In the second edition, he noted that even the ruins had gone:

> Passing onward, Old Rome was soon reached. A busy place it was in days of yore, with its row of homely cottages, schoolhouse, and distillery; but now it is a deserted village in very truth, for the cottages are all removed, the husbandman having passed his plough over their very sites.

Everything else along the main road-side had gone, apart from the school building and the schoolhouse. No longer required for education purposes, it was converted into a cottage, the solitary remnant of another old village.

42

Pennyvenie

★

Pennyvenie was an old mining community that was enlarged in the early twentieth century. It was located to the north-east of Dalmellington in the valley of the Cummock Burn. The oldest miners' houses were the Colliers' Row, which was later to be named Camlarg Cottages. Colliers' Row was located at the corner of the New Cumnock road, where a stream flows from Ben Beoch down into the glen. The houses were arranged on a north-south axis, with gardens between them and the burn. The five houses were owned by the Dalmellington Iron Company, and in 1914 were occupied by four colliers (John MacAllister, James Murphy, William MacLung and David Watson) and a labourer (John Duncan) and their families. The houses probably dated from the early eighteenth century, for on General Roy's map of Scotland from around 1750 there are 'coalpits' indicated in this vicinity.

New miners' houses were erected at Pennyvenie, being completed in December 1912. Twenty houses were built at Low Pennyvenie, twelve in the first row and eight in the second row. They were often referred to as the Pennyvenie Terraces. The first row was built alongside the road, facing across to the bing of Pennyvenie Number 1 pit. The second row was located back from the road, overlooking Little Camlarg in the glen below. The new cottages were constructed by William Hunter of Ayr.

Further up the glen seven houses were erected at Clawfin for Dalmellington Iron Company in 1910. This comprised of three houses at Glenview, built to house the managers of local pits, and four houses at Sighthill. The first managers to occupy Glenview were James Sharp, manager of Clawfin and Pennyvenie Number 4 pits, who lived in cottage number one. Next door was Thomas Menzies, manager of Benbain and Beoch pits. Cottage number three was occupied by Robert Dempster, manager of Pennyvenie Numbers 2 and 3. Glenview was named from the fact that the houses had an attractive outlook over the Cummock Burn valley to the moors and Mains Hill beyond. The houses were located behind the first row of Pennyvenie.

106. Pennyvenie – Collier's Row

Sighthill was built alongside the road from Dalmellington to New Cumnock, between the Colliers' Row and the first row. The cottages were the ones that were closest to Pennyvenie Colliery, number 2 and 3 pits. Each house had a projecting porch, surmounted by a gablet, and to either side were windows lighting the bedroom and front room of the houses.

At High Pennyvenie 22 houses were built in a row, and a further ten houses in a row at Craig View. These were often referred to as Clawfin, from the nearby farm. The High Pennyvenie rows were in two terraces, positioned on the northern side of the road, overlooking the Pennyvenie Number 4 pit bing. As with most Pennyvenie houses, the cottages were built in terraces, but here there were pairs of houses sharing a gablet facing the road, under which were the two front doors. In 1914, the occupations of the head of each household was as follows: colliers – 14; miners – 3; oversmen – 2; blacksmith – 1; labourer – 1 and mine manager – 1 (Thomas Chambers).

The Craig View Houses were built further east, nearer to Clawfin farm, on the opposite side of the road. The houses were in the course of erection at the start of the First World War. When the *Third Statistical Account of Scotland* was being compiled in 1951, the houses at Pennyvenie were described as being 'distinctly good'.

Pennyvenie School was built by the side of the main road, between it and the Pennyvenie Burn. The school only educated infants up to the age of nine years, after which they went to Dalmellington school. In 1951 there were twenty pupils on the roll. In 1967 cracks appeared in the walls of the school building, and it was soon deemed to be unsafe. The school was demolished in 1968.

There was a congregation of the Church of Christ at Pennyvenie, existing in the 1940s. This met in the home of one of its members and it also ran a Sunday School.

Most of the male residents worked in the Pennyvenie pits, the first of which was sunk in 1868. This was located to the north of the road, opposite the second terrace of Pennyvenie. Pits numbered 2 and 3 were located to the west of the Colliers' Row, and Number 4 was located to the east, at High Pennyvenie. Five and six were sunk near to Pit Number 2. Pit Number 7 was sunk in 1939 (but was delayed by the war) and operated until 6 July 1978, the last deep mine in the area. It had the distinction of being the first pit in the Doon valley to have pithead baths, which opened in January 1939, providing a great boost to the

107. Pennyvenie – Wren's Nest and Sighthill Row

miners as well as their wives, who no longer had to provide tin baths in front of the fire each night when they returned home.

108. Pennyvenie – Sighthill Row

Adjoining Pennyvenie Number 7 was the famous 'burning bing'. The coal spoil which was dumped in a tall bing was to self-ignite and internally the bing was to burn for many years. Even in the dead of winter, when deep snow covered much of the Doon valley, the bing was clear of snow, and the precipitation was converted into steam, visible for miles around.

A good number of the new residents of Pennyvenie moved in from other mining communities in the area. One family was the Carlyles, who moved from Benquhat. A gravestone in Dalmellington cemetery recalls how many families lost children – the stone was erected by James and Sarah Carlyle in memory of the two children who died at Benquhat – James died in September 1885 aged 5 years and Jane, who died at Benquhat three months later aged eighteen months. A third child survived longer – David died in 1903 aged 20 years. They moved to Pennyvenie, but James died there in 1915, aged 27.

Most of the rows at Pennyvenie were emptied in the 1960s, leaving only Sighthill in occupation for much longer. Some of the old houses at Craig View stood for a good number of years, being adapted for use by the farmer. The roof was removed in 1991 and when the open cast coal mine took over much of the district, the remains of the row were cleared away.

The old row of houses at Sighthill was eventually demolished in 2012 to allow the creation of a large opencast coal site.

109. Pennyvenie Terrace

43

Sourlie

*

The village of Sourlie was located about half a mile north along Lochlibo Road (the Glasgow road) from Girdle Toll, north-east of Irvine. The first buildings in the village were erected on the west side of the road, exactly at the milestone indicating Glasgow 23 and Irvine 2¼. The first houses date from the early nineteenth century, perhaps around 1815 – in 1820 there were six households living here. By the time the Ordnance Survey carried out their map-making surveys in 1856, the community had about nine houses. Two of these formed a small semi-detached property, located by the roadside. The other six formed a T-shaped group, built at an angle to the main road.

Sourlie Coal Pit, Number 26, was sunk in the late nineteenth century, just to the south-west of the first houses at Sourlie. It was built adjoining the railway which allowed the coal to be transported out by rail. The mines at Sourlie were owned by Archibald Finnie of Kilmarnock, as were the houses. Littlestane Cottage was occupied by the mines manager, William Rodger in 1900.

With the sinking of a new pit, accommodation for the workers was needed. To the south of the old Sourlie houses a row of mineworkers' homes was built. Located alongside the main road, they were built immediately south of the old semi-detached houses. The houses were probably built in two stages, for the first eight houses were also semi-detached homes, each of which had a tiny front garden and a larger one to the rear. The rear garden, rather than being a place of relaxation, faced directly over the pithead buildings.

To the south again were two more blocks of houses. The first had a terrace of four houses, the second was a terrace of six homes. Again, there were gardens to the front and rear of the homes. These eighteen houses formed what was known as Low Sourlie Row.

Very similar in style to the second phase of semi-detached homes was a row of houses built on the opposite side of the road, a few hundred yards to the south, in the gusset between two roads. Here were ten houses, formed in five blocks of two. In the back gardens of this row were two wells, used for drawing water. The rows to the north obtained their water from a well located at the foot

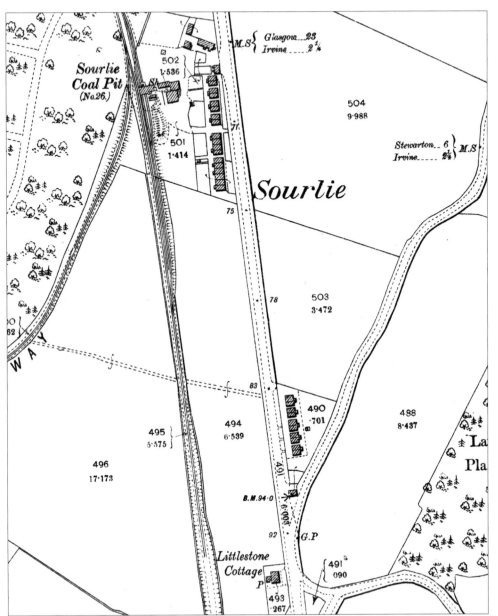

110. Sourlie from 1896 Ordnance Survey map
Reproduced by permission of the National Library of Scotland

of the gardens of the original T-planned row. This was known as Sourlie High Row.

Immediately to the south of the Low Row, on Lochlibo Road, was an old toll cottage, positioned exactly in the road gusset. This was known as Sourlie Toll.

In 1819, prior to the arrival of the railway to Irvine, which did not take place until 1839, the 12th Earl of Eglinton proposed creating a railway from Sourlie and Doura westwards to the Ardrossan harbour in order that coal could more readily be exported. The plans caused panic among the councillors of Irvine, who were concerned at the possible loss of trade through their harbour. The line was never laid, however.

The lack of church provision in Sourlie and other miners' rows to the north-east of Irvine was of concern, not only to the church itself, but also to the burgh council. In 1829 the council subscribed three guineas towards a fund to employ an assistant to Rev John Wilson of Irvine Parish Church to provide services at Sourlie. This was to counter, 'the extreme ignorance as to religion that prevailed among a very numerous class of parishioners about Bartonholm and Sourlie.'

The houses at Sourlie were cleared away by the Second World War. Most of the residents were given council houses at Girdle Toll, established in 1934 by Ayr County Council, on the outskirts of Irvine. According to the *New Statistical Account* of Irvine parish, written just seventeen years after Girdle Toll had been created, 'What really troubles Girdle Toll is the lack of community spirit. When the men were in the hamlets and villages, they worked in the neighbouring pits and usually met at some bridge or other spot where they had their discussions, and there was a nearby inn where they might consort. Now the miners for whom the village was originally intended have got scattered, and only about a score of them remain.' From 1983-1986 surface mining of coal took place in the vicinity, the land later being landscaped.

44

Southhook

*

The village of Southhook was separated into two distinct parts. They were located on the farm of Southhook, in the parish of Dreghorn, separated by the Glasgow & South Western Railway line linking Kilmarnock with Irvine. At one time there were four rows of houses, two in each community, and they belonged to three different owners.

Heading west from Knockentiber, the Garrier Burn is crossed by the Plann Bridge, leaving Kilmaurs parish behind. On the right, running parallel with the stream, was Hayside Row, owned by Robert Marshall of Knockentiber. This row had nineteen two apartment houses in it, though it was built in two stages. The older part of the row had twelve houses, and these were erected with stone. The remaining seven houses were added, and by this time brick was used to construct them. The difference in quality between the two was reflected in the rent payable – the older stone houses cost 2s. per week, the newer brick ones 2s. 6d.

Inside the cottages the rooms were fairly small. The kitchen measured around 12 feet square, and adjoining it was a second room, measuring around 12 feet by 9 feet. The floor of the kitchen in the stone buildings was finished with brick tiles, and the room had a wooden floor. The brick houses had wooden floors throughout, which was much more comfortable.

Residents in Hayside Row shared five dry closets, each having the luxury of a door for privacy. There were also three wash-houses, again shared by the tenants, but each house came with a coalhouse. The ashes from the fires were dumped onto two ash-pits. Some ashes were spread on the roadway which passed along the front of the row, though this in general was muddy and full of holes. In bad weather the rain lay in deep puddles. Ten feet in front of the row was an open drain, into which dirty water passed, described in November 1913 as being 'choked and evil smelling'.

Lining the side of the road that crossed the Plann Bridge, on the opposite side from Hayside Row, was Southhook Row. The cottages here were eleven in number, and a pathway passed round them on all sides. Beyond the path, on the south side of the row, were gardens.

Southhook Row had the advantage of a water pump, located at the eastern end of the row, where water could be drawn. This, however, still had to be carried back to the houses.

Across the road from Southhook Row were two isolated buildings. One of these, located in the wide bend that the road described, was the mission hall, used on a Sunday for religious services, but at other times of the week for community events and meetings.

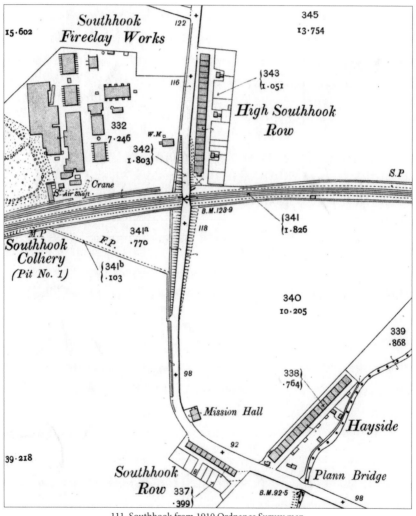

111. Southhook from 1910 Ordnance Survey map
Reproduced by permission of the National Library of Scotland

A few hundred yards after the bend in the road, the railway line was crossed by a bridge. On the immediate right to the north of this was High Southhook Row. Originally there were two rows here, the southern being the longest. This comprised of twenty two-apartment houses, built of brick. It is thought that they were erected around 1875 and were the property of the Southhook Coal Company. The houses in this row were smaller than those at Hayhill, the rooms measuring 10 feet by 9 feet. The kitchens, at 12 feet square, were similarly sized.

Inside the houses, the residents complained that they were rather damp, and that it was difficult to heat them. In wet weather it was noted that water often leaked through the roof. The kitchen had a brick floor, and only the room had floorboards.

Residents at High Southhook Row had to pay 2s. per week for rent. In addition to the houses, they were supplied with three shared closets and ash pits, located in front of the row. Water was obtained from a pump positioned at the road junction, itself supplied from a well at the nearby mine. However, in summer months, this often ran dry. To the rear of the row were small garden plots for each household.

To the north of the High Southhook Row was a second row, comprising of ten houses. This shared two closets, and like the larger row had gardens to the rear. This row did not last as long as the other row, for it was demolished sometime between 1895 and 1908.

Most of the residents of Southhook worked at the local pits or fireclay works. Originally smaller mines existed, which came and went over a short period, but sometime between 1895 and 1908 the Southhook Colliery Number 1 Pit was sunk, immediately across the road from the High Row. Adjoining this was the Southhook Fireclay Works, where bricks, basins, tiles, and glazed blocks were manufactured.

Today, there is nothing to indicate that Southhook ever existed. The two Southhook Rows have totally gone, the site of them returned to agriculture and, the last time I visited, a fine crop of barley was growing where once folk lived. Only at Hayside was a small field of rougher grass which gave a clue that this piece of ground once had houses on it. Even the extensive Southhook Fireclay Works has gone, and it takes a considerable amount of imagination to picture the considerable works that once existed there.

45

Swinlees

★

To the north of Dalry a road strikes north from the main Kilbirnie road, heading for the Glen of Rye and over the pass to Largs. From Burnside the road starts to climb, and almost two miles from Dalry reaches Swinlees farm. Two thousand yards further on, where a road strikes left into Swinlees roadstone quarry, one arrives at the site of Swinlees village. On the left side of the road is a hawthorn hedge, with a tree here and there. Today nothing indicates that a community existed in this field, but it was once of a considerable size. Only aerial photographs of the site of the community show anything different – for the grass strip adjoining the road is of a different colour.

The houses at Swinlees were all located on the west side of the road, climbing up the hillside. There were two rows of houses, the rows almost joined together, and one – the southern one – was set back slightly from the other. The front of the houses looked onto the road, and a wide view over the Garnock valley towards Kilbirnie and Beith, but when the houses were here the landscape would not have been so pleasant, for in the valley below were dozens of small mines and pits, digging coal and ironstone from the earth. Behind the houses the fields rose up to the eminence of Carwinning Hill, its summit containing a prehistoric fort, named in honour of the local St Winning.

The residents of Swinlees Row were employed in the local ironstone pits, of which there were many in the district. Immediately in front of the southern row, across the road, was an ironstone pit which appears to have been active in 1856, when the Ordnance Survey produced their detailed maps of the district. At the southern end of the village, on the same side as the row, was a second ironstone pit. Iron ore, or haematite, was discovered early on in the district, and in the immediate area the ironstone strata was reckoned to be from 15-20 feet thick. Also on the lands of Swinlees, at the time owned by Mr Paton of Swinlees House, copper ore was discovered in a band 2 feet thick, producing from 30 to 75 per cent. According to Cornish miners, who had inspected the ore, it appeared as being 'very favourable'.

On the hillside to the west of the village were a number of limestone quarries, still in operation in the 1850s. Others were located at the north end of the village. A possible older community of houses existed at the northern end of Swinlees, but on the opposite side of the road. This was known as Blair Row, having been erected on the lands of South Hourat, at the time the property of the Blairs of that Ilk, but by 1856 some of the houses were in ruins.

Swinlees appears to have been a short-lived community for by 1899 there were no houses left. Even the Ordnance Survey maps of that time do not indicate that they were in ruins, all remnants of them having been cleared away. It is said that a number of houses erected at Darnconner in the parish of Auchinleck had roofs which had been taken from miners' houses at Dalry. It is possible that they came from here.

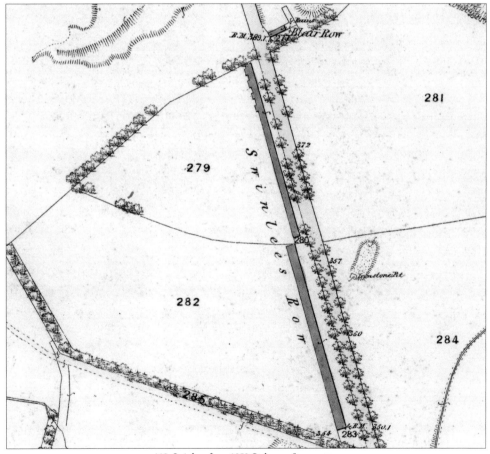

112. Swinlees from 1858 Ordnance Survey map
Reproduced by permission of the National Library of Scotland

46

Tarholm

✱

The small village of Tarholm was located on a holm, or floodplain of the River Ayr, south-west of Annbank. It was never a large community, gaining its name from tar works that used to exist there.

Archibald Cochrane, the 9th Earl of Dundonald (1748-1831), established a tar distilling works at this place in the late eighteenth century. He was a keen developer of such businesses, for another tar works he set up was established at Muirkirk, where the famous road-maker, John Loudoun MacAdam was employed. At Tarholm, Dundonald used locally-mined coal, and the distilling equipment was housed in a large barn-like building. How successful, or for how long the business operated is unknown, there being little recorded about it.

There were two main rows of houses in Tarholm, one on each side of the public road. Each, however, was located a few hundred yards back from the road. On the east side of the road, near to Tarholm Bridge, was a small row of three houses. These are shown on the 1860 Ordnance Survey map as being fair-sized in plan, but were little more than single-storey thatched buildings. Across a track that passed by the southern gable end of the row a short footpath led to a well from where drinking water was drawn.

The larger row at Tarholm was located on the other side of the road. The 1860 map indicated eight houses here, though one of them appears to have been roofless. At the southern end of the row a well was used to draw water. To the north-west side of the row, away from the public road, was an area of gardens or allotments. By the time the 1898 map was surveyed, this large row appears to have been rebuilt, for the row now comprised ten houses, all joined together. The gardens had been relocated to the front of the houses, stretching to the public road.

One of the rows at Tarholm was called the Slate Row, no doubt from its roof, the other row probably being older and covered with thatch. At one time a single cottage was located between the two rows, with a small garden to the rear. This was gone by the 1896 map.

The roadway through Tarholm crosses the River Ayr by means of Tarholm Bridge. This is quite an unusual structure, having three sandstone piers rising from the riverbed and two stone abutments. On these is a concrete deck. The parapets of the bridge are also of cast concrete, but this has been formed into balusters, making a more attractive structure than it may otherwise have been. A few of the balusters have become damaged, revealing the iron wire down the centre, used as reinforcement. Two previous bridges have occupied this site, which was one of the more notable crossings of the Ayr this far downstream.

Although Tarholm was a very small community, it used to be able to rustle up enough boys and men to take on the nearby lost village of Craighall at football. The contest was held on Patrick's Park, a local field, which was set out for the match.

113. Tarholm – Long Row around 1920

In 1930 the existing houses at Tarholm were still fully occupied. By now they were owned by John Roland Bell of Enterkine House. The properties were leased to William Baird & Company, who rented the properties to its employees. At the time, these were Robert MacCroskie (drawer), Adam Mackie (labourer),

William Buchanan (collier), Mrs Sweden (widow), James MacCroskie (miner) Samuel Jess (miner), Henry Currans (collier), Mrs Isabella Aitken (widow), James Sweden (fireman) and Andrew MacCroskie (collier).

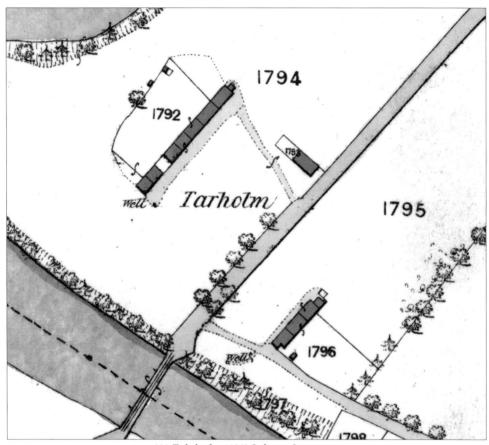

114. Tarholm from 1860 Ordnance Survey map
Reproduced by permission of the National Library of Scotland

The houses at Tarholm were demolished in the early 1930s, the residents being allocated new council houses in Annbank or elsewhere. Sometime after the houses were demolished a couple of more recent buildings were erected in their place. One of these, Stanalane cottage, a modern red brick building with a red tiled roof, is located where the Wee Row once was. On the other side of the road is Tarholm Nursery, noted for its leeks and other plants, brought on in the glasshouses that are built over the northern end of the Big Row. The opposite end of the Row is where the present Riverslea cottage stands.

47

Thornton

★

The small village of Thornton was located around half a mile to the west of Crosshouse, on the road to Irvine. There were two terraces of houses, forming one long Thornton Row, stretching from Holm farm westward to Holm Bridge. The houses dated from sometime in the first half of the nineteenth century, being indicated on the Ordnance Survey map of 1860. At the time, the nearby farm was known as Holmes.

The Thornton Colliery comprised of a number of small coal pits, dotted across the countryside to the west of Crosshouse. The pits did not survive long, and once one was closed a new one was sunk in a different part of the parish. Thus, pits existed at Laurieland (where a row of twelve houses was built), at Carmel Bank, with miners' houses built at Farmfield Toll on Laigh Milton Road, and at Thornton itself.

The eastern terrace, which stretched westward from the Holm farm road, had fourteen houses in it, all built in a single line with no gaps. Each house had a garden, located between the house and the road. The western terrace was built adjoining the first row, and it also contained fourteen houses. Unlike the first row, the houses in this row were not all of equal size, seven of them being larger. Some of the houses were linked, such as numbers 1 and 2, for William Hood, whereas numbers 19 and 20 were divided, to give numbers 19½ and 20½.

The source of water for the row was originally a well that was located next to the burn, but by 1908 piped water had been brought to the community, and two water taps or pumps were located in front of the rows, one serving each.

In 1875 most of the residents in Thornton were from Cornwall, men brought north to work in the pits when the local supply was poor, or else the men were on strike. The houses were noted as being old and damp, with only one closet of four apartments for the whole row, at the time comprising 21 houses, located abutting the gable end of one of the rows. Rent was 1s. per week for single-apartment houses, and 2s. for double houses.

In 1913 inspectors from the Ayrshire Miners' Union visited the community and at that time noted that there were 27 houses. There were fourteen single-apartment houses – built of brick, but white-washed to improve the appearance. Internally, the houses had a room that measured 15 feet by 12 feet. The rent was 1s. 3d. per week.

The two apartment houses were built of stone, and were probably the older buildings in the community. These had a kitchen that measured 10 feet square, plus a room that measured 10 feet by 12 feet. The rent payable was 1s. 10d. per week. The floors of most of the houses had uneven brick tiles on them, but underneath the bed these were not used – flattened earth being all that there was.

The residents had the use of four closets and three ash pits. There was no washing-house, and no coal houses. The residents, to improve conditions in the community, had built a number of washing boilers, but these were open to the elements.

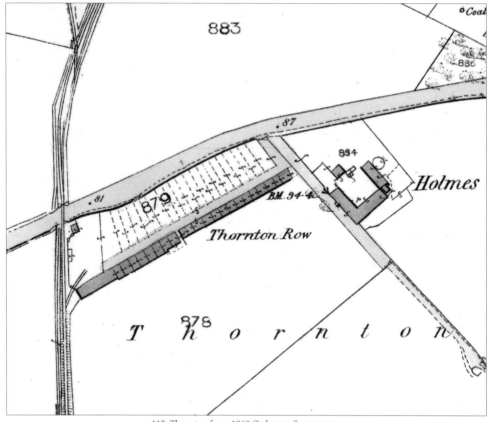

115. Thornton from 1860 Ordnance Survey map
Reproduced by permission of the National Library of Scotland

The two-apartment houses suffered from subsidence, their floors being lower than the level of the road. This often resulted in the homes being flooded during wet weather, sometimes several inches of water covering the floors.

Thornton was owned by Messrs Archibald Finnie & Sons. This company was to be taken over by J. & R. Howie after 1920.

The rows at Thornton were demolished in the early 1930s, the residents being rehoused in new county council houses that were erected in Crosshouse. By 1937 maps only showed a small field of 1.7 acres where once the houses and gardens were located.

48

Tongue Bridge

★

Tongue Bridge Row, or just Tongue Row as it was sometime referred to, was located at an angle to the roadway from Drongan to Patna. The houses were built in one continuous terrace, striking uphill from the main road, facing the Tongue Burn.

The oldest houses formed a single line, seventeen homes in total, though these were of three different sizes. Nearest the road were eight houses of the same size. Adjoining these were five houses which were narrower in plan, followed by four houses. The homes were erected prior to 1857, perhaps being built around 1850, when the pits opened. The walls were erected of stone, which may have been obtained from a small freestone quarry that is shown on old maps, by the side of the burn that flows from the Carline Knowe.

Most of the men from Tongue Bridge were employed in the Bowhill pits, which were located on the moor to the south of the community. Operated by the Dalmellington Iron Company, the mines worked ironstone, which was taken to Waterside ironworks for smelting. The houses at Tongue Bridge were also owned by the Dalmellington Iron Company.

Sometime before 1896 the row of houses was extended, when a second row, almost perpendicular to the first row, was constructed at the head of the hill. Again, these houses were all joined together, and at the corner a building occupied the apex. The older houses appear to have been rebuilt as well, for the first block of eight houses was reconfigured into twelve homes. The five narrow houses were subdivided once more, to form eight homes. The final group of four were halved to form eight houses.

The new row had nine similar-sized houses in it, plus the corner building, and another home joining the angled row to the original row. This made a total of 39 houses.

As the years passed, many of the smaller homes were converted into one, when a doorway was knocked through the wall separating them. This, in many cases, returned the houses to their original size.

The west side of the houses faced directly onto the open moor, the northern extremity of Dunston Hill, whereas the eastern side faced onto the roadway. There were two buildings that acted as wash-houses for the whole community, located between the roadway and the Tongue Burn, and the residents had the luxury of a reasonably-sized allotment. To get their water, there were two water pumps, one half-way up the long row, the other half way across the short row. To supplement the water supply, many residents had wooden barrels at their front door, into which rainwater was collected.

The miners at Tongue Bridge were a Christian lot, and having no place of worship nearby (the parish kirk was at Dalrymple, almost five miles down the glen), arranged to use two of the houses for meetings. These, number 22 and 23, were converted into a Mission House. By 1928 it was referred to as the Institute.

116. Tongue Bridge looking south

The community was large enough to support a junior football team for a short time. The Cumnock and Mauchline Football Associations ran various tournaments in which local teams competed. One of these, formed just after the end of the First World War, was Tongue Row. Of its success, or otherwise, there are few records.

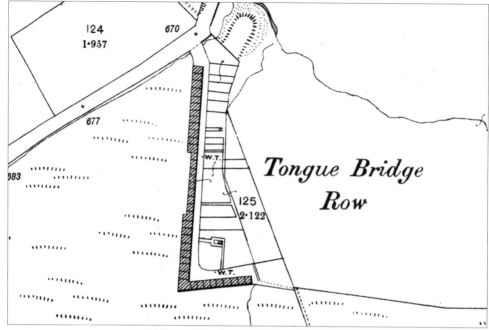

117. Tongue Bridge from 1896 Ordnance Survey map
Reproduced by permission of the National Library of Scotland

By 1928 most of the houses at the upper end of the row were uninhabited, only the lower and older houses remaining occupied. The remaining residents of Tongue Bridge were rehoused in the 1930s, some of them in Polnessan, others to Dalrymple. Today, there is very little to indicate that a community once existed here. If one passes through the farmer's gate the line of the old roadway is still there on the ground. To the left the old gardens can be visualised, a number of old trees marking the outline of one plot, and amongst the ground can be found a line of bricks that formerly edged a pathway. Further up the brick foundations of a wash-house can be seen. The houses have totally gone, but at the far end of the row, where the track crosses the Tongue Burn, the parapets display bricks stamped DICO, remembering the company that first built the rows here.

49

Trabboch

★

Compared with most of Ayrshire's lost villages, Trabboch was a comparatively new community. The houses were erected in the 1880s by John Galloway & Company to house their workers, employed in the Trabboch and Drumdow pits. Also, compared with many other miners' rows, Trabboch was more of a model community, if it can bear that degree of honour, for the houses all had their own gardens, there were regular pumps for each row, and community facilities were provided. The village was later to become the property of William Baird & Company, Ltd.

The name Trabboch, however, has a far longer history. The name comes from Trabboch Castle, an ancient fortified dwelling whose shattered remnants still stand in a field, just over one mile to the east. The castle was originally a seat of the Boyd and Douglas families, as well as being the caput of an ancient barony, but the building was long abandoned. An old tradition claims that the castle and barony were granted by Robert the Bruce to the Boyds of Kilmarnock in recognition of their services at the Battle of Bannockburn.

By the time Trabboch village was established, the lands of Trabboch had been broken up, and much of the estate was owned by the Boswells of Auchinleck. Trabboch village was laid out on the fields east of the Stair to Coalhall road, positioned at approximately right angles to the main road. There were four rows of houses, the southernmost being the longest.

The long row at Trabboch, usually referred to as the First Row, contained five separate terraces of houses, each having eight houses in it. The west-most terrace, however, had nine houses, and at its western end, adjoining the public road, was a Reading Room. This was later to become the Mission Hall. Most of the houses had only two apartments in them, though the end house in each block had three apartments. The two apartment houses had a kitchen that was 14 feet by 12 feet in size, the other room just 12 feet by 6 feet. The three apartment houses had a similar floor-space. Residents had to pay 2s. per week for rent, paid to the owners of the rows. A few houses were joined together to form larger dwellings, such as 10 and 11 First Row, occupied in 1915 by Roger

MacClelland, miner, who was to become the proprietor of the village store, once Baird's gave it up. The occupiers of the other houses in the First Row were generally listed as miners, though there were a few 'colliers', labourers, surfacemen, fireman, and miners' widows too.

South of the row, and across the roadway that passed in front of the houses, were gardens, at the bottom of which were coal-houses and a small dry-closet. There were also five wash-houses, centrally placed across the road from the terraces, in front of which was a water pump. This had fresh water, piped from the reservoir at Loch Bradan.

The Second Row had two terraces of homes, both of which had nine houses in them. Again, across the roadway were pumps, wash-houses and gardens. The first house was occupied by Sam Leckie, insurance agent. The second house was used as a Mission Hall, the cost of which was covered by William Baird & Company. A brethren assembly was formed at Trabboch in 1900. The group seems to have folded around 1945.

118. Trabboch – remains of wash house

Rows number three and four were almost exact copies of the second row, each having two terraces of nine houses. Again, most of the houses were occupied by miners, roadsmen, labourers and surfacemen, terms used to describe various occupations in the pits. By 1930, the second house in Row Four was converted into a workshop. Although the rows had fair-sized gardens associated with each house, this was not always regarded by the tenants as a luxury. In fact, the mine owners often inspected the gardens to ensure that they were being maintained, and if they were not, the miner would be sent from his work to correct the problem, thus losing his wages from the shift.

The houses at Trabboch were constructed of facing brick, though the lintels over the doors and windows were of stone. The lintels and door and window openings all had chamfered corners, hinting at a slightly more thought-out plan for the houses than was normal in miners' rows.

At the western end of the four rows were larger cottages, built onto the gable, and angled to the principal row. These had four apartments each. The kitchen was a reasonable size, and the main room measured 9 feet by 8 feet. The rent for these cottages was more, being 2s. 6d. per week.

At the side of the road, next to the bottom of the long row, was Trabboch Store, a double-storey building built of stone. This was for a time owned by Roger MacClelland and he sold provisions to the residents. At one time, when the mine owners had considerable control over the residents and their properties, there were gates at the end of each row. Local grocers, milkmen and butchers who wished to take their carriages up the rows to sell their wares had to purchase a key for the lock, paying a fee of £1 per annum. Another shop by the 1930s was Maitland & Holland's.

A mobile shop belonging to the co-operative at Annbank (a branch of the Kilmarnock Equitable Co-operative Society) regularly visited Trabboch, and most of the residents were members, getting an annual dividend on purchases made.

Passing to the west of the village, across a couple of fields, was the Ayr and Cumnock branch railway. On this for a number of years was Trabboch Station, from where passengers could join trains heading from Ayr to Edinburgh. Most residents would be unable to afford the fare, however.

Trabboch pit was located to the south-west of Trabboch rows, the shaft sunk around 1880. There were two simple headframes on the surface, as well as a collection of buildings housing various works. The pit was established by John Galloway & Company of Ayr.

The Galloway family had been coalmasters for a good number of years. William Galloway was a coalmaster in Ardrossan in the early 1800s. His son, John Galloway (1825-1889), may have started the business, hence the company's name. However, it was his son, James William Galloway (1856-1907), who moved to Trabboch House and lived there for a number of years. Two of his children at least were born at Trabboch House, James Norman (born in 1888) and Margaret Kerr (born in 1885). Robert Clark (born in 1891), was probably also born at Trabboch House. They had two elder brothers, John (born 1881) and George Maxton (born in Ayr in 1883). James Galloway presented a trophy to Stair Curling Club in 1892 (known as the Points Cup), and he was appointed as Honorary President at the annual general meeting on 1 November 1895.

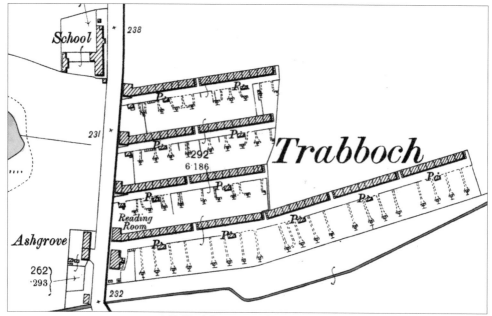

119. Trabboch from 1896 Ordnance Survey map
Reproduced by permission of the National Library of Scotland

Galloway's honorary position may have been because by 1894 the mine had been taken over by William Black & Sons of Glasgow, owner of the nearby Drongan Castle Colliery. At the time, the pit employed 61 men below ground and a further nineteen on the surface. This company became part of United Collieries Ltd, of Glasgow. In 1898 the pit had 81 miners working below ground, plus a further 21 on the surface. The manager at the time was David Paterson.

The number of workers increased, peaking in 1901 at 154 working below ground. Trabboch Colliery was closed in May 1908.

Trabboch had at its peak a population of around 430. By 1930 William Baird had given up ownership of the houses at Trabboch, and they reverted to the landowner, by this time Lord Talbot de Malahide.

When the local mines had closed, the residents of Trabboch had to travel to find work in other pits. For many years, a good number of miners walked from their homes to Trabboch Station, catching a train which let them off at Skares Station, near Cumnock, where they worked in Whitehill pit. Others worked in the nearby Burnockhill Pit. At least two residents of the village lost their lives at Burnockhill - Andrew Strachan, who was killed by a fall of stone from the roof on 20 November 1919, and Hugh Mitchell, killed by a stone fall in March 1923.

Predating the rows, in 1863 a school building had been erected to serve the needs of the children belonging to Stair parish. As such, it was named Stair Public School. This was located at the north end of what became the village, on the opposite side of the main road from where the rows were to be built. A single-storey building, it was extended a few times. The main school building

120. Trabboch School today

had the schoolmaster's house built on to its northern end. In 1902 the school building was altered to plans prepared by Allan Stevenson. He also carried out alterations to the schoolmaster's house in 1906. In 1910-14 the school building was extended, again the work of Allan Stevenson.

The roll of the school varied over the years, but at one time was almost as high as 200 pupils. The school was closed in 1969, the last headmistress being Miss Brown, and today really forms the only building of Trabboch to survive. It was converted into a community centre for the district.

As with almost all small villages, Trabboch had its own junior football team, known as Trabboch Thistle. In 1900-01 they won the Cumnock & District Cup. One of the players was to sign for Celtic on 29 May 1901 – this was Hugh Watson (born 1882), who played back. He broke his leg in 1904, bringing his Celtic career to an end and missing an opportunity to play for Scotland. He later played for Kilmarnock and Belfast Celtic.

The houses at Trabboch were deemed to be unfit for modern living and thus it was decreed that the residents had to be rehoused. At the time the new community of Drongan was being built, originally planned to be a new town with a possible population of up to 19,000 residents, and the folk of Trabboch were gradually housed there. Many would have preferred to remain at Trabboch, perhaps with the addition of running water and electricity in their houses, or perhaps in new homes erected at the site, but the council officials preferred a new start. As the folk moved out, the rows were gradually removed. Some, however, remained standing for some years, before they were eventually razed to the ground.

The *Third Statistical Account of Scotland*, written in 1951, noted that the houses at Trabboch were 'due for demolition as soon as the 430 mining folk living in them can be re-housed in the new township which is being planned at Drongan. Conditions are pretty raw. There are no inside water taps, no proper sanitary arrangements and no scavenging service. The houses are lit by paraffin oil lamps.'

50

Woodside

★

The village of Woodside comprised of a row of 37 houses along the eastern side of the minor road that links Belston, east of Ayr, with Stair. The oldest of the six rows of houses was the fourth from the Ayr end. This existed prior to 1857, when the Ordnance Survey first produced detailed maps of the county. However, it isn't shown on Roy's map of the mid-1700s. This row had thatched roofs, again indicative of its age, though by 1913 it was described as being of a 'poor type'. The row of houses was named Woodside, being located on the other side of the road from a long shelterbelt of trees.

The original rows were erected by George Taylor & Co., of Ayr Colliery, to house miners employed in the Sundrum pits. In 1875 the village had from eighteen to twenty single-apartment houses and a few room and kitchen cottages. The newest houses had wooden floors, the older ones being of brick. There were no wash houses or coal-sheds and every property used the single ash-pit. Water came from a field drain, which supplied good clear water at most times, but this became discoloured during heavy rain.

By 1895 there were an additional six rows at Woodside. Three of these were erected on the Ayr side of the first row, and further three to the east. Around the houses, to the front and rear, were paths, but these were unpaved and had dirty open syvors, although the paths were generally clean.

Approaching the village from Broadwood farm, the first row on the right comprised of six houses, set back from the roadway a bit. To the rear were gardens and various outhouses. The second row also had six houses in it, similar in style to the first. Two wash-houses were shared by these rows, each row of six houses having a wash-house, and every three homes sharing a dry-closet. When the inspectors from the Royal Commission on Housing visited in 1913 they found that the closets were filthy: 'They are all placed at the back. There are no locks on any of the closet doors, and some of the closets were unspeakably dirty. The womenfolk complained bitterly against the lack of closet accommodation.'

In the front of the close between the second and third row was a water pump, raising water from a well in the ground. This was the only source of water in the village itself, although there was a second well a few hundred yards along the road south of the community.

The third row was the smallest at Woodside, only having four houses in it. As with the first two rows, this was typical of the newer homes at Woodside. Facing the street, each house had a single door, and to one side there was a vertical window opening, in which was placed a sliding sash window. The roofs were slated, and along the ridge were chimneys.

All of the houses in the first three rows appear to have been the same size. This was quite small, each house having a single room measuring 15½ feet by 12½ feet internally. The colliers paid a rent of 1s. per week to live there.

The old row followed. Although initially thatched, this row was later slated, but little was done to improve the inside of the houses.

The fifth row at Woodside had six houses in it, the two nearest Ayr being smaller in size, compared to the other four, comprising of a single apartment. The remaining houses were double-apartment ones, though each of the rooms was small. The kitchen measured 12 feet by 11 feet, the room 10½ feet by 9 feet. The sixth row had five houses, again facing the roadway. The two-apartment houses had a rent of 1s. 6d. per week in 1913.

The seventh row at Woodside was located to the right, at angles to the main road, facing onto a minor track that led eastwards to the old mine. This row had four houses in it.

The inspectors from the Royal Commission who called in 1913 noted that the gardens at Woodside were all in good condition, the residents taking a keen

121. Woodside from south-west

interest in them. They also remarked that 'the people here are of a good type, and deserve better accommodation.'

By 1923 Woodside was owned by William Baird & Co. Ltd, and there were 29 houses, some houses being joined together to form larger ones. Most of the homes were still occupied by miners and other colliery workers. Among the surnames of the families who lived there were the Wales's, Youngs, Shimmans, Kerrs, Truesdales, MacIntyres, Wilcoxes, and Alexanders.

One family who remained at Woodside for decades was the Hays. James 'Dun' Hay was born in the rows on 9 February 1881. He was a keen football player, playing for Annbank, and soon his skill was recognised by Ayr Football Club, where he played from 1902. In 1903 Jimmy Hay signed for Celtic for £50, his skill being noted and he actually acted as team captain from 1906 until 1911. During this time, he was part of the team that won the league cup on six successive seasons. Hay's dexterity on the field resulted in him being called up to play for his country, and he was capped for Scotland eleven times between

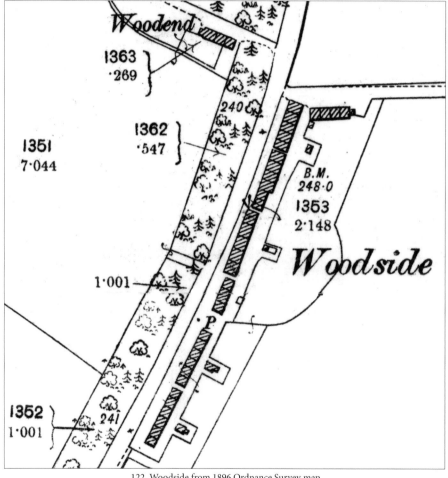

122. Woodside from 1896 Ordnance Survey map
Reproduced by permission of the National Library of Scotland

1905 and 1914. On three occasions he captained the team. In 1911 Hay signed for Newcastle United, remaining with the English team for four years, before returning to play for the 'Honest Men' in 1915. James Hay died in Ayr on 4 April 1940 and was buried in the town's Holmston cemetery.

A close-knit group, 'Woodsiders' were keen to celebrate various events, which they did by building bonfires on the summit of the low hill to the south known as Raith Hill. From the top of the hill extensive panoramas could be had of Ayr beach and over to Arran. As the sun set, and the light from the bonfire intensified, the residents often danced to accordion music, returning home when the blaze had died to embers.

Apart from great celebrations such as Victoria's jubilees, the end of the Great War, and New Year, bonfires may have been lit for special events. One of these took place when Woodsider, Tommy Cuthbert, was honoured by being given the British Empire Medal for his services in the war.

Baird sold the village of Woodside in 1926 to the estate of Mrs Crystabel Mary Hamilton. In February 1928 the trustees decided to offer the residents of Woodside the chance to buy their homes, something that appears to have been unusual. Within a year almost all of the houses had been sold, apart from four houses that were uninhabitable. Those houses that had been merged were sold as one, and in the case of numbers 25, 26 and 17, they were bought by Hugh Shimmons. He also owned numbers 21-22, perhaps originally occupied by his

123. Woodside in decline

father, Samuel Shimmons. Number 13-14 Woodside was purchased by Thomas Stewart for £12 10s., but he was also liable to pay an extra £4 4s. 9d. for rates and other expenses. With the residents of Woodside now owning their properties, they tried to make improvements that previous landowners didn't bother about. The fronts of the houses were whitewashed, the pathways cleaned and the drains cleared.

Although the residents of Woodside were now owner-occupiers, the condition of the houses meant that they were only habitable for another twenty years or so. Most of the residents gradually moved out, some to Ayr, but most to Tarbolton. In 1948 a Woodside Reunion was held, when former residents, plus the last of those still domiciled there, met to enjoy a social evening of reminiscences. Some of the meetings were held in the Claud Hamilton Memorial Hall in Coylton, such as the third reunion, which may also have been the last. On that night 110 folk enjoyed the entertainment and chat, from young toddlers to octogenarians.

When the *Third Statistical Account of Scotland* was published in 1951, Woodside was 'marked down for demolition'. This eventually took place in March 1954. Today, drivers along this minor road would hardly recognise the fact that Woodside existed, apart from the strange arrangement of trees which formerly marked the edges of the gardens.

Appendix

★

Village	Parish	Grid Reference
Alton	Loudoun	NS 501387
Annicklodge	Irvine	NS 355421
Barleith	Riccarton	NS 457360
Bartonholm	Irvine	NS 304411
Benquhat	Dalmellington	NS 464096
Beoch	New Cumnock	NS 522101
Borestone	Dalry	NS 297513
Burnbrae	Tarbolton	NS 412232
Burnfoothill	Dalmellington	NS 433105
Byrehill	Kilwinning	NS 299424
Cairntable	Dalrymple	NS 432139
Carsehead	Dalry	NS 302497
Coalburn	New Cumnock	NS 573140
Commondyke	Auchinleck	NS 576223
Craigbank	New Cumnock	NS 598122
Craighall	Coylton	NS 391222
Craigmark	Dalmellington	NS 473073
Darnconner	Auchinleck	NS 576240
Doura	Kilwinning	NS 345425
Drumsmudden	Ochiltree	NS 466175
Ellerslie	Kilmaurs	NS 406377
Fardalehill	Kilmaurs	NS 409383
Fergushill	Kilwinning	NS 332434

Garrallan	Old Cumnock	NS 542191
Gasswater	Auchinleck	NS 615233
Glenbuck	Muirkirk	NS 749296
Glengyron	Old Cumnock	NS 557193
Glenlogan	Sorn	NS 570256
Grievehill	New Cumnock	NS 644168
Hagsthorn	Kilbirnie	NS 300518
Kerse	Dalrymple	NS 419127
Kersland	Dalry	NS 304505
Knockshoggle	Coylton	NS 417231
Knowehead	Galston	NS 468364
Lethanhill	Dalmellington	NS 436103
Loudounkirk	Loudoun	NS 494494
Meadowside	Sorn	NS 547247
Montgarswood Bridgend	Sorn	NS 532275
Mosshouse	Auchinleck	NS 603223
Neiphill	Kilmarnock	NS 406370
Old Rome	Dundonald	NS 392358
Pennyvenie	Dalmellington	NS 500070
Sourlie	Irvine	NS 343415
Southhook	Dreghorn	NS 387399
Swinlees	Dalry	NS 202532
Tarholm	Tarbolton	NS 394222
Thornton	Kilmaurs	NS 386383
Tongue Bridge	Dalrymple	NS 429133
Trabboch	Stair	NS 439219
Woodside	Coylton	NS 421223

Bibliography

★

The following bibliography lists only some of the hundreds of references used to compile this volume.

Adamson, Archibald R., *Rambles Round Kilmarnock*, with an introductory Sketch of the Town, Kilmarnock Standard, Kilmarnock, 1875.

Baird, J. G. A., *Muirkirk in Bygone Days*, W. Shaw Smith, Muirkirk, 1910.

Barber, Derek, *Steps through Stair – a History of Stair and Trabboch*, Stair Parish Church, Stair, 2000.

Farrell, Robert, *Benwhat and Corbie Craigs: a Brief History*, Cumnock & Doon Valley District Council, Lugar, 1983.

Faulds, Rev M. H., and Tweedie, William (Junior), *The Cherrypickers – Glenbuck, Nursery of Footballers*, Cumnock & Doon Valley District Council, Lugar, 1981.

Kirkwood, Rev J., *Troon and Dundonald*, Mackie and Drennan, Kilmarnock, 1876.

Loudoun, Craufuird C., *A History of the House of Loudoun and Associated Families*, Craufuird C. Loudoun, Kilmarnock, 1995.

MacJannet, Arnold, *The Royal Burgh of Irvine*, Civic Press, Glasgow, 1938.

MacKerrell, Thomas, & Brown, James, *Ayrshire Miners' Rows 1913*, Ayrshire Archaeological and Natural History Society, Ayr, 1979.

MacQuillan, T. Courtney, *The 'Hill – its People and its Pits*, Cumnock & Doon Valley District Council, Lugar, 1988.

Moore, John, *Among Thy Green Braes*, Cumnock & Doon Valley District Council, Lugar, 1977.

Moore, John (editor), *Gently Flows the Doon*, Dalmellington District Council, Dalmellington, 1972.

Paterson, Barbara E., *The Social and Working Condition of the Ayrshire Mining Population*, Ayrshire Archaeological and Natural History Society Collections, Vol. 10, Ayr, 1972.

Powley, Adam, & Gillan, Robert, *Shankly's Village: The Extraordinary Life and Times of Glenbuck and its Famous Footballing Sons*, Pitch Publishing, Durrington, 2015.

Reid, Denholm T., *Old Annbank and Mossblown*, Stenlake Publishing, Catrine, 2005.

Reid, Donald L., *Yesterday's Patna and the Lost Villages of Doon Valley*, Donald Reid, Beith, 2005.

The Lost Mining Villages of Doon Valley: Voices and Images of Ayrshire, Donald Reid, Beith, 2012.

Smith, David L., *The Dalmellington Iron Company: its Engines and Men*, David & Charles, Newton Abbot, 1967.

Statistical Account of Ayrshire, William Blackwood, Edinburgh, 1842.

Strawhorn, John, & Boyd, William, *Third Statistical Account of Scotland – Ayrshire*, Oliver & Boyd, Edinburgh, 1951.

Wark, Gavin, *The Rise and Fall of the Mining Communities in Central Ayrshire in the 19th and 20th Centuries*, Ayrshire Archaeological and Natural History Society, Ayr, 1999.

Wilson, Arthur, *Mining Lays, Tales and Folk-Lore*, Paterson's Printing Press, Perth, Australia, 1944.

Index

★